# Advocacy *and* Awareness *for* Archivists

# ARCHIVAL FUNDAMENTALS SERIES III

Peter J. Wosh, Editor

1 **Leading and Managing Archives and Manuscripts Programs**
Peter Gottlieb and David W. Carmicheal, Editors

2 **Arranging and Describing Archives and Manuscripts**
Dennis Meissner

3 **Advocacy and Awareness for Archivists**
Kathleen D. Roe

4 **Reference and Access for Archives and Manuscripts**
Cheryl A. Oestreicher

5 **Advancing Preservation for Archives and Manuscripts**
Elizabeth Joffrion and Michèle V. Cloonan

6 **Selecting and Appraising Archives and Manuscripts**
Michelle Light and Margery Sly

7 **Introducing Archives and Manuscripts**
Peter J. Wosh

# Advocacy *and* Awareness *for* Archivists

**Kathleen D. Roe**

**The Society of American Archivists**
**www.archivists.org**



Printed in the United States of America.

**Library of Congress Control Number:** 2019942808

ISBN: 978-1-945246-16-6 (paperback)
eISBN: 978-1-945246-17-3 (epub)
eISBN: 978-1-945246-23-4 (pdf)

Graphic design by Sweeney Design, kasween@sbcglobal.net.

# Table of Contents

FOREWORD

# The Evolution of a Book Series

The Society of American Archivists (SAA) first conceived the notion of developing and publishing "manuals relating to major and basic archival functions" in the early 1970s. Charles Frederick Williams (popularly known as C. F. W.) Coker (1932–1983), a former US Marine Corps captain and North Carolina state archivist who recently had been appointed to head the Printed Documents Division of the National Archives and Records Services, edited the initial Basic Manual Series. The first five basic manuals, which appeared in 1977, illustrated the ways in which archivists defined and classified their core concepts at that historical moment:

- *Archives & Manuscripts: Appraisal & Accessioning* by Maynard J. Brichford
- *Archives & Manuscripts: Arrangement & Description* by David B. Gracy II
- *Archives & Manuscripts: Reference & Access* by Sue E. Holbert
- *Archives & Manuscripts: Security* by Timothy Walch
- *Archives & Manuscripts: Surveys* by John Fleckner

The entire series accounted for only 163 pages of text, which included numerous illustrations, graphics, sample forms, charts, and bibliographic insertions. Each 8.5" by 11" softbound pamphlet contained three holes, punched down the left side, for easy insertion into a loose-leaf binder that might be handily referenced at an archivist's desk. Individual volumes sold for $4, though SAA members received a $1 discount.

Archivists operated within a far different cultural, legal, and professional framework during the early and middle years of the 1970s. In 1973, the same year that SAA began work on the Basic Manual Series, IBM introduced the Correcting Selectric II typewriter as its major technological breakthrough, thereby eliminating the need for such popular tools as rubber erasers, correction fluid, and cover-up tape. This revolutionary product seemed destined to alter the nature of document creation forever. During this period, a few archivists had begun grappling with the challenges of something known as "machine-readable records," but a bibliographer who surveyed this puzzling development could still confidently conclude in a 1975 *American Archivist* article that "only a few archival establishments" appeared to be "developing programs for accessioning" such materials. Other momentous—and occasionally unsettling—changes appeared on the horizon. A new copyright law, which was enacted by Congress in 1976 and became effective on New Year's Day 1978, contained significant implications for how archivists would manage collections and serve researchers. Richard Nixon's resignation in 1974 prompted the promulgation of new legislation in 1978 that declared for the first time that presidential and vice presidential records are public documents. Professionally, the archival landscape seemed to be shifting as well. The Association of Canadian Archivists launched an exciting new journal, *Archivaria*, in winter 1975/1976, a development destined to deepen the discipline's intellectual discourse. Regional archival associations formed, became fruitful, and multiplied in the United States. In addition, a new era in archival education began as library schools and history departments inaugurated archives-based graduate programs in the late 1970s, ultimately resulting in a highly credentialed and formally trained corps of professional practitioners.

Such transformations, and many others too numerous to mention here, convinced the Society of American Archivists that only an active publications program that regularly refreshed the existing literature could provide its membership with easy access to rapidly changing trends and best practices. SAA accordingly published the Basic Manual Series II—a second set of five volumes—in the early 1980s:

- *Archives & Manuscripts: Exhibits* by Gail Farr Casterline
- *Archives & Manuscripts: Automated Access* by H. Thomas Hickerson
- *Archives & Manuscripts: Maps and Architectural Drawings* by Ralph E. Ehrenberg
- *Archives & Manuscripts: Public Programs* by Ann E. Pederson and Gail Farr Casterline
- *Archives & Manuscripts: Reprography* by Carolyn Hoover Sung

Over the years, SAA published scores of other titles, each illustrating the rich diversity of archival work: administration of photo collections, conservation, machine-readable records, law, management, a basic glossary, collections of readings on archival theory and practice, and books specific to archives in a variety of institutional settings (i.e., colleges and universities, businesses and corporations, religious and scientific institutions, museums, government agencies, historical societies, etc.). Even with the proliferation of publications, the bedrock of archival practice rested on the core knowledge represented in the basic manuals, which were reconceptualized and rechristened between 1990 and 1993 as the Archival Fundamentals Series:

- *Understanding Archives and Manuscripts* by James O'Toole
- *Arranging and Describing Archives and Manuscripts* by Fredric M. Miller
- *Managing Archival and Manuscript Repositories* by Thomas Wilsted and William Nolte
- *Selecting and Appraising Archives and Manuscripts* by F. Gerald Ham
- *Preserving Archives and Manuscripts* by Mary Lynn Ritzenthaler
- *Providing Reference Services for Archives and Manuscripts* by Mary Jo Pugh
- *The Glossary of Archivists, Manuscript Curators, and Records Managers* by Lynn Lady Bellardo and Lewis Bellardo

A second iteration of the seven books in this revamped series appeared roughly fifteen years later as the Archival Fundamentals Series II:

- *Understanding Archives and Manuscripts* by James O'Toole and Richard J. Cox
- *Arranging and Describing Archives and Manuscripts* by Kathleen D. Roe
- *Managing Archival and Manuscript Repositories* by Michael Kurtz
- *Selecting and Appraising Archives and Manuscripts* by Frank Boles
- *Preserving Archives and Manuscripts* by Mary Lynn Ritzenthaler
- *Providing Reference Services for Archives and Manuscripts* by Mary Jo Pugh
- *A Glossary of Archival and Records Terminology* by Richard Pearce-Moses

Mary Jo Pugh and Richard J. Cox edited these multivolume compilations, which almost instantaneously became required texts in archival education courses and necessary additions to archivists' bookshelves. The Archival Fundamentals Series I and II differed in scope and scale from the initial Basic Manual Series. For example, John Fleckner's comprehensive treatment of surveys did not appear in need of revision and dropped out of the series. Security became incorporated into a broader manual on preservation. SAA commissioned an introductory overview of the field, added a new book that focused on managerial issues, and developed a glossary with the goal of defining and historicizing key archival concepts. Beginning in the 1970s, both Archival Fundamentals Series I and II incorporated and delineated the evolving descriptive standards that defined professional practice, dissected the contentious debates surrounding appraisal and deaccessioning that enlivened archival discourse in the 1980s, and reflected the growing emphases on an expanding user base and more complex reference services that revolutionized reading rooms and repositories in the late twentieth century.

This third edition—Archival Fundamentals Series III—contains important continuities and significant departures from its predecessors:

- A new book, *Advocacy and Awareness for Archivists* by Kathleen D. Roe, reflects an increased understanding that these functions undergird all aspects of archival work.
- The management volume, *Leading and Managing Archives and Manuscripts Programs* edited by Peter Gottlieb and David W. Carmicheal, has been reconfigured to focus especially on leadership and to provide readers with opportunities to explore their individual managerial styles.
- *Advancing Preservation for Archives and Manuscripts* by Elizabeth Joffrion and Michèle V. Cloonan addresses digital challenges and focuses on such current issues as risk management, ethical considerations, and sustainability.
- *Arranging and Describing Archives and Manuscripts* by Dennis Meissner, *Reference and Access for Archives and Manuscripts* by Cheryl A. Oestreicher, and *Selecting and Appraising Archives and Manuscripts* by Michelle Light and Margery Sly may appear familiar topics to readers of the previous two series, but each book illustrates the innovations in thought and practice that have transformed these archival functions over the past fifteen years.
- A general overview volume which I am preparing, *Introducing Archives and Manuscripts*, provides a broad introduction to the historical, philosophical, and theoretical foundations of the profession.

One contribution that constituted a cornerstone of the previous series has been reformatted to maximize its currency and usability. Although not part of the Archival Fundamentals Series III, the *Dictionary of Archives Terminology* (dictionary.archivists.org) will replace *A Glossary of Archival and Records Terminology* and will be maintained and updated as a digital resource by SAA's Dictionary Working Group.

We hope that undergraduate and graduate students, new professionals, seasoned archival veterans, and others in the information science and public history fields will find the seven volumes in the Archival Fundamentals Series III helpful, provocative, and essential to both their intellectual life and their daily work. As Richard J. Cox observed in his preface to an earlier edition of the series, the time has long passed "when individuals entering the archival profession could read a few texts, peruse some journals, attend a workshop and institute or two, and walk away with a sense that they grasped the field's knowledge and discipline." This series provides an entry point and a synthetic distillation of a much broader literature that spans an impressive array of academic disciplines. We encourage you, of course, to do a deeper dive into each of the individual topics covered here. But we also remain confident that this series, like its predecessors, provides an honest and accurate snapshot of archival best practices at the end of the second decade of the twenty-first century.

The authors, of course, deserve full credit for their individual contributions. The Archival Fundamentals Series III itself, though, constitutes a collaborative enterprise that benefited from the work of SAA Publications Board members, editors, and interns throughout the past decade. These individuals helped to define the series parameters, reviewed proposals and manuscripts, and shepherded various projects to conclusion. Special shout-outs (in alphabetical order) are owed to: Bethany Anderson, Jessica Ballard, Roland Baumann, Cara Bertram, Mary Caldera, Amy Cooper Cary, Jessica Chapel, Paul Conway, J. Gordon Daines, Todd Daniels-Howell, Sarah Demb, Jody DeRidder, Keara Duggan, Margaret Fraser, Thomas J. Frusciano, Krista Gray, Gregory Hunter, Geoffrey Huth, Petrina Jackson, Joan Krizack, Christopher Lee, Donna McCrea, Jennifer Davis McDaid, Kathryn Michaelis, Nicole Milano, Lisa Mix, Tawny Nelb, Kevin Proffitt, Christopher Prom, Mary Jo Pugh, Aaron Purcell, Colleen Rademaker, Caryn Radick, Dennis Riley, Michael Shallcross, Mark Shelstad, Jennifer Thomas, Ciaran Trace, Anna Trammell, Joseph Turrini, Tywanna Whorley, and Deborah Wythe. Nancy Beaumont has been an inspirational executive director for SAA, as well as a brilliant editor in her own right. Abigail Christian, SAA's editorial and production coordinator, has skillfully shepherded design and layout. Teresa Brinati, keenly insightful and good-humored as always, remains the epitome of competent leadership and has transformed the SAA publications program into a model for professional associations. It has been a privilege and great fun to work with everyone on this project.

PETER J. WOSH
Editor, Archival Fundamentals Series III
Society of American Archivists

1

# Introduction to Advocacy and Awareness

Never doubt that a small group of thoughtful, committed citizens can change the world; indeed, it's the only thing that ever has.

—*Margaret Mead*

## Advocacy and Awareness Is Fundamental to Archives

Archivists invest countless hours, resources, and energy in the work of identifying, caring for, and making available evidence from the past to support the information needs of current and future users. Those needs reflect an astonishing array of purposes, including the following:

- An oral surgeon used archival resources to pursue his grandfather's missing murderer, ultimately leading to the return of that person to jail in Montana.[1]
- In his Public Broadcasting Service series *Finding Your Roots,* Henry Louis Gates Jr. brought the realities of slavery to the rapper Nas by sharing with him the bill of sale for his enslaved third great-grandmother.[2]
- Historian Ron Chernow used extensive archival resources to write his biography *Alexander Hamilton,* bringing new perspectives to Hamilton's role and importance in American history.[3] His work then inspired composer/actor Lin-Manuel Miranda to create the multiple-award-winning Broadway show *Hamilton.*
- During the disaster at the Quecreek coal mine in Pennsylvania, archival maps were used to locate the abandoned shaft where nine miners were sheltering, leading to their rescue.[4]

As this range of examples demonstrates, archives and the work of archivists are foundational to addressing so many information needs. Yet those contributions are too little understood or valued for the real impact and opportunities they provide.

Advocacy and awareness-building are critical activities for archivists who want to increase the use of archival records, bring resources and attention to institutions that hold them, gain support and respect for the professional archivists who manage them, and broaden the understanding of the value of archives and archivists. These outcomes can be accomplished only with focused, intentional advocacy and awareness efforts that demonstrate the role and contributions of archives.

> Archives change lives. Archives improve lives. Archives enrich lives. Archives save lives. Archives connect lives. Archives empower lives.
>
> *—Society of American Archivists, 2015*

This volume is included in the Society of American Archivists' (SAA) Archival Fundamentals series because advocacy and awareness are, in fact, essential activities that underpin the work of the archives profession. As a professional group, as members of an archives staff, or as individual archivists, we have too often failed to incorporate fundamental advocacy and awareness efforts as part of the archival endeavor. Processing backlogs, digitizing records, or responding to reference questions quite naturally take priority; conducting effective advocacy and awareness initiatives is set aside in the face of what are perceived as more pressing needs. But archival practice is not linear or one-dimensional. Archivists must invest in advocacy and awareness to ensure the health, understanding, and use of and respect for archives and archivists.

## Developing an archival advocacy frame of mind

Although new to the Archival Fundamentals Series, advocacy and awareness are, in fact, not new functions to archivists and the archival endeavor. In the past, archivists have pursued focused efforts that have included the founding of the National Archives, concerted actions taken to prevent the closure of the Georgia Archives, promotion of legislation on copyright that recognizes archival concerns, and the sponsorship of American Archives Month. SAA and regional archival organizations periodically provide training on advocacy and awareness. SAA participates in the National Coalition for History to pursue federal and national-level advocacy. And archivists have certainly been aware of and carried out advocacy or awareness efforts in individual repositories. Examples of past and current efforts appear throughout this volume to suggest directions and opportunities for archivists to take action on behalf of their institutions and profession.

> Advocacy is a frame of mind.
>
> *—Nancy Amidei, 2010*

The need for archivists to focus on advocacy and awareness has been raised consistently in past decades by David B. Gracy II, Elsie Freeman Finch, Larry J. Hackman, and others. Those individuals and efforts have encouraged many archivists to recognize the need to focus clearly and directly on the implementation of advocacy and awareness efforts as a regular, planned, and expected component of the mission of individual institutions, as well as for the archival profession.

All archivists, whether those pursuing graduate studies, "front-line" archivists, or senior management, should take responsibility for incorporating advocacy and awareness into their responsibilities—and they need to do so actively. Conversations at professional conferences, in social media, and archival literature regularly reflect concern about the limited understanding of or respect given to the archival profession. That manifests itself in many ways regarding the archival profession as well as archival collections.

As Dr. David Gracy noted in his 1984 presidential address, archives and archivists are often subject to misconceptions about their basic role and functions.[5] Nearly every archivist has found it necessary to counteract the common misperceptions on archives involving words and phrases such as *dusty, old, hidden away*, and *housed in the attic* and a litany of terminology that bedevils the profession. Newspaper articles, however well-meaning, often characterize archivists as individuals who "have long spent their careers cloistered, like the objects they protected."[6] That undervaluing of archivists also has a direct economic impact on individual members and the status of the profession. Although there is often an expectation of an advanced degree for entry-level archivist positions, salaries are not comparable to those in other professions requiring less education. This has been a regular topic of discussion in professional forums for decades.[7] Managers to whom archivists and their employing institutions report need to become aware of, and value, the extensive skills and competencies required for archival work.

> For more than a decade archivists and administrators of historical agencies have been aware of the acute problem of maintaining competitive salaries for their respective professions.
>
> —*Philip P. Mason, 1967*

Advocacy and awareness initiatives are essential to counteracting misperceptions and to establishing a firm understanding of the essential evidence that archives hold and the role of archivists in ensuring that information is identified, preserved, and made widely available to a range of current and future users.

Although archivists have been involved in advocacy, awareness, and even lobbying since the establishment of this profession in the United States, those activities have not generally been acknowledged as an essential function in archival education or as an ongoing job responsibility. Archivists often have an overload of daily work and a surfeit of experience, training, or encouragement to undertake such efforts in a focused way.

> Behind . . . expressions of enthusiasm rests a dis-ease, a suspicion that these activities, however useful and laudatory, do not fit readily into the mainstream of activities we call archives administration, rendering them at the outset dubious. Why do these programs more often than not appear to be episodes or events rather than programs in the ongoing sense?
>
> —*Elsie Freeman Freivogel, 1978*

## What is in this manual

This manual provides a basic guide to the principles and practices underpinning every advocacy or awareness endeavor, regardless of the focus, scope, time frame, or resources needed for those efforts. It is intended to provide methods and examples of approaches that will assist archivists and archival organizations in pursuing advocacy in active and productive ways. Because awareness and advocacy should be part of an archivist's core skill set, this volume focuses on providing:

- Basic definitions and principles of advocacy and awareness drawn from the literature and the practices of professions and groups that have long been involved in advocacy and awareness in their respective areas of interest;
- Background on previous advocacy and awareness efforts to support archives and archivists, demonstrating both productive approaches and "cautionary tales" that may help inform future efforts;
- Practical steps and methods for developing advocacy and awareness initiatives, including defining goals, developing effective plans, identifying audiences, developing compelling messages, gathering essential data and evidence to support the effort, and implementing advocacy and awareness initiatives;
- Examples of a wide range of advocacy and awareness efforts conducted by the archives community, to foster ideas and share what has been learned from successes and challenges that may benefit other initiatives;
- Charts and brief forms to complete with your own ideas, experiences, or thoughts to help develop or refine an advocacy/awareness focus for you, your institution, your professional association, or a project; and
- Resources to assist you in taking the next steps in advocacy and awareness.

## Defining Terms

When discussing efforts to draw attention to archives, archival records, archival issues, archivists, and the archives profession, our professional community uses a variety of terms, including *advocacy, awareness, lobbying, outreach/external advocacy,* and *inreach/internal advocacy.* Although these terms are sometimes used rather loosely, the definitions for each exist in the literature and practice of other groups involved in seeking change for a wide range of causes and situations.

Three core terms describe the *actions* being taken to effect change: *awareness, advocacy,* and *lobbying.* Each represents an increasingly specific level of focus and action. (See Figure 1.) Those are coupled with two additional concepts, *outreach/external advocacy* and *inreach/internal advocacy,* that reflect the audience at which the actions are directed. Definitions and examples of these terms follow.

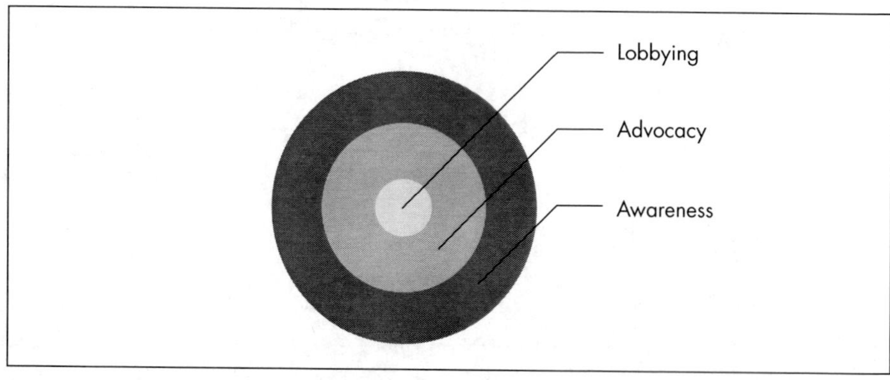


**FIGURE 1.** Actions to Effect Change

**Source:** David W. Carmicheal and Kathleen D. Roe, "Advocacy and Awareness for Archivists Workshop," 2008, reproduced by permission of the author and David W. Carmicheal.

| | Specificity | Message | Audience | Outcome |
|---|---|---|---|---|
| **Awareness** | Very general | Understand us. Change your perception of us. | Anyone | Better knowledge |

**FIGURE 2.** Defining Awareness

**Source:** David W. Carmicheal and Kathleen D. Roe, "Advocacy and Awareness for Archivists Workshop," 2008, reproduced by permission of the author and David W. Carmicheal.

## Awareness

***Awareness*** is the most general of the three types of action. Awareness involves efforts and initiatives to share information about archives to raise the general knowledge about the existence of archival collections, the institutions that hold them, and the professionals who manage them. (See Figure 2.)

Although many individuals have some idea of what archives are, their perceptions can be a bit hazy and, unfortunately, inaccurate. Those perceptions generally are not negative. In fact, they usually reflect an idealized vision of archives as "treasure chests" holding fragile items of famous individuals for rare and special purposes. One has only to observe visitors at the National Archives who stand before the exhibits of the Declaration of Independence or the Constitution "oohing and ahhing" over these iconic documents. However rewarding it may seem, that sense of veneration or privilege does not translate into use of, or appreciation for, the extensive range of purposes that archives can support. Awareness is essential in providing a more balanced, informed view of the many values of archival records, the work of archivists, and the archival institutions they serve.

> Many people are unfamiliar with archives, so their value is not readily apparent. Archivists are quick to point out the historical value of the records. . . . For some, history is a warm and fuzzy diversion that can be cut in light of hard, cold, budgetary needs.
>
> —*Richard Pearce-Moses, 2013*

One of the most consistent awareness activities undertaken in the United States at the national level is American Archives Month. Established initially by archivists in New York City as Archives Week, since 2006 American Archives Month (October) has provided a focused opportunity for archivists and archival institutions to raise awareness of the value of archival records, institutions, and the profession.[8]

Around the country, archivists pursue a wide range of efforts to remind and demonstrate to the public the role and importance of archives. Professional organizations have been very active in promoting American Archives Month, both through their own activities and by providing ideas and support to the archival community. SAA provides guidance on public relations as well as resources and ideas for activities, in addition to sponsoring "Ask an Archivist" day on Twitter.[9] Since 2010, the Council of State Archivists (CoSA) has sponsored Electronic Records Day to highlight the need for attention to the challenges of ensuring the preservation of archival electronic records.[10] A number of state archives select a theme and distribute a statewide poster with individual institutions sponsoring related activities.[11] Other professional organizations and individual institutions host public events, tours, lectures, and contests to celebrate American Archives Month.

Many institutions have traditionally pursued a range of activities to raise the public's awareness of their archival collections and the records they hold. These have typically included:

- "Milestones" such as centennials of a business or college's establishment or such popular events as the Olympics or other sporting events;[12]
- The acquisition of a significant collection of materials, such as the James Baldwin papers by the New York Public Library's Schomburg Center for Black Culture;[13] and
- Recognition months or days, such as Women's History Month, Veterans Day, Martin Luther King Jr. Day, or International Archives Day.[14]

Archivists have sought to raise general awareness about archives and archivists through individual actions as well, focusing on developing "elevator speeches" that prepare them to describe archives and the work of archivists in simple, approachable language.[15]

At the same time, archival organizations have begun to develop position and issue statements to clearly define, raise awareness about, and advocate for a variety of public policy concerns ranging from federal funding for archives to privacy, freedom of information, copyright and fair use, and accessibility of government records. They have also taken positions on issues affecting archival records, repositories, and archivists themselves, such as dramatic cuts in funding or closure of archival facilities, lack of diversity and inclusion within records and institutions, and use of nongovernment email for public business. Setting forth such statements provides a foundation for archivists, through their professional organizations, to have articulated positions in advance that have been vetted by the groups' governing bodies. When specific incidents occur, discussion has already taken place and advocacy efforts can be initiated in a timely and more effective manner.[16]

The focus of awareness activities, then, is to raise interest in and understanding of archives. The intended audience may be the general public or a more targeted group, such as university students, administrators, business executives, or government officials. The purpose of awareness efforts is to achieve a more informed understanding of archives, their potential uses, and their value to society. Although the audience and goals of awareness efforts are more general and not targeted at producing a specific, tangible action or outcome, awareness may set the stage for more specific advocacy efforts.

> Successful archives are those that can be relevant to those who need, value and use them, and continuously reach out to new audiences.
>
> —*Norehan Jaaffar, 2016*

## Advocacy

***Advocacy*** is defined as giving a focused, purposeful message to a targeted audience in order to effect a positive change. (See Figure 3.) This function moves beyond the general goals of awareness because it involves working toward an explicit change.

In SAA's *Many Happy Returns,* Larry Hackman notes that advocacy activities are "consciously aimed to persuade individuals to act on behalf of a program or institution."[17] Unlike the less-targeted awareness, advocacy is characterized by a conscious, focused effort to move a group or person to act in order to accomplish a goal on behalf of archives and archivists.

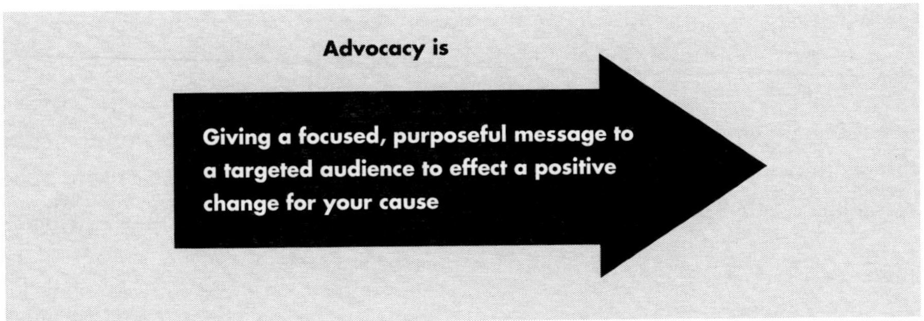


**FIGURE 3.** Defining Advocacy

**Source:** David W. Carmicheal and Kathleen D. Roe, "Advocacy and Awareness for Archivists Workshop," 2008, reproduced by permission of the author and David W. Carmicheal.

Advocacy efforts may range in size, purpose, extent, resources, and time frame needed to achieve them. A university archives and special collections may plan a focused effort to engage the university's public relations office in using its materials for alumni relations. A regional library's history collection may launch an advocacy effort to engage local Latinx community organizations to preserve their records to ensure a more inclusive historical record. Special collections staff might recommend that the records be donated to the library or alternatively provide advice on the establishment of a community archives, depending on the advocacy goal. A business archives may develop an ongoing advocacy plan to gain and maintain the compliance of corporate departments in scheduling records and ultimately turning over those that are designated as permanently valuable. Or a historical society may undertake efforts to expand its user base to include teachers who are developing classroom instructional materials.

Well-planned and carefully executed advocacy is also essential at a broader level for archives and archivists. At the institutional level, it is important for most archives to develop and maintain a long-term advocacy effort to gain support for the program as a means of ensuring its fiscal and operational health and management. For professional organizations, advocacy can address a wide range of critical professional issues. Some archival examples include copyright law, privacy legislation, standards of practice, archival education criteria, graduate program accreditation, adequate salary compensation, workplace diversity, or selection and acquisition criteria for a more broad-based historical record.

Every advocacy effort should begin with development of a well-defined goal, a clear sense of the audience to whom the appeal will be made, and a set of actions that are most likely to achieve the goal. Advocacy efforts are more focused and explicit in their execution and results than are awareness efforts. (See Figure 4.) Regardless of the extent and scope of an effort or whether its

| | **Specificity** | **Message** | **Audience** | **Outcomes** |
|---|---|---|---|---|
| **Awareness** | Very general | Understand us. Change your perception of us. | Anyone | Better knowledge |
| **Advocacy** | More specific | Help us in a specific way. | Targeted | Specific, positive change |

**FIGURE 4.** How Advocacy and Awareness Differ

**Source:** David W. Carmicheal and Kathleen D. Roe, "Advocacy and Awareness for Archivists Workshop," 2008, reproduced by permission of the author and David W. Carmicheal.

accomplishment takes a few months and limited resources or several years and extensive resources, advocacy is an essential component of effectively managing an archival program or carrying out the work of a professional organization. Effective advocacy may mean the difference between an archives program closing or remaining viable. Writ larger, it may help to ensure that archives and archivists function as the critical information infrastructure and resource for our society and democracy. Table 1 offers some examples that illustrate how awareness and advocacy differ.

**Table 1. Awareness vs. Advocacy**

| Awareness | Advocacy |
|---|---|
| A university archives creates an exhibit of yearbooks and student life during the 1960s for Alumni Weekend. | A university archives creates an exhibit of yearbooks and student life during the 1960s for Alumni Weekend. Staff are present to interact with alumni from that time period regarding whether they are willing to donate their records or to participate in oral histories of their experience for the archives' collection. |
| During Women's History Month, a regional historical society holds a series of lectures by women's historians from nearby universities and creates an online exhibit highlighting letters from early women settlers in the region. | A regional historical society has individual and group meetings with local women politicians, educators, and leaders of civic, social, and charitable organizations to develop a documentation plan for increasing the society's holdings relating to women. |

## Lobbying

**Lobbying** is generally defined as "to conduct activities aimed at influencing public officials and especially members of a legislative body on legislation."[18] (See Figure 5.) The importance of a citizen's right to lobby is, as some commentary notes, embedded in and protected by the First Amendment of the U.S. Constitution's provision that "Congress shall make no law . . . abridging . . . the right of the people peaceably to petition the Government for a redress of grievances."[19]

Although individuals use the term *lobbying* informally to describe advocacy efforts, it actually has a specific definition that clarifies appropriate usage of that term. Lobbying involves explicit efforts to influence policymakers to take a specific position on legislation, such as "Congresswoman Chase, would you please vote in favor of the current bill supporting net neutrality?"

Archivists should be familiar with the parameters of "lobbying" as defined by the federal government. Those who work in, or who plan to lobby, state or local governments should determine

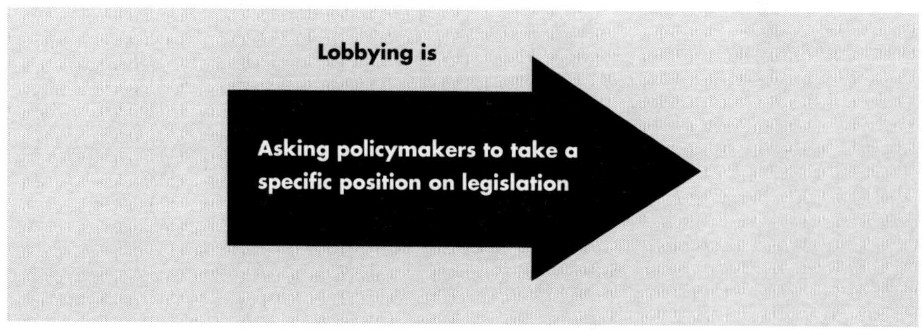


**FIGURE 5.** Defining Lobbying

**Source:** David W. Carmicheal and Kathleen D. Roe, "Advocacy and Awareness for Archivists Workshop," 2008, reproduced by permission of the author and David W. Carmicheal.

| | Specificity | Message | Audience | Outcomes |
|---|---|---|---|---|
| Awareness | Very general | Understand us. Change your perception of us. | Anyone | Better knowledge |
| Advocacy | More specific | Help us in a specific way. | Targeted | Specific, positive change |
| Lobbying | Very specific | Take a position on specific legislation. | Legislators | Support for specific legislation |

**FIGURE 6.** How Awareness, Advocacy, and Lobbying Differ

**Source:** David W. Carmicheal and Kathleen D. Roe, "Advocacy and Awareness for Archivists Workshop," 2008, reproduced by permission of the author and David W. Carmicheal.

whether there are additional parameters that must be observed, either as a voter or as a member of an organization.

The Internal Revenue Service provides guidance on lobbying, which it defines as "attempting to influence legislation," in information provided to organizations with nonprofit 501(c)3 status.[20] It distinguishes between two practices: direct lobbying and grassroots lobbying. Although lobbying is not completely forbidden, a nonprofit may not lobby as a "substantial" part of its activities. The IRS defines direct lobbying as "attempts to influence a legislative body through communication with a member or employee of a legislative body, or with a government official who participates in formulating legislation," distinguishing it from grassroots lobbying, which it defines as "attempts to influence legislation by attempting to affect the opinion of the public with respect to the legislation and encouraging the audience to take action with respect to the legislation."[21] The IRS website provides guidance for measuring the extent of lobbying activity to determine whether an organization is, in fact, meeting the criteria.

Although lobbying is limited, if not prohibited, for nonprofits, there is no ban on carefully targeted advocacy relating to federal legislation and, comparably, state legislation. (See Figure 6.) Both individual archivists and nonprofit or government archives organizations should be aware of parameters before lobbying. Some organizations specifically forbid staff members from involvement in lobbying activities. Most archives organizations or their parent organizations have policies about staff involvement in lobbying, even if the focus is not directly related to the institutional mission (such as lobbying on copyright law). Archivists should be careful to clarify the policies or permissions necessary from their employing institutions. This often involves discussion with the institution's legal counsel before involvement in lobbying activities.

Although lobbying may not be permitted for some individuals, as the IRS explains, providing information or advocating with legislators or government officials can be acceptable. For

**Table 2. Advocacy vs. Lobbying**

| Advocacy | Lobbying |
|---|---|
| • Informing your member of Congress about how a federal grant has allowed your institution to create digital collections<br>• Inviting your member of Congress to the opening reception for an exhibit funded by a federal grant<br>• Informing your member of Congress about the impact of Freedom of Information legislation on your researchers | • Asking your member of Congress to vote in favor of the reauthorization legislation of a federal grants program<br>• Emailing an action alert/call to action asking your researchers and colleagues to contact their members of Congress to ask them to vote for (or against) a specific piece of copyright legislation |

example, it may be appropriate to inform or educate a legislator or public official on the potential impact of a policy but not appropriate to ask that legislator or public official to vote in a specific way. Table 2 offers examples that distinguish advocacy from lobbying.

Professional archivists' organizations, as well as individual archivists and archival institutions, have been involved in federal legislative advocacy and lobbying on a range of issues, including grant funding, the status of the National Archives, privacy, Freedom of Information legislation, and fair use and copyright. Most organizations have clearly defined policies on when or whether they will pursue legislative advocacy or lobbying, as well as acceptable roles for staff or leaders. Not all individuals or institutions will handle this in the same manner. For example, in recent efforts to advocate for restoration of federal funding for the National Historical Publications and Records Commission, archivists were given a range of instructions by their employing institutions, including the following:

- Advocating by providing information to Congress on the value of NHPRC is acceptable for individual staff members using their institutional affiliation.
- Advocating by providing information to Congress on the value of NHPRC is acceptable for individual staff members, but they may not use their institutional affiliation, letterhead, or institutional email.
- Advocating will be done by the institutional leadership but is not permissible for individual staff members.
- Advocacy is acceptable, but lobbying is not. To ensure that this is handled in compliance with institutional policy, staff members should have their communications reviewed.
- No participation in either advocacy or lobbying is acceptable.

The importance and long-term impact of various federal programs and legislation can be critical for most archivists, archival programs, and the constituents they serve. Involvement on issues at the national level need not be avoided automatically, but it does require being informed on the parameters for doing so legally and within the practices and policies of an institution.

## Inreach and outreach

Awareness, advocacy, and lobbying are all directed at effecting change in support, understanding, or action relating to archival records, archival institutions, or archivists and the archives profession. Those actions can be directed via *inreach,* focused on an internal audience, or *outreach* to a range of external audiences.

***Inreach,*** or ***internal awareness/advocacy***, refers to "the activities conducted by an archives within its parent institution to raise awareness and gain support for its programs."[22] The need to justify the existence and contributions of a cultural heritage program is far too common for archivists, as it is for our colleagues in libraries, museums, and other cultural institutions. Inreach can provide opportunities for archivists to do this through more general awareness-raising efforts or with focused advocacy initiatives.

Archivists have found that their institutional leaders and managers sometimes have limited understanding of the value of archival programs for their own institution. This was most dramatically demonstrated in the report "The Image of Archivists: Resource Allocators' Perceptions," a qualitative study prepared by Social Research, Inc., and commissioned by SAA's Task Force on Archives and Society in 1984. Based on interviews with some 44 managers/resource allocators for government, university/college, business, and historical organizations with archives programs, the report included conclusions such as, "Archivists are perceived as quiet professional [*sic*], carrying out an admired but comparatively subterranean activity."[23] The Task Force on Archives and Society urged the archives community to address such perceptions directly, but archivists continue to be concerned about this issue decades later.

> Archivists need to develop skills to deal with resource allocators in terms they will respond to. They must identify the appropriate people to reach and educate.
>
> —*The Status of Virtue: Resource Allocators' Perceptions, 1984*

Many archivists have found it important to pursue internal advocacy or awareness efforts to explain the contributions and value of their archival program. For example, business archivists have noted the value to them in raising the awareness with their public relations and legal departments.[24] Many state archives are placed in government structures, such as the secretary of state's office or the department of education, where the value of archives and records management must be demonstrated to public officials whose focus is on managing elections, funding schools, or registering businesses. Even in college and university archives that are placed in a library where the director values the role of information and service to the university community, the needs, professional practices, and opportunities provided by archives and special collections may have to be made clear and distinct from library approaches. For many archivists, effective inreach can be important for program support and may be needed on an ongoing basis.

> Corporate archivists have always known that their function adds value, but the language of archives is not suited to demonstrating that archives are strategic to their firm.
>
> —*Paul Lasewicz, 2015*

***Outreach,*** or ***external awareness/advocacy***, refers to a wide range of efforts to "provide services to constituencies with needs relevant to the repository's mission, especially underserved groups, and tailoring service to meet those needs."[25] This broad definition encompasses an extensive variety of audiences and possible activities. External constituencies might include those who can benefit from the information in archives: academics; university, high school, or elementary school students; genealogists; artists and writers; journalists; land surveyors; lawyers; scientists; and many other professional, personal, or avocational users. Outreach to those groups is similarly varied in approaches, from exhibits, conferences, and training events to publications, websites, and festivals—and a vast array of other approaches.

Not all outreach activities are specifically directed to accomplishing awareness or advocacy goals. Yet each provides an opportunity to incorporate, at a minimum, improving awareness of the value of archives. For example, an online exhibit on the Harlem Hellfighters might be created to recognize Black History Month. With some additional planning, it could be designed to explicitly raise awareness of the contributions of African Americans to U.S. military efforts and the need for more donations of African American materials to an archival repository.

Similarly, efforts to use historical records as part of a classroom curriculum not only educate students in critical and historical thinking skills, but the opportunity can be taken to provide onsite visits or information that helps them to understand the role and value of archival institutions and the work of archivists. That awareness can translate into understanding of and support for archives in the future.[26]

## Why Archives Matter

Advocacy, awareness, and lobbying efforts on behalf of archives and archivists should be based in a firm understanding of and ability to convey a message about why archives matter. The various ways in which that message can be conveyed and by whom are addressed more specifically in Chapter 5.

### Starting with "why"

In his book *Start with Why: How Great Leaders Inspire Everyone to Take Action,* Simon Sinek observes that most people are comfortable and capable of talking about what they do and how they do it. This is characteristic of archivists, just as it is of other professional groups. We talk about preservation techniques, discuss the merits of software for managing our digital collections, compare our implementations of Encoded Archival Description, and debate appraisal methods. Those are all necessary professional discussions that energize and engage us, but they are about issues that are internal to "what" we do and "how" we can most effectively undertake our work. These subjects, which may provide some interesting insights into our work processes or address a curiosity, are not likely to provide a compelling understanding for non-archivists of the value of our collections and the profession. Sinek asserts that to inspire others, we must connect or reconnect with "why" each of us values the work we do. In giving voice to that "why," we might inspire others to understand, value, and support our work.[27]

> Dr. [Martin Luther] King wasn't the only man in America who was a great orator. He wasn't the only man in America who suffered in pre-civil rights America. In fact, some of his ideas were bad. But he had a gift. He didn't go around telling people what needed to be changed in America, *he went around and told people what he believed. . . . And people who believed what he believed took his cause and made it their own.* (emphasis added).
>
> —*Simon Sinek, 2013*

Individual archivists generally know why they value archives but speak about it infrequently. There is no single, definitive "response" that will serve all situations and purposes, but considering thoughts shared by other archivists may be useful. In a post on the National Archives UK blog, archivist Laura Cowdrey wrote:

> Archives are not mute, dead things. They scream with a million human voices. And as such, they tell us more about ourselves than we could ever imagine. They tell us what it means to be human in any age, and what makes us the way we are today.[28]

Archivist Rob Spindler provides additional thoughts on the topic: "I believe archives make a difference by helping us all become more self aware and compassionate people as we compare our own lives to those of others past and present."[29]

Further ideas are expressed through some examples of responses to SAA's call for archivists to express why archives are important. (SAA limited the number of words, not just to be clever, but to try to get at the essence of what makes archives important.)[30]

- "Archivists Support Accountability, Identity, Memory."[31]
- "Archivists are warriors for democracy."[32]
- Archives are "evidence for accountability and rights."[33]
- Archives are "the evidence behind the narrative."[34]
- "Actively preserving and sharing communities."[35]
- "Enabling diverse access to history!"[36]

These answers underscore the importance of archives. When linked with specific examples of data or compelling stories or experiences of users, they provide a clear demonstration of the value that others can understand and support. Answers to the question "Why archives?" will vary based on individual beliefs, the focus of collections, and cultural context. Nonetheless, for archivists to move forward in efforts to advocate or raise awareness about archives and archivists, being able to articulate what each sees as the value and impact of archives provides an essential foundation. Take a moment to write your own statement in response to the question "Why archives?"

Archives are important because:

________________________________

________________________________

________________________________

In addition to personal statements, or summaries like elevator speeches, archivists—through the profession's literature—have asserted many reasons that archives have value. The SAA *Glossary of Archival and Records Terminology* notes that archivists have discussed a number of value types, all intended to address "the usefulness, significance, or worth that determines a record's retention."[37] By revisiting the range of values identified during appraisal that led to the decision to retain records permanently, archivists can glean important evidence to share in advocacy and awareness efforts.

> Archives are central to good governance.
>
> Archives and records are the tools by which governments can make themselves accountable and demonstrate their democratic credentials. Well-managed archives and records are the means by which a country can understand the who, when, where, how, and why of government actions. They enable the delivery of human rights and the ability for a government to explain and defend its actions. Good management also ensures efficient, timely government.
>
> —*International Council on Archives, "Why Archiving?," 2016*

## Moving forward with advocacy and awareness

Much of the information provided here will not be surprising or complicated for those who make the decision to pursue advocacy and awareness efforts. However, making the commitment to advocacy and awareness does require individual archivists, institutions, and professional organizations to focus on the change needed, invest the time to develop a plan, and then pursue an approach that will engage the audience and result in real change. There are many ways to approach advocacy and awareness. This volume provides a basic set of principles and practices that will help you adopt an "advocacy frame of mind" and encourage you to do the work that will bring about the change you seek.

## NOTES

1 Council of State Archivists, *The Importance of State Archives* (Albany, NY: Council of State Archivists, 2013), 3, www.statearchivists.org/files/7114/4071/0454/Importance_of_State_Archives.pdf, captured at https://perma.cc/W8KK-SEWM.

2 *Finding Your Roots*, season 2, episode 6, "Nas' Enslaved Roots: "A Receipt for a Human Being," aired on PBS.org on October 27, 2014, https://www.pbs.org/video/finding-your-roots-nas-enslaved-roots-receipt-human-being/, captured at https://perma.cc/8TPY-DGWR.

3 Ron Chernow, *Alexander Hamilton* (New York: Penguin/Random House, 2005).

4 Council of State Archivists, *Importance of State Archives*, 3.

5 David B. Gracy II, "Archives and Society: The First Archival Revolution," *American Archivist* 47 (Winter 1984): 6–10. In his address, Gracy noted some of the mistaken versions of the word *archivist*, including *orchidvist*, *activist*, and *archivisor*.

6 Alison Leigh Cowan, "Leaving Cloister of Dusty Offices, Young Archivists Meet Like Minds," *New York Times*, April 28, 2013, www.nytimes.com/2013/04/29/nyregion/archivists-bringing-past-into-future-are-now-less-cloistered.html, captured at https://perma.cc/HCB4-C993.

7 A range of examples are available regarding this issue, including Philip P. Mason, "Economic Status of the Archival Profession 1965–66," *American Archivist* 30 (January 1967): 102–155; David Bearman, "Survey of the Archival Profession," *American Archivist* 46 (Spring 1983): 233–241, which includes data on education and salaries; Victoria Irons Walch, Nancy Beaumont, Elizabeth Yakel, Jeannette Bastian, Nancy Zimmelman, Susan Davis, and Anne Diffendal, "A*CENSUS (Archival Census and Education Needs Survey in the United States)," *American Archivist* 69 (Fall/Winter 2006): 291–419, www2.archivists.org/sites/all/files/ACENSUS-Final.pdf, captured at https://perma.cc/6AN6-Y3DN; and Danna C. Bell, "The Jobs Thing . . .," *Off the Record* (blog), February 4, 2014, https://offtherecord.archivists.org/2014/02/04/the-jobs-thing/, captured at https://perma.cc/97T5-DQS8.

8 Larry J. Hackman, "Archives Week in the United States?," *SAA Newsletter*, March 1991, 14.

9 Society of American Archivists, Committee on Public Awareness, "Ask An Archivist Day," updated September 12, 2018, www2.archivists.org/initiatives/askanarchivist-day, captured at https://perma.cc/Q8WF-HMGT.

10 Council of State Archivists, "Electronic Records Day," www.statearchivists.org/programs/state-electronic-records-initiative/electronic-records-day/, captured at https://perma.cc/LW47-C9EY.

11 Council of State Archivists, "Archives Month Posters," www.statearchivists.org/programs/archives-month/archives-month-posters/, captured at https://perma.cc/YUU6-CS8N.

12 Jenny Schooley, "Coca Cola Connects Past and Present at Public Event," *Archival Outlook* (May/June 2010), 12.

13 New York Public Library, "The Schomburg Center for Research in Black Culture Acquires Papers of Renowned Literary Icon James Baldwin," news release, April 12, 2017, www.nypl.org/press/press-release/april-12-2017/schomburg-center-research-black-culture-acquires-papers-renowned, captured at https://perma.cc/X9S9-W9US.

14 International Council on Archives, *International Archives Day 2017*, www.youtube.com/watch?v=XGx6UIs3WGs, captured at https://perma.cc/N2RU-YE2F.

15 Society of American Archivists, Committee on Public Awareness, "Crafting Your Elevator Speech," updated December 15, 2017, www2.archivists.org/advocacy/public-awareness/elevator-speech, captured at https://perma.cc/8YG7-YKTT.

16 See Appendix C for a summary of SAA issue briefs and policy and position statements.

17 Larry J. Hackman, "Introduction," in *Many Happy Returns: Advocacy and the Development of Archives*, edited by Larry J. Hackman (Chicago: Society of American Archivists, 2011), vii.

18 "Lobbying," *Merriam-Webster.com,* www.merriam-webster.com/dictionary/lobbying, captured at https://perma.cc/89B2-4ADC.

19 Farlex, "Lobbying," *The Free Dictionary*, http://legal-dictionary.thefreedictionary.com/Lobbying, captured at https://perma.cc/4HTW-YF32.

20 U.S. Internal Revenue Service, "Lobbying," www.irs.gov/charities-non-profits/lobbying, captured at https://perma.cc/MKG9-29HG.

21 U.S. Internal Revenue Service, "'Direct' and 'Grass Roots' Lobbying Defined," www.irs.gov/charities-non-profits/direct-and-grass-roots-lobbying-defined, captured at https://perma.cc/8KNQ-N8P6.

22 Society of American Archivists, "Word of the Week: inreach," *Dictionary of Archives Terminology,* 2014, http://us3.campaign-archive2.com/?u=56c4cfbec1ee5b2a284e7e9d6&id=9cd3d5044d, captured at https://perma.cc/2UHV-AVL6.

23 Sidney J. Levy and Albert G. Robles, *The Image of Archivists: Resource Allocators' Perceptions* (Chicago: Social Research, Inc., 1984), p. iv, https://babel.hathitrust.org/cgi/pt?id=mdp.39015071447299;view=1up;seq=3, captured at https://perma.cc/DD9L-VBNE.

24 Society of American Archivists, Business Archives Section. "Advocating Business Archives Toolkit," www2.archivists.org/groups/business-archives-section/advocating-business-archives-toolkit, captured at https://perma.cc/N867-R363.

25 "Outreach," *A Glossary of Archival and Records Terminology*, 2005, www2.archivists.org/glossary/terms/o/outreach, captured at https://perma.cc/9TU6-QMAB.

26 Society of American Archivists, "Celebrating the American Record with Young People," *American Archives Month Public Relations Kit* (October 2007), http://files.archivists.org/advocacy/AAM/YoungPeople.pdf, captured at https://perma.cc/79HZ-BVME.

27 Simon Sinek, *Start with Why: How Great Leaders Inspire Everyone to Take Action* (New York: Penguin Books. 2009).

28 Laura Cowdrey, "Why do you love to #explorearchives," *Blog,* The National Archives, November 15, 2014, http://blog.nationalarchives.gov.uk/blog/love-explorearchives/.

29 Rob Spindler, "#WhyIAmAnArchivist," *Archival Outlook* (March/April 2015): 13, www.bluetoad.com/publication/?i=251532, captured at https://perma.cc/6FJ4-U5K8.

30 Society of American Archivists, "Call to Action #9: #Archivesin5words," A Year of Living Dangerously for Archives, 2015, www2.archivists.org/living-dangerously/archivesin5words, captured at https://perma.cc/B2WY-AA6M.

31 Laura Millar, (@MillarLaura), Twitter, June 16, 2015, https://twitter.com/search?q=%23archivesin5words.

32 Kelly Stewart, (@kellyannewithe), Twitter, June 16, 2015, https://twitter.com/search?q=%23archivesin5words.

33 James Lowry, (@JamesLowryRAI), Twitter, June 17, 2015, https://twitter.com/search?q=%23archivesin5words.

34 Maureen Callahan, (@meau), Twitter, June 11, 2015, https://twitter.com/search?q=%23archivesin5words.

35 Purdue University Archives, (@PurdueArchives), Twitter, June 11, 2015, https://twitter.com/search?q=%23archivesin5words.

36 Maarja Krusten, (@ArchivesMaarja), Twitter, June 11, 2015. https://twitter.com/search?q=%23archivesin5words.

37 Society of American Archivists, "Word of the Week: value," *Dictionary of Archives Terminology,* 2016, http://us3.campaign-archive1.com/?u=56c4cfbec1ee5b2a284e7e9d6&id=11c3422d1b, captured at https://perma.cc/2VAT-PKZX.

2

# Advocacy and Awareness in the "Real World" of Archives

Archivists have been involved in advocacy and awareness efforts throughout the history of our profession. This chapter does not provide a comprehensive history of those advocacy and awareness efforts but does give examples of the kinds of initiatives and issues undertaken in the past, as well as approaches to them.

Tracing our profession's past advocacy and awareness efforts can be challenging. Although some are reflected in the archival literature, many others take place in real time but are not well documented (if recorded at all). The "backstory" of how change was engineered cannot always be discussed in a public forum. This overview of archival advocacy and awareness draws from existing literature and online resources so that you can pursue specific examples or issues in more depth. In *Many Happy Returns,* Larry J. Hackman calls for the development of case studies to provide best practices and resources for the profession more widely.[1] Although there is a modestly growing literature addressing archival advocacy and awareness, a very real need for those case studies and articles remains.

Such nineteenth-century bibliophiles and historians as Jared Sparks and Peter Force drew attention to the importance of manuscripts and archives by actively collecting colonial and early statehood historical sources and producing documentary editions. Their work ultimately provided the basis for many early historical societies and manuscript collections.[2] The interest in developing a separate, professional focus on archives is evident in the American Historical Association's establishment of a Public Archives Commission (PAC) in 1901. This led to the 1909 Conference of Archivists meeting sponsored by the PAC as part of the American Historical Association. It was the first time a self-identified group of archivists met in the United States. This movement for a professional identity for archivists led to the creation of the Society of American Archivists (SAA) as an independent body.[3]

Since the development of a distinct archives profession, there has been some attention in the literature to a range of advocacy and awareness efforts. Issues and experiences that reflect these past practices and directions include:

- The role of advocacy and awareness in establishing archival institutions ranging from government, business, and institutional archives to archival collections focusing on specific issues or groups;
- Awareness and advocacy drawing attention to the role and value of archives and the archives profession; and
- Legislative and policy advocacy initiatives with which archivists and the archival community have been involved at the regional and national levels.

Whether these efforts have been successful, faced ongoing challenges, or failed to accomplish their purposes, archivists have undertaken a variety of efforts to strengthen and expand the capacity and reach of archives and the profession. These examples illustrate some of the approaches used either implicitly or explicitly to advocate for, and raise awareness about, archives and address the real-world challenges that archivists have faced since the inception of the profession.

## Advocacy and the Creation of Archival Institutions

### Establishing the U.S. National Archives

The effort leading to the creation of the U.S. National Archives is a nearly textbook demonstration of the essential practices necessary for effective and successful advocacy. As early as the 1890s, plans for a national Hall of Records were developed, and a 1903 law authorized the purchase of a site and construction of a building. No real progress was made, however, until J. Franklin Jameson came on the scene and demonstrated incredible personal tenacity, the ability to engage supporters, and the political acumen to navigate the federal bureaucracy.[4] Jameson went to Washington in 1905 as director of the Department of Historical Research at the Carnegie Institution of Washington with the express purpose of carrying out a plan he had developed to ensure the preservation, management, and use of records of the federal government. It took more than 30 years for Jameson to accomplish his goal.

The key to Jameson's success was his focus on engaging influential groups to support his effort. He advocated with scholarly and historical organizations that were opinion leaders and with nationally respected individuals who were willing to advocate strongly with members of Congress on behalf of a national archives. He enlisted groups with national recognition, including such scholarly associations as the American Historical Association, as well as patriotic and veterans groups like the Daughters of the American Revolution and Sons of the American Revolution. He reached out to the state and regional constituencies of members of Congress by gaining the active support of state and regional historical organizations, such as the Wisconsin Historical Society, the Tennessee Historical Society, and the Massachusetts Historical Society, as well as influential individuals like Thomas M. Owen, who had established the Alabama Department of Archives and History.

Jameson made progress in Congress through direct meetings with key members of the House and Senate. He enlisted his influential supporters to meet with their representatives in Congress to press the case for a national archives. To increase awareness, his colleagues also wrote newspaper editorials, published articles in periodicals, and encouraged others to join in this effort. Waldo Gifford Leland attributed Jameson's ultimate success to his prestige as a scholar and his dedication to a goal that would not benefit him directly and personally. In 1934 the National Archives was authorized by law and appropriations were provided for a building. Because this was a decades-long effort, Leland's emphasis on Jameson's "patient and tactful persistence" is particularly apt.[5]

## Establishing the first state archives: The Alabama Department of Archives and History

Alabama was the first state to create an independent government archives that was not part of a state library, secretary of state's office, or state historical society. As with Jameson and the U.S. National Archives, one skilled and motivated individual was the prime mover—in this case, Thomas McAdory Owen.[6]

Owen was motivated by a personal interest in identifying and collecting sources for Alabama history. He failed in his initial effort to get the Alabama legislature to establish a commission that would study and make recommendations on resources for the state's history. Undeterred, Owen then focused on developing a cadre of key leaders in support of his plan. Owen himself was a member of a prominent Alabama family and was married to Marie Bankhead Owen, a member of the powerful Bankhead family.[7]

Despite Owen's ability to draw on strong family connections, he needed to find additional approaches to gain the support necessary to achieve his goal. Owen developed a progression of organizations to undertake the lobbying necessary to create an independent state archives. He first convinced key individuals to rejuvenate the moribund Alabama Historical Society as a potential source for advocacy. He convinced Governor Joseph Forney Johnston to assume the role of president while Owen himself took the role of secretary. He used that position to launch a publicity campaign to raise the visibility of the organization, growing the membership to more than 300 individuals and reaching out—strategically—to encourage many state legislators to join. The Alabama Historical Society then advocated for the creation of the Alabama History Commission as part of state government. The Commission, with Owen as chair, subsequently drafted a bill to create an independent Department of Archives and History with the unique mandated responsibility of preserving and making available state government records.[8] The bill was passed in 1901 after a strong advocacy campaign by the supporters Owen had enlisted. In the next decade, similar independent state archives agencies were created in Mississippi, Arkansas, South Carolina, and North Carolina.

## From eclectic collecting to a college archives: Oberlin College

The development of a formal archives program at Oberlin College followed a general pattern that is evident in other universities and colleges. Like many of those institutions, Oberlin College valued its past but relied on an eclectic Oberliniana collection in its library, with institutional records being kept by the secretary of the college. As with the development of a number of other archives, advocacy by a key motivated individual was critical to addressing that situation. In the 1960s Eileen Thornton—who was, at the time, head of the college library—recognized the need to develop a professionally focused program with appropriately trained staff. She developed a core message, used strategic alliances, appealed to institutional reputation and pride, gained credibility through outside expertise, and took advantage of institutional history to make the college archives a reality.[9]

Thornton developed a message that would resonate with the college's leaders by focusing on the need for strong management of both the college archives and historical records to support scholarship by faculty and students. She cultivated a relationship with and support from the college secretary, who was responsible for administrative records. She also organized an ad hoc committee to define the problems and needs of a college archives—a committee that included history professor Thomas LeDuc, who had written an article on college archives for the *American Archivist* in 1943.

To gain credibility and further demonstrate the importance of a college archives, Thornton brought in an archives expert, Dr. Philip P. Mason from Wayne State University, to conduct an assessment and provide a report and recommendations. Mason's report emphasized the rich resources at Oberlin and appealed to institutional pride by pointing out that hundreds of other colleges and universities had developed strong archives programs since World War II. The final impetus that spurred the college administration to approve the creation of a college archives came with the need to write the definitive institutional history.[10]

## Establishing archives for underrepresented groups and topics

Successful archival advocacy does not rely solely on gaining the support of administrators or individuals with political power. During the past several decades, archives have increasingly addressed the need to ensure that the documentation of underrepresented groups and topics is preserved and made available. Advocating with and involving the communities and individuals whose history is "missing" from the archival record has been key to a number of successful efforts to establish archives with a strong focus on an underrepresented topic or group or, more recently, to work with communities to create and maintain their own archival collections outside of institutional archives programs.

> The unions of America have a large stake in presenting an accurate story of organized labor and the contributions which it has made.
>
> —*Philip P. Mason, 1964*

In the early 1960s, the Labor History Archives was established at Wayne State University to ensure that the voices of organized labor and workers were documented and made available for research. In establishing the Archives, Dr. Philip Mason worked directly with current and former union officers and members to gain from their perspectives and knowledge of union history and records and garner support for the effort. Many organizations have members with a particular interest in their history, and their involvement can be crucial. The Labor History Archives drew on the involvement and expertise of Newman Jeffrey, a former United Auto Workers (UAW) staff representative who had surveyed research institutions in the United States to determine the extent of union records in collections. Mason and Jeffrey also collaborated with the director of the UAW's Education Department, Carroll Hutton, who had important contacts with all of the UAW locals. Hutton reached out to those locals regarding their records, which provided a "legitimacy" and connection with trusted union leadership that gave the Archives staff credibility as they sought to acquire records. It resulted in the acquisition of significant records from the locals as well as private collections of union members.[11]

Raising awareness of an archives' importance to a community that has experienced prejudice and stereotyping benefits from personal communication and support in order to assure that community that the archives program will be respectful and trustworthy. The New York Public Library's Schomburg Center for Research in Black Culture was the first repository to collect materials relating to black gay and lesbian individuals, such as Glenn Carrington and Assotto Saint, as well as groups such as Gay Men of African Descent. Those collections, which were acquired between 1977 and 1998, were substantially expanded into the Black Gay and Lesbian Archive at the Schomburg Center through the focused work of Steven Fullwood. As a member of the Schomburg Center staff who was involved in black gay and lesbian cultural circles and communities, he devoted considerable time and personal connections to building the collection in the early 2000s.

> I was in the right place and time to do this work.
>
> —*Steven G. Fullwood, 2009*

He communicated with a range of people, organizations, and businesses via email and listservs, and he wrote articles for various newsletters and magazines. He connected with people at their community events and organizations, attending dozens of black queer events. Fullwood notes the value of making a direct appeal to individuals, asking them to donate to the archives and taking the time to nurture relationships with a full complement of information specialists, artists, writers, professionals, and community organizers. While those individuals understood the limited representation in libraries and archives historically and the need to address this, personal outreach and direct communication were essential to raising the awareness and confidence of black gay and lesbian community organizations and individuals in donating their materials to a repository.[12]

## Milestones and acquisitions as a motivation for establishing archives programs

Institutional milestones such as anniversaries or the acquisition of a major collection have provided archivists and other key individuals with opportunities to advocate for the establishment of an archives program or raise awareness about and garner increased support for an existing program.

In preparation for its fiftieth anniversary, Nationwide Insurance Companies hired a part-time archivist. That event provided the archivist, Karen Benedict, with the opportunity to advocate with management and other key departments regarding the continuing value of an archives program, leading to the establishment of a corporate archives.[13]

Although Harvard University has a large existing library and archives program, the Archives for Women in Medicine was established in response to a call by the dean of the medical school, Dr. Joseph Martin, for events or special projects to commemorate the start of the new millennium in 2001. Because the involvement of women in Harvard's medical community was very recent, a Joint Committee on the Status of Women collaborated with Harvard's Countway Library Center for the History of Medicine to assess the extent of collections that reflected the role of women. Given the disappointing results—they found that only 20 of 900 faculty collections had been created by women and only one of those had been processed—an advocacy effort was launched to establish the Archives for Women in Medicine as part of the medical school's Countway Library. Advocacy and awareness activities then focused on obtaining both donations of records and funding for the archives.[14]

These historical examples provide useful insights for contemporary archivists. Those interested in either creating archival collections or programs or reawakening interest in existing ones can find useful guidance in methods that have been successful to date. A committed individual who has the energy and vision to pursue the goal, and either has or develops the credibility to do so, is essential. Enlisting outside supporters, whether community members, researchers, or institutional leaders, is also important. Connecting to a need that others can clearly recognize or addressing an issue of concern demonstrates the value of the proposed archives. A final essential component is devoting the time (which may be years) to nurturing relationships, sharing key messages, and convincing key individuals to support the proposed archives program.

## Awareness and the Archives Profession

Archival institutions have traditionally offered a range of outreach activities, including lecture series, exhibits, tours, workshops, brochures, bibliographic instruction, and programs with teachers to raise awareness about the archives' holdings and the work of their staff members. Web pages and digital collections also raise awareness about archival institutions. Social media has expanded outreach tools to include blogs, Facebook pages, Twitter, Instagram, Pinterest, and Flickr. Many of these outreach efforts implicitly raise awareness of archival holdings and institutions, but, for the most part, this does not result from intentional planning and direct goals. This sort of oblique approach to raising awareness has dominated archival outreach for much of the twentieth century. Since the 1980s, many initiatives have been launched to assist and encourage archivists to focus explicitly on raising awareness about archival institutions, archival collections, and the work of archivists and the archives profession generally.

### The SAA Task Force on Archives and Society

In 1983, SAA President Dr. David Gracy II challenged the organization's members and leaders with the following admonition: "The misconception by our publics and by those with the power to allocate resources to our repositories strikes at the heart of our existence and ability to function."[15] With Gracy's energetic urging, the SAA Council created a Task Force on Archives and Society charged with providing tools and guidance to help archivists, institutions, and the archives profession develop skills and tools for raising public awareness, understanding, and support for archival work.

> Archivists are viewed as quiet professionals, carrying out an admired but practically frivolous activity.
>
> Resource allocators respect documents and collections but they view them as objects rather than sources of information. Some resource allocators suggest that promoting the use of archives is not very important.
>
> —*Task Force on Archives and Society, 1985*

The Task Force's work resulted in a range of activities and products that helped guide public awareness initiatives. Of particular impact—and the source of much discussion—was the report by Social Research, Inc. (*The Image of Archivists: Resource Allocators' Perceptions,* commonly called "The Levy Report" after primary author Sidney Levy). The assessment provided sobering information on the perception of archivists and the archival function.[16] It was presented at the Society of American Archivists' Annual Meeting plenary and followed by sessions for commentary and discussion by members. The report also served as a key resource for subsequent plans developed by the Task Force.

The Task Force's work led to the creation of a Committee on Public Information, which, during its tenure, created or initiated various public awareness tools and activities:[17]

- Brochures for use by archivists: "Who Is the 'I' in Archives" and "Archives: What They Are, Why They Matter"
- A workshop on marketing aimed at archivists
- Program sessions for annual meetings focusing on public awareness and marketing
- Establishment of the J. Franklin Jameson Advocacy Award[18]
- Encouragement for the development of a manual by Elsie Freeman Finch, *Advocating Archives: An Introduction to Public Relations for Archivists* (1994)

The Committee on Public Information was discontinued in 1998 as part of a larger reorganization of SAA committees recommended by the Committee on Goals and Priorities and the Task Force on Organizational Effectiveness.[19] In 2014, however, SAA returned its attention to public information when it created the Committee on Public Awareness (COPA). COPA is responsible for providing advice on opportunities for developing initiatives to raise awareness about the value of archives and archivists as well as undertaking initiatives on behalf of SAA. Its *ArchivesAWARE!* blog provides ideas and information to stimulate action among the archival community.[20] In addition, COPA has sponsored #AskAnArchivist Day on Twitter as part of American Archives Month.[21] Its website continues to provide resources and initiatives to encourage and inform the profession on awareness opportunities.

## American Archives Month

In October 1989 the Archivists Roundtable of Metropolitan New York held the first Archives Week, an approach to raising awareness that has had a long-term impact on archival awareness. The Roundtable sponsored a collaborative effort, Family Heritage Day, providing the public with information on understanding and preserving family photographs, letters, and other documents and memorabilia. Individual institutions throughout the city offered exhibits, lectures, tours, and panel discussions aimed at broadening public awareness.[22] The idea caught on rapidly throughout New York State and other geographical regions, expanding from one week to a full month of public awareness activities. In 2006, SAA began active promotion of American Archives Month, providing an American Archives Month Kit with materials to assist with planning, tips on media relations, and ideas for activities, especially for working with young people and examples from other repositories.[23]

A wide range of collaborative and individual institutional activities have been conducted in the years since the inception of Archives Week/Month, including the following:

- SAA has sponsored such initiatives as "I Found It In The Archives," which asked users to tell the stories of their discoveries while researching in an archives, and #AskAnArchivist Day, a Twitter chat in which archivists and repositories make themselves available and encourage people to ask questions about archives and get answers from archivists.[24]
- An "archives bazaar" or "archives fair" is held in a number of cities and states—including Austin, Houston, Los Angeles, Sacramento, Oregon, and Vermont—with dozens of local archives participating to draw attention to their collections and services and promote the diverse cultural heritage resources available to the public in their area.
- The Rochester Museum and Science Center in New York State sponsored "Rochester's Unknown Ones," an original theater piece based on archival primary sources. It focused on telling the stories of the active African American community that Frederick Douglass found when he moved to Rochester, New York, in 1847.[25]
- In 2015 the University of Maryland Libraries raised awareness about its new Filipino American Community Archives by holding the first Istorya-DC Symposium.[26]
- The National Archives has pursued a wide variety of activities over the years, including a free virtual Genealogy Fair, blog posts on the presidential libraries, and a collaboration with the Academy of American Poets to create original poems inspired by records held in the Archives.[27]

In the nearly three decades since its inception, American Archives Month has become a staple of public awareness efforts in the archives community. There is periodic discussion of coordinating efforts around a "theme," but to date that has functioned best at a regional or state level. No one single organization has served as a national coordinator. Instead, individual institutions, regional or state groups, and various professional organizations have developed approaches to address particular needs or goals for public awareness.

## Collaborating with national awareness campaigns

Archival institutions and professional organizations have also collaborated with a number of national awareness campaigns that focus on issues relating to archives. In 2005 the American Library Association, the Library of Congress, and the Institute of Museum and Library Services launched Preservation Week, a national effort to raise public awareness about collecting and preservation. SAA was an early supporter, along with Heritage Preservation and the American Institute for Conservation of Historic and Artistic Works.[28] For more than a decade, the archives community has focused on pursuing activities on May 1 ("May Day") to encourage "doing something, even if it's something simple—to save our archives" from both natural and human-created disasters.[29]

Archivists and archival organizations have also become involved in Sunshine Week, an initiative of the American Society of News Editors and the Reporters Committee for Freedom of the Press.[30] Since 2005, government records repositories and professional organizations have used this opportunity to raise awareness about issues relating to transparency and access to records. The Council of State Archivists (CoSA) has participated by posting on social media during Sunshine

Week to draw attention to electronic records issues.[31] For a number of years, the National Archives has hosted lectures and programs that focus on Freedom of Information and access issues.[32]

Many archival institutions regularly take advantage of nationally designated recognition months (such as Black History Month, Women's History Month, and Hispanic Heritage Month) to raise awareness. Archivists frequently use social media sites—Twitter and Facebook, in particular—as well as online exhibits to share information focusing on individual collections or institutional holdings.

National awareness days and months provide archivists with general awareness opportunities, but the profession and individual institutions may benefit from focusing on them as routes to collaboration and communication with new audiences. The effectiveness of these efforts might be increased by collaborating with individuals or groups connected to the issues/topics of focus to either improve documentation of underrepresented groups or issues or to raise the awareness of those who might use information held by archives. For example, Mental Health Awareness Month provides an opportunity to connect with a range of mental health support organizations providing services to individuals and families as well as consumer/ex-patient/survivor groups, most of which are poorly documented in the archival record at this time. Public policy researchers on mental health issues could benefit from connecting with archival organizations that hold records relating to previous research work undertaken in universities, medical institutions, and government. These national day/month recognitions provide an entrée for pursuing deeper advocacy and awareness with more communities and issues.

## Legislative and Policy Advocacy for Archives and History

Since the emergence of the archives profession in the early 1900s, archivists, archival institutions, and professional archival organizations have repeatedly been involved in a range of legislative and policy advocacy initiatives. As the literature reflects, the archives community has focused its professional attention on issues of theory, archival functions, and practical implementation. On occasion, situations, events, and issues have propelled the community to advocate for action relating to legislation or policy. Many efforts have involved issues at the national level and have required focused efforts to undertake a purposeful advocacy campaign to achieve specific changes or to speak against issues that were deemed harmful to archives and the profession.

The establishment of a U.S. National Archives involved years of sustained advocacy efforts. Since then, continued situations and challenges at the national level have resulted in collaborative advocacy, including the fight for the National Archives to be an independent agency and efforts to address the appointment of the Archivist of the United States. Both individual archivists and their professional organizations have undertaken considerable advocacy efforts regarding such issues as federal funding for archives, fair use and copyright, privacy, access and freedom of information, management of electronic records, and presidential records.

> Development of an advocacy program takes patience, perseverance, and resources. Successful lobbying is seldom ad hoc or short term.
>
> *—Page Putnam Miller, 1988*

The three national archival organizations—the Society of American Archivists, the Council of State Archivists,[33] and the National Association of Government Archives and Records Administrators—have taken roles in national and, as appropriate, regional advocacy at varying levels based on their organizational mission and membership. CoSA and SAA, as well as a number of regionals, became members of the National Coalition for History to advocate with the federal government and Congress in collaboration with more than fifty other history, museum, and cultural organizations.[34] Although archivists and professional organizations have periodically focused on legislative and public policy advocacy, their efforts have not had the emphasis or resources for embedded advocacy that sister professional organizations, such as the American Library Association and the American Alliance of Museums, have developed.[35]

Much of the discussion that follows focuses on national issues, largely because they have involved a wide range of archivists and organizations and are better documented in terms of approaches to advocacy. It is important to note that state and local organizations and archival institutions have taken on critical leadership in state- and community-based issues and supported national efforts. The literature on advocacy efforts at the national, regional, and local level is sparse and typically describes a current effort. Summary or evaluative discussion of archival efforts remains fairly limited; there is a very real need for these efforts to be documented and shared through the professional literature.

## The National Archives' independence efforts

When established in 1934, the U.S. National Archives was an independent agency. In 1949, it was placed under the General Services Administration (GSA), was renamed the National Archives and Records Services (NARS), and was given additional responsibility for records management. The GSA is essentially a "housekeeping" agency focused on efficiencies and processes of government operations. Its leadership did not understand or support the cultural mission of preserving the nation's documentary heritage. Concern escalated in the archives community that GSA management failed to recognize not only budgetary and personnel needs for archives and records management but the need for expert commentary/involvement with legislation affecting records, such as the Privacy Act.[36] For many years, issues and concerns about the politicization of the Archives by the GSA prompted ongoing calls for return of the National Archives to independent status.[37]

In 1980, Robert M. Warner was appointed Archivist of the United States by President Jimmy Carter. Dr. Warner had a strong reputation in the archives community for his leadership of the Bentley Historical Library at the University of Michigan, his extensive professional involvement in SAA (as a Fellow, President, and Executive Secretary), and as an author on archives topics. He assumed the role with a firm knowledge of the need to address the issue of returning the National Archives to independent status.[38] His appointment was critical to accomplishing this change because he had both professional knowledge of the needs and functions of an archival institution and considerable diplomatic and advocacy skills to carry out the necessary actions and enlist effective supporters.

As the Archivist of the United States, Warner could not lead the independence movement directly. Nonetheless, he took an active role in encouraging and coordinating the effort. An internal "secret committee" met to discuss strategy on how to influence Congress and how to enlist and coordinate with supporting organizations.[39] This guidance was essential to providing supporters with accurate information about the federal government rules and practices that they needed to work with (or around!) to be effective and to ensure a coordinated message. Supporters included the National Coordinating Committee for the Promotion of History, the American Historical Association, the Society of American Archivists, the National Association of Government Archives and Records Administrators, the American Library Association, the National Genealogical Association, and the National Coalition to Save Our Documentary Heritage. Substantial efforts by those groups resulted in enlisting influential members of the Senate and House to sponsor legislation, including Senators Mark Hatfield (R-OR), Charles Mathias (R-MD), and Thomas Eagleton (D-MO) and Representatives Jack Brooks (D-TX), Frank Horton (D-NY), and Glenn English (D-OK).[40] That legislation, Public Law 98-497, was passed by Congress and signed by President Ronald Reagan in October 1984, bringing to fruition a decade-long effort.[41] The National Archives then became known as the National Archives and Records Administration (NARA).

As with the initial founding of the National Archives, it was necessary to conduct a concerted campaign over time, and the success of this advocacy effort could be attributed to a number of factors. The internal guidance from NARA was critical to developing a focused message on why independence was essential, as well as for clarifying the bureaucratic processes that needed to be addressed. In addition, advocacy was focused on key congressional members of both political parties who became "champions" for NARA independence. The effort also enlisted the involvement of key professional organizations of both users (historians and genealogists) and information and history professionals. Advocacy was undertaken by recognized, "name" individuals and supplemented by large numbers of contacts from constituents. Finally, the campaign for NARA independence was sustained consistently for a number of years until sufficient support and pressure yielded the needed result.

## Advocacy on the appointment of the Archivist of the United States

Following the passage of legislation granting NARA's independence, Dr. Warner announced his resignation and return to the University of Michigan.[42] One of the key components of the NARA legislation was the proviso that the U.S. Archivist be a nonpartisan professional, making it one of only two senior presidential appointments with such a requirement. In the years since the passage of that law, the archives community has been involved in a number of advocacy efforts when those nominated for appointment did not have that critically important qualification.

Following Dr. Warner's resignation, John Agresto, who was then acting chair of the National Endowment for the Humanities, was nominated for the position of Archivist of the United States. This raised a furor among archives and history professional organizations because of his lack of qualifications and the presidential administration's failure to consult with these interested groups on the selection. They also asserted that the nomination of an individual with no archival credentials as the first to head the newly independent agency set a bad precedent.[43]

The Society of American Archivists joined the American Historical Association, the American Association for State and Local History, the National Council on Public History, the Federation of Genealogical Societies, and others in opposition. The SAA leadership passed resolutions on both the specific nomination of Agresto and the selection process.[44] Pressure on this nomination continued for many months. Advocates visited key members of Congress and provided testimony at congressional hearings. Editorials questioning the appointment appeared in the press, including the *Washington Post*, the *New York Times,* and the *Boston Globe*.[45] Archivists and historians suggested several alternate names, including Don W. Wilson, the director of the Gerald R. Ford Presidential Library and Museum. Ultimately, Agresto withdrew his name from nomination and, months later, President Reagan nominated Wilson as Archivist of the United States. The organizations that had advocated for a professional archivist appointment supported the nomination, and Wilson assumed the role.[46] Wilson's nomination was a productive result of collaborative advocacy involving both vocal opponents and an effective presence in the mainstream press.

Despite this initial victory, challenges have continued in subsequent nominations for the Archivist of the United States. After Wilson's resignation in 1993, no action was taken on a nomination until 1995. At that time, the presidential administration floated the names of three nominees, and SAA representatives met with each of them. Two—Nicholas Burckel, associate dean at Washington University Libraries and a past president of SAA, and Raymond Smock, Historian of the U.S. House of Representatives—were approved by SAA.[47] The third, former Kansas governor John W. Carlin, was not supported. SAA, the American Historical Association, several regional archival associations, and other history and genealogy organizations again advocated with the White House and Congress on the need to appoint an Archivist with professional qualifications. Nonetheless, the Clinton administration forwarded the nomination of John Carlin. SAA testified at Senate hearings, and a range of editorials and newspaper articles opposing the nomination appeared in print and on radio.[48] Despite strong opposition by professional organizations, the Carlin nomination was approved. Subsequently, SAA invited Carlin to join the association and attend annual meetings, which he did. Maygene Daniels, who was SAA president at the time, noted that, while unsuccessful in blocking the appointment, SAA gained considerable experience in this extensive foray into advocacy at the federal level.[49]

In 2004 issues regarding the nomination for Archivist of the United States emerged again. The George W. Bush administration nominated Professor Allen Weinstein for the position without holding public hearings or seeking professional review of his qualifications. Sixteen national and regional organizations from the archives, library, and history communities prepared a public statement objecting to the nonconsultative process. This coalition included the groups that had advocated regarding previous appointments (e.g., Society of American Archivists, the American Historical Association, the Organization of American Historians, the American Library Association, and the American Association of State and Local History) but also drew in many new voices, including the American Association for Law Libraries, the Association of American University Presses, and a range of state and regional archival organizations.[50] The opposing groups called for open hearings and raised objections to the nomination process, as it had provided no opportunity to meet with interested parties as in the past. Further, the groups stressed that the candidate did not meet the qualifications stated in the National Archives law.[51] Again, despite concerted advocacy efforts, Dr. Weinstein was confirmed in February 2005.[52]

With the 2008 resignation of Allen Weinstein, the archives, history, genealogy, and library communities again faced the issue of who might be selected and how. The Obama transition staff met with representatives of national archives and related organizations to seek input on candidates and qualifications for the Archivist position.[53] A collaborative statement, "Qualities of a Successful Candidate," was developed by SAA, CoSA, the National Association of Government Archives & Records Administrators (NAGARA), the Academy of Certified Archivists, ARMA International, and the National Coalition for History.[54] The collaborative group also submitted testimony to the House Committee on Oversight and Government Reform's Subcommittee on U.S. Census, Information Policy, and the National Archives for its hearing on challenges faced by a new Archivist of the United States.[55] President Obama subsequently nominated David Ferriero, who at the time was director of the New York Public Libraries. After the initial consultation on qualifications, however, no opportunity was provided for constituent groups to interview the candidate. As a result, SAA chose to take no position on the nomination.[56] Ferriero was confirmed in 2009.

Although SAA, other archives organizations, and related information and user-oriented organizations have striven to speak out on the position of Archivist of the United States, recent appointments have proceeded with or without professional support. The position is a presidential appointment, and the archives community rarely has a "seat" at the table with presidential transition teams or appointment processes. It is similarly rare that the archives community, or even its leading members, are consulted regarding qualifications or suggestions for potential appointments. Most often, the archives community finds itself in a position of reacting to the announcement of a potential appointee; having to mount a campaign against an already named individual is extremely difficult. Monitoring current developments and challenges to institutions such as the National Archives as well as key institutions at the state and regional levels is an essential task that archivists and their professional organizations need to pursue as a regular responsibility for timely statements and advocacy to be effective. SAA's Council, along with the Committee on Public Policy and several component groups such as the Issues and Advocacy Section, have been striving to do this in a more organized fashion.[57]

## Advocating for federal funding

*NHPRC.* With creation of the National Archives in 1934, the National Historical Publications Commission was established to make recommendations on the publication of the nation's documentary record. It did so, focusing on the publication of documentary editions of the Founding Fathers' writings, but until 1964 it did not receive funding to award grants. In 1974, its scope was expanded to include grants for records and archives projects, and its name was changed to the National Historical Publications and Records Commission (NHPRC).[58]

Funding of $10 million was authorized for the NHPRC for documentary editions and records/archives projects. Although that is a modest amount, especially in comparison to funding for libraries and museums awarded through the Institute of Museum and Library Services, it was appropriated annually for many years. In 2001, President George W. Bush's budget proposal included substantial cuts to the NHPRC, and that pattern has continued frequently in subsequent years.[59] The archives community has been involved in regular efforts directed at Congress to advocate for the restoration of funding to the NHPRC as the House and Senate respond to the president's proposed budget.[60] Advocacy with the relevant House and Senate committees and key leaders has resulted in restoration of funding every year (to date).

This has served as an opportunity for archivists, particularly through SAA, CoSA, NAGARA, and regional archives associations, to develop advocacy capacity in the organizations themselves and among their individual members. One element that has strengthened advocacy is building collaborative relationships with the National Coordinating Committee for the Promotion of History/National Coalition for History, the Association of Documentary Editors, the American Historical Association, and other history and genealogy groups. Archivists and their professional organizations have become more adept at undertaking grassroots campaigns of letters and visits with members of Congress. The regularity of proposed cuts has resulted in development of resources for ongoing advocacy efforts to ensure rapid response when and if cuts or elimination of the NHPRC are again proposed.[61]

*Preserving the American Historical Record Act.* Recognizing the limitations of funding available through the NHPRC even when fully funded, in 2006, CoSA, SAA, and NAGARA agreed to expand their work beyond funding for the NHPRC to seek introduction of a bill, dubbed the "Preserving the American Historical Record Act," to authorize $50 million in funding to be distributed by formula to states for re-granting to institutions within each state for historical records projects.[62] Launched in 2009, this action introduced archives organizations to an expanded scope of federal advocacy work. It involved gaining support from key members of the House and Senate to develop and introduce a bill, obtaining additional sponsors in Congress and endorsements from related professional organizations, and conducting a multi-year advocacy campaign.[63]

With the deepening fiscal crisis at that time, the congressional sponsors recommended suspending the effort after 2010. As with other advocacy efforts, despite lack of success, the bill effort did provide a "training ground" for archivists to gain experience with federal legislation, learn more about the intricacies of advocacy, establish connections with members of Congress and their staffs, and gain perspectives that are useful for future advocacy efforts.

## Advocacy on national policy issues

Congress passed the Presidential Records Act of 1978 (PRA) to prevent former President Richard Nixon from destroying, selling, or taking a large tax break for donation of his presidential records. The act applied to all presidents taking office after 1981. By tradition, presidents previously were believed to "own" their presidential records and thus could make decisions on their disposition and access. Although the PRA was supported by archives, history, and library organizations, the Watergate scandal was the major force behind its passage. Weaknesses and loopholes in the law led to issues related to its execution by subsequent presidential administrations.[64]

In 2001 George W. Bush signed Executive Order 13233, which overrode portions of the PRA that allowed the Archivist of the United States to release presidential and vice-presidential records 5 years after the end of an administration, with the option that the president could extend that an additional 7 years (i.e., a total of 12 years) for sensitive materials, except for classified records. Instead, this executive order permitted presidents to veto release of their own presidential documents for even more than 12 years after their administrations had ended. Further, it asserted that vice-presidential privilege should allow for similar control over the release of records created by that office. It also gave designated representatives or family members the right to make these decisions on behalf of the president or vice president.[65]

A lawsuit was filed by Public Citizen on behalf of the Organization of American Historians, the American Historical Association, the National Security Archive, and the Reporters Committee for Freedom of the Press.[66] The archives community followed the filings and counter-filings over the subsequent 6 years, and SAA issued action alerts at key points to urge opposition to the Executive Order.[67] Ultimately a federal district court judge struck down the section of EO 13233 that permitted the former president and vice president to indefinitely delay the release of records. However, the constitutionality of the Executive Order was not ruled on, nor did the court address the legality of allowing heirs or designees to control release of records.[68]

## Continuing national advocacy challenges

During the past three decades, the archives community has increased its efforts to advocate on the national level in regard to presidential appointments for the Archivist of the United States, for federal funding, and on a range of policy issues. Recently, the national archival organizations have collaborated to both advocate on these issues and to develop a cadre of experienced archivists that can make visits and interact directly with members of Congress. The first "Archives on the Hill" day was coordinated by the Society of American Archivists, the Council of State Archivists, the National Association for Government Archives and Records Administrators, and the Regional Archival Association Consortium during their joint annual meeting in Washington, D.C., in 2018.[69] Teams of more than seventy archivists were assembled to meet with nearly fifty members of Congress or their staff members on key committees. A coordinating team provided basic information on conducting meetings and conveying the message on archival concerns relating to federal funding and electronic records management. Information packets were also created on those issues for dissemination at the meetings. Following the event, resources were further refined to support future advocacy efforts.[70]

While encouraging efforts to expand capacity are underway, it has been—and remains—challenging. The profession does not have a consistent, ongoing base of support ("champions") in Congress or the White House who consider it either valuable or essential to consult with the archival community on key appointments, issues, legislation, or funding. If archivists believe that this must change, they (as individuals) and their professional organizations will have to invest in assessing options; reviewing the successes, challenges, and approaches used by sister professions; determining a multi-year approach; and committing finances and staff and volunteer time to advancing a national agenda for archives. Although progress has been made in addressing needs and issues at the federal level, considerable work remains to be done to develop the infrastructure and increase the involvement of the archives community.

## State and institutional advocacy efforts

Although efforts at the national level are more frequently documented in the archival literature, there have been significant advocacy issues at the state, regional, and institutional levels. Particularly in times of fiscal constraint, archival repositories face closure or crippling reductions in funding. In other cases, advocacy has taken place to ensure that essential records not only survive but are appropriately accessible to the public for research and use. The following examples demonstrate some of the situations that have developed and the approaches that have been used to address the issues.

- *Saving the Philadelphia Savings Fund Society's archival collection.* In 1993, when the Philadelphia Savings Fund Society (PSFS) went into receivership, Philadelphia-area archivists were concerned about the fate of the Society's historically important records dating to 1816. Recognizing that these collections were not likely to be given much consideration, archivists in the Philadelphia area organized to ensure that the holdings would be preserved as a collection and not be sold off as the PSFS assets were liquidated. They launched an effort to advocate directly with the Federal Deposit Insurance Corporation, which was appointed as the receiver. Archivists and researchers wrote letters and sought support from such national groups as SAA. A well-orchestrated information campaign helped draw attention to the archival collections, and they were ultimately donated to the Hagley Museum and Library.[71]

- *Speaking Out for the Center for Black Music Research, Columbia College of Chicago.* Bringing national attention to an archival issue can be an effective advocacy approach, particularly when the effort involves both researchers and professional archivists. In February 2012, as part of efforts to respond to fiscal problems, Columbia College's Office of Provost/Academic Affairs approved plans to eliminate the Center for Black Music Research. The CBMR is recognized as a significant collection of archival, rare, and special materials, including sheet music, sound recordings of jazz pioneers, and unpublished works of Negro spirituals arranged for instrumental and choral ensembles. Calls for action emerged from the research community as well as the press.[72] On learning of the impending action, the SAA Archivists and Archives of Color Roundtable developed a letter template for members to send to Columbia College and created a Change.org petition against the closing. The widespread concern led to a rethinking of the Center's administrative structure and relationships, but ultimately the decision was reversed and the collection survived.[73]
- *Keeping Public Records Public: NYC Mayoral Records.* At the end of his administration, Mayor Rudolph Giuliani did not transfer his mayoral records to the New York City Department of Records and Information Services, as previous mayors had. Instead, his mayoral records were moved out of city custody to the oversight of the Rudolph W. Giuliani Center for Urban Affairs and stored in a private warehouse. Members of the Archivists Roundtable of Metropolitan New York, along with leading historians from the Gotham Center and lawyers, called attention to this issue with a press conference, news articles, petitions, grassroots letter-writing, and threat of legal action.[74] In response, Giuliani and his staff claimed that he was having "private archivists" process the records without influence from him or his advisers. After considerable pressure and attention, Giuliani's mayoral records ultimately were returned to the Department of Records and Information Services after processing by a private consulting organization.[75]
- *Forming a Coalition to Advocate for the Georgia Archives.* The Georgia Archives, which reported to the secretary of state, had experienced a number of years of devastating budget cuts and staff reductions during fiscally challenging times.[76] The Coalition to Save the Georgia Archives formed to advocate for restoration of funding and draw attention to the value of that institution. In September 2012, when Georgia Secretary of State Brian Kemp announced that the Georgia Archives would be closed to the public, a group of advocates was ready to take immediate action. The Coalition included the Society of Georgia Archivists, Friends of Georgia Archives and History, the Georgia Genealogical Society, and the Georgia Historical Records Advisory Board, among others. The group circulated information via social media accounts on Facebook and Twitter and created an online petition. Fortunately, Archives Month (October) was approaching, and the Georgia governor traditionally had signed a proclamation about the Month with archivists from the state in attendance. Leaders of the

Coalition attending the ceremony with Governor Nathan Deal brought with them a printed copy of the petition—which had more than 10,000 signatures in the first week—as well as copies of hundreds of supportive letters to share with him. A rally in support of keeping the Georgia Archives open was held at the State Capitol and was attended by more than 300 individuals, including archivists, historians and genealogists, concerned citizens, and local officials, such as the mayor of Morrow, Georgia, where the Archives is located.[77]

The group also launched a broad and carefully orchestrated advocacy campaign. They raised funds to hire a government affairs consulting group, Joe Tanner and Associates, to provide advice and training on their effort. They developed an impressive set of PowerPoint™ slides addressing the legal, fiscal, and research value of the Georgia Archives holdings.[78] The issue received press coverage in the *Atlanta Journal-Constitution* and regional newspapers, as well as in such national newspapers as the *New York Times.* The group also orchestrated a grassroots effort entailing meetings with and letters to state legislators to press their case. The extensive campaign led Governor Deal to transfer the Georgia Archives from the Secretary of State's Office to the University System of Georgia's Board of Regents, where the function of creating research resources and working with users is better understood. He further empaneled a working group that included representatives of archival organizations to advise on the transfer.[79] This initiative is among the most effectively conducted archival advocacy campaigns, and, fortunately, its thorough documentation in a special issue of *Provenance, Journal of the Society of Georgia Archivists* provides a blueprint for future efforts.[80]

## Archival advocacy and awareness: What does our past tell us?

As noted throughout this chapter, the archival literature on advocacy and awareness initiatives is not extensive. In some cases, it may have seemed to be unwise or impolitic to relay the very real details of how advocacy or awareness efforts were carried out. In others, chronicling the steps and roles may have been seen as unproductive once the work was done. Nonetheless, the stories of various efforts can provide insights on approaches used and elements that have been productive or that have posed serious challenges.

It is important to note that the advocacy efforts described here were often reactive. They may have been a response to an immediate issue or critical conditions or may have sought to change a longer-term situation viewed as negative. These have ranged from the need to establish an archives to saving archival records of an institution, restoring or obtaining critical funding, or addressing a challenge to preservation or access. Efforts to raise awareness about archives and archivists are considerably fewer at the national or collaborative level, except for American Archives Month. Although one often hears archivists express concern about the lack of appreciation for the work of archivists and the archives profession, an often myopic focus on individual archival institutional processes and practices has too often taken precedence. Giving attention to advocacy and awareness remains an important need for archives, archivists, and archival organizations.

In reviewing the available information from past efforts, the common characteristics of the more successful ones suggest the importance of the following elements:

- A key individual or group who initiates or leads the effort and remains engaged for whatever period of time needed;
- A clearly defined purpose that conveys a compelling message;
- Key and influential individuals who will take action as well as mobilizing individuals to speak up in support;
- Collaboration with allied institutions in the library, historical and genealogical communities, and developing coalitions that cross disciplinary boundaries;
- Flexibility to change approaches to meet situations or conditions, or to involve individuals whose support is essential; and
- Relentless focus and dedication to "staying the course" for what may be many years of advocacy and/or awareness activity.

Advocacy and awareness have not traditionally been part of archival education and training or included among the expected competencies for archivists. Efforts to date demonstrate a range of situations in which those skills are essential to individual archivists, archival institutions, and the archives profession. The remaining chapters of this volume provide information gained from past initiatives in archives as well as insights from other professions and efforts to help highlight approaches, best practices, and skills that the archives community needs to become more adept and successful in advocacy and awareness efforts.

## NOTES

1 Larry J. Hackman, ed., *Many Happy Returns: Advocacy and the Development of Archives* (Chicago: Society of American Archivists, 2011).

2 George H. Callcott, "Antiquarianism and Documents in the Age of Literary History," *American Archivist* 21 (January 1958): 17–29.

3 Peter J. Wosh, Richard Cox, Charles J. Dollar, and Rebecca Hirsch, "Founding Brothers: Leland, Buck, and Cappon and the Formation of the Archives Profession," *American Archivist* 74 (January 2011): 1–27.

4 Fred Shelley, "The Interest of J. Franklin Jameson in the National Archives: 1908–1934," *American Archivist* 12 (April 1949): 99–130.

5 Waldo Gifford Leland, "John Franklin Jameson," *American Archivist* 19 (July 1956): 195–201.

6 Alden Monroe, "Thomas Owen and the Founding of the Alabama Department of Archives and History," *Provenance, Journal of the Society of Georgia Archivists* 21 (2003): 22–35.

7 Marie Bankhead Owen was the daughter of Senator John H. Bankhead and the sister of U.S. Senator John H. Bankhead II and Representative William B. Bankhead, who was later Speaker of the House of Representatives.

8 Monroe, "Thomas Owen."

9 Roland L. Baumann, "Oberlin College and the Movement to Establish an Archives 1920–1966," *Midwestern Archivist* 13, no. 1 (1988): 27–38.

10 Baumann, "Oberlin College."

11 Philip P. Mason, "Preserving Labor's History," *American Federationist* 71 (January 1964).

12 Steven G. Fullwood, "Always Queer, Always Here: Creating the Black Gay and Lesbian Archive in the Schomburg Center for Research in Black Culture," in *Community Archives: The Shaping of Memory*, ed. Jeannette Bastain and Ben Alexander (London: Facet Publishing, 2009), 235–249.

13 Elizabeth W. Adkins and Karen Benedict, "Archival Advocacy: Institutional Archives in Corporations," in Hackman, *Many Happy Returns,* 45–66.

14 Giordana Mecagni, "Starting the Archives for Women in Medicine: Advocacy in Creation, Survival—and Beyond?," in Hackman, *Many Happy Returns,* 200–214.

15 Gracy, "Archives and Society," 8.

16 Levy and Robles, *The Image of Archivists.*

17 James Fogerty, "Committee on Public Information Dispels Myths," *SAA Newsletter*, July 1989: 4–5.

18 Donn C. Neal, "From the Executive Director's Desk," *SAA Newsletter*, July 1989: 3.

19 Society of American Archivists Task Force on Organizational Effectiveness, "Final Report to Council," 1997, www2.archivists.org/governance/taskforces/reports/tfoe, captured at https://perma.cc/WE87-9J82.

20 Nick Pavlik, ed., *ArchivesAWARE!* (blog), Society of American Archivists, Committee on Public Awareness, https://archivesaware.archivists.org/, captured at https://perma.cc/JBZ9-LK6D.

21 Society of American Archivists, Committee on Public Awareness, "#AskAnArchivist Day," updated September 12, 2018, www2.archivists.org/initiatives/askanarchivist-day, captured at https://perma.cc/Q8WF-HMGT.

22 "Archivists Declare a Week for Peering into the Past," *New York Times,* October 4, 1990, www.nytimes.com/1990/10/04/garden/archivists-declare-a-week-for-peering-into-the-past.html, captured at https://perma.cc/N33M-D48K.

23 Society of American Archivists, "American Archives Month: The Power of Collaboration," www2.archivists.org/initiatives/american-archives-month-the-power-of-collaboration, captured at https://perma.cc/4A62-CPGX.

24 Society of American Archivists, "I Found It In the Archives!," October 2012, www2.archivists.org/initiatives/i-found-it-in-the-archives, captured at https://perma.cc/AR2H-T7MQ; Society of American Archivists, Committee on Public Awareness, "#AskAnArchivist Day."

25 Society of American Archivists, "American Archives Month 2010," www2.archivists.org/initiatives/american-archives-month-the-power-of-collaboration/american-archives-month-2010, captured at https://perma.cc/BUV5-SJ7M.

26 The Tagalog word for *story* is *istorya*. An annual symposium is co-sponsored by the Rita M. Cacas Foundation, Inc. (RMCF), and the Filipino Cultural Association (FCA). Society of American Archivists, "American Archives Month 2015," www2.archivists.org/initiatives/american-archives-month-the-power-of-collaboration/american-archives-month-2015, captured at https://perma.cc/Z7WC-GKLE.

27 U.S. National Archives, "National Archives Virtual Genealogy Fair 2018," www.archives.gov/calendar/genealogy-fair, captured at https://perma.cc/8CYA-NGVW.

28 American Library Association, "Preservation Week," www.ala.org/alcts/preservationweek/sponsors, captured at https://perma.cc/NJC7-DTG4.

29 Society of American Archivists, "Preservation Week: Saving Heritage and Memories," updated April 26, 2016, www2.archivists.org/initiatives/mayday-saving-our-archives/preservation-week-saving-heritage-and-memories, captured at https://perma.cc/8V7T-8DBP.

30 American Society of News Editors, "Sunshine Week," 2018, http://sunshineweek.rcfp.org/, captured at https://perma.cc/D2L9-J7PH.

31 Council of State Archivists, "Advocacy," www.statearchivists.org/programs/advocacy/, captured at https://perma.cc/2RRX-BCDV.

32 U.S. National Archives, Office of Government Information Services, "Sunshine Week," www.archives.gov/ogis/outreach-events/sunshine-week, captured at https://perma.cc/69RZ-RF6U.

33 The Council of State Archivists initially operated as the Council of State Historical Records Coordinators.

34 "National Coalition for History Launched," *Archival Outlook* (January 24, 2003). The National Coalition for History was established in 1982 as the National Coordinating Committee for the Promotion of History, a nonprofit organization that advocated on behalf of the history community. Archives and archival records were recognized early as an essential issue for NCCPH/NCH advocacy.

35 American Library Association, "Advocacy, Legislation & Issues," www.ala.org/advocacy/, captured at https://perma.cc/2NYJ-DL5G; American Alliance of Museums, "Advocacy Resources," http://aam-us.org/programs/advocacy/advocacy-resources, captured at https://perma.cc/9PSB-2WLX.

36 Walter Robertson Jr., "NARS: The Politics of Placement," *American Archivist* 39 (October 1976): 485–492.

37 Kaitlin Errickson, "An Independent National Archives," *Pieces of History* (blog), U.S. National Archives, March 29, 2016, https://prologue.blogs.archives.gov/2016/03/29/an-independent-national-archives/, captured at https://perma.cc/P4AN-LCGJ.

38 Society of American Archivists, "Robert M. Warner Named Archivist of the U.S.," *SAA Newsletter,* July 1980: 1.

39 Robert M. Warner, "Secrecy and Salesmanship in the Struggle for NARA's Independence," *Prologue* 37, no. 1 (Spring 2005), www.archives.gov/publications/prologue/2005/spring/archivist-warner.html, captured at https://perma.cc/499S-ZTXC.

40 Society of American Archivists, "National Archives Independence a Reality at Last," *SAA Newsletter,* November 1984: 1.

41 Dr. Warner maintained a diary during this effort and later published a detailed account that provides considerable insight into the federal legislative process and advocacy. See Robert M. Warner, *Diary of a Dream: A History of the National Archives Independence Movement, 1980–1985* (Metuchen, NJ: Scarecrow Press, 1995).

42 Society of American Archivists, "National Archives."

43 Society of American Archivists, "U.S. Archivist Nominated," *SAA Newsletter* (March 1986): 1.

44 Society of American Archivists, "Council Resolution," *SAA Newsletter,* July 1986: 16; Society of American Archivists, "Selecting an Archivist of the U.S.," *SAA Newsletter,* March 1987: 3.

45 "Archivist Nomination Politicized?," *SAA Newsletter,* September 1986: 1, 3.

46 Society of American Archivists, "U.S. Archivist Wilson Sworn In," *SAA Newsletter,* January 1988: 1.

47 Timothy Ericson, "U.S. Archivist Search Continues," *Archival Outlook* (May 1995): 10.

48 Society of American Archivists, "Senate Testimony Transcript Regarding the U.S. Archivist," *Archival Outlook* (July 1995): 6–7.

49 Maygene Daniels, "President's Message," *Archival Outlook* (July 1995): 1.

50 Society of American Archivists, "Statement on the Nomination of Allen Weinstein to Become Archivist of the United States," April 14, 2004, www.archivists.org/statements/weinstein.asp, captured at https://perma.cc/U9U4-RYJK.

51 Timothy Ericson, "Choosing the Next Archivist of the United States," *Archival Outlook* (May 2004): 3, 19.

52 Timothy Ericson, "Weinstein Confirmed as Archivist of the United States," *Archival Outlook* (March/April 2005): 6.

53 "SAA, Coalition Partners Meet with Obama Transition Team," *Archival Outlook* (January/February 2009): 4.

54 "Joint Statement on 'Qualities of a Successful Candidate' for Archivist of the United States," Society of American Archivists, December 19, 2008, www2.archivists.org/statements/joint-statement-on-qualities-of-a-successful-candidate-for-archivist-of-the-united-states, captured at https://perma.cc/WQ2U-JVHZ.

55 Leland J. White, "Hearing Focuses on Challenges Facing Next U.S. Archivist," *Archival Outlook* (July/August 2009): 19.

56 Peter Gottlieb, "SAA and the U.S. Archivist," *Archival Outlook* (November/December 2009): 3.

57 Society of American Archivists, "Public Policy," updated February 8, 2018, www2.archivists.org/advocacy/publicpolicy, captured at https://perma.cc/5S4U-Y4N3.

58 Kathleen Williams, "The NHPRC: Extending the Archives' Reach," *Prologue* 41, no. 2 (Summer 2009), www.archives.gov/publications/prologue/2009/summer/nhprc.html, captured at https://perma.cc/FLG2-XQDZ.

59 Bruce W. Craig, "Washington Beat," *Archival Outlook* (July/August 2001): 24.

60 Examples of calls to action on the NHPRC can be found on the SAA website by searching for "NHPRC advocacy."

61 See, for example, Society of American Archivists, "Issue Brief: Federal Grant Funding for Archives," updated May 22, 2017, www2.archivists.org/statements/issue-brief-federal-grant-funding-for-archives, captured at https://perma.cc/KN52-QCEJ; SAA/CoSA/NAGARA, "Issue Brief: Adequate Funding of Government Archives and Archival Programs, November 20, 2014, www2.archivists.org/statements/issue-brief-adequate-funding-of-government-archives-and-archival-programs, captured at https://perma.cc/732G-GBP2; and Society of American Archivists, "Backgrounder: Funding for the National Historical Publications and Records Commission," June 15, 2017, www2.archivists.org/statements/backgrounder-funding-for-the-national-historical-publications-and-records-commission, captured at https://perma.cc/2P4F-TNH4.

62 Council of State Archivists, "Preserving the American Historical Record (PAHR)," www.statearchivists.org/programs/advocacy/legislation/, captured at https://perma.cc/XBY6-ELVM; and Society of American Archivists, "Preserving the American Historical Record," 2009, updated March 26, 2016, www2.archivists.org/initiatives/preserving-the-american-historical-record, captured at https://perma.cc/QS32-3ESS.

63 PAHR was developed with particular advice and assistance from Representative Maurice Hinchey (D-NY) and was cosponsored by Representative John McHugh (R-NY) and Senators Orrin Hatch (R-UT) and Carl Levin (D-MI).

64 "Issue Brief: Presidential Records Act of 1978," 2014, *Society of American Archivists,* www2.archivists.org/statements/issue-brief-presidential-records-act-of-1978, captured at https://perma.cc/A62A-ZWS4.

65 Bruce P. Montgomery, "Presidential Materials: Politics and the Presidential Records Act," *American Archivist* 66 (Spring/Summer 2009): 102–138.

66 Public Citizen is a nonprofit consumer advocacy organization. For information on the public interest issues Public Citizen addresses, see www.citizen.org/about/about-us.

67 Steven L. Hensen, "Call to Action on Executive Order 13233," 2001, updated November 10, 2010, www2.archivists.org/news/2001/call-to-action-on-executive-order-13233, captured at https://perma.cc/TH78-PFHZ.

68 Leland J. White, "NCH Washington Year in Review," *Archival Outlook* (January/February 2008): 17.

69 "Archives on the Hill," 2018, www2.archivists.org/am2018/attend/archives-on-the-hill, captured at https://perma.cc/WFK7-U7Y9.

70 Society of American Archivists, "Archives, Public Policy & You: Advocacy Guide," updated September 26, 2018, www2.archivists.org/advocacy/advocacy-guide, captured at https://perma.cc/E9JG-GM45.

71 Anne R. Kenney, "From the President's Desk," *Archival Outlook* (May 1993): 3.

72 Howard Reich, "A Blow to Black Music in Chicago," *Chicago Tribune*, March 5, 2012.

73 Steven D. Booth, "Bridge Over Troubled Water: How the Archivists and Archives of Color Roundtable Created Change at the Center for Black Music Research," *Archival Outlook* (November/December 2012): 4–5.

74 "The Giuliani Papers," Gotham Center for New York City History, February 16, 2002, www.gothamcenter.org/past-special-projects/february-21st-2015, captured at https://perma.cc/6WDQ-V8KZ.

75 Andrew Zajac, "How Giuliani Tried to Control His NYC Legacy," *Chicago Tribune*, October 28, 2007.

76 David W. Carmicheal, "The Georgia Archives Budget: An Unfolding Crisis," *Provenance, Journal of the Society of Georgia Archivists* 31, no.1 (January 2013): 7–13.

77 Kaye Lanning Minchew, "Lessons Learned While Saving the Georgia Archives," *Provenance, Journal of the Society of Georgia Archivists* 31 (January 2013): 16–21.

78 Coalition to Preserve the Georgia Archives, *Our Georgia Archives, Our Georgia History—Is It Worth Saving?*, January 2013, www2.archivists.org/sites/all/files/GA_archives_deck_Jan-2013.pdf, captured at https://perma.cc/G3Q2-KLRG.

79 Minchew, "Lessons Learned."

80 "Special Issue on Advocacy," *Provenance, Journal of the Society of Georgia Archivists* 31, no. 1 (2013).

3

# Developing Goals for Advocacy and Awareness Initiatives

Advocacy should begin well before you need to ask for something.

—*Lewis Bellardo, 2011*

Archivists will find many opportunities for advocacy and awareness efforts. Some will support and further the mission and strategic directions for the archives or its parent organization. Other initiatives may support increasing the understanding of and attention to the value of archives and the archives profession more broadly. Whether an initiative is done on a proactive basis or opportunistically in reaction to events, acquisitions, natural disasters, political developments, or social issues that may draw attention to archives and archivists, some level of thoughtful preparation is essential.

## Connecting Advocacy and Awareness Goals to Mission and Strategic Plans

It is important to think about advocacy and awareness and to explicitly connect advocacy or awareness goals to existing organizational mission statements and/or strategic plans. Regardless of where the archival program exists within an organizational hierarchy, its own mission and plans should reflect and connect to those of the larger institution. Few, if any, archival institutions have the luxury of staff and fiscal resources to explore nonessential efforts. Aligning advocacy and awareness goals explicitly with institutional directions helps to justify the use of resources for an effort, enlist support from institutional or organizational leadership, and demonstrate the value to staff members, colleagues, and others who will be instrumental in the effort.

For example, a number of archival institutions are interested in developing programs to use archival materials in K–12 classrooms.[1] To advocate with institutional managers for the resources to do this, the initiative needs to demonstrate how it supports the institutional mission. In a regional historical society whose mission is to engage and inform residents about the history of their community, an initiative with teachers might be presented as an effective way to reach younger members of the community and encourage their engagement with and pride in that community. An additional benefit or by-product is the potential to engage students' parents and families as well. For a college offering teaching degrees, the connection to mission might be characterized as supporting instructional pedagogy for education majors. For a state government archives whose mission is to support the functions of state government, training teachers in the use of historical records in the classroom supports their ability to meet state curriculum and testing mandates. For a corporate archives, a school curriculum involving information about the company could demonstrate to corporate management how it can show its community-mindedness and involvement.

To consider an example from an academic setting, Iowa State University's Special Collections wanted to raise awareness about its film collections because users were unaware that this resource existed. Staff members determined that they could pursue their goal by uploading the most requested films to YouTube. They linked that effort explicitly to the Special Collections institutional mission:

> To identify, select, preserve, create access to, provide reference assistance for, and promote the use of rare and unique research materials that support major research areas of Iowa State University.[2]

With this strategy, the goal became more relevant for the institution's administration because it highlighted the importance of supporting the research areas of Iowa State University. Although it might be a "noble" goal to make resources available to researchers nationally or internationally regardless of their academic affiliation, that is not the institution's primary mission, nor is the administration funded or held accountable for accomplishing that larger goal. Certainly, other researchers would find the resources valuable as well, but to justify the value of Special Collections within the ISU mission, this effort focused on raising the visibility of the ISU film collections by promoting a selected group of films already identified as having "popular" content. By putting a selected group of films on YouTube, ISU could potentially draw inquiries about what additional film resources, as well as other formats, might exist in Special Collections. Because this initiative was tied to the institutional mission, it could also be used to demonstrate to the administration how the archival collections make a positive contribution to the institution's overall priorities and directions.

## Defining the Purpose and Goal

Every advocacy or awareness initiative should be based on a defined goal with a clearly articulated purpose. You may decide to undertake initiatives specifically motivated to advocate for or raise awareness about your institution or the archives profession. For example, staff members of a college special collections department may want to raise professors' awareness of their resources to increase use by students in particular courses. You also may identify an advocacy/awareness goal as part of a larger project on which you or your institution are working. A regional historical society hoping

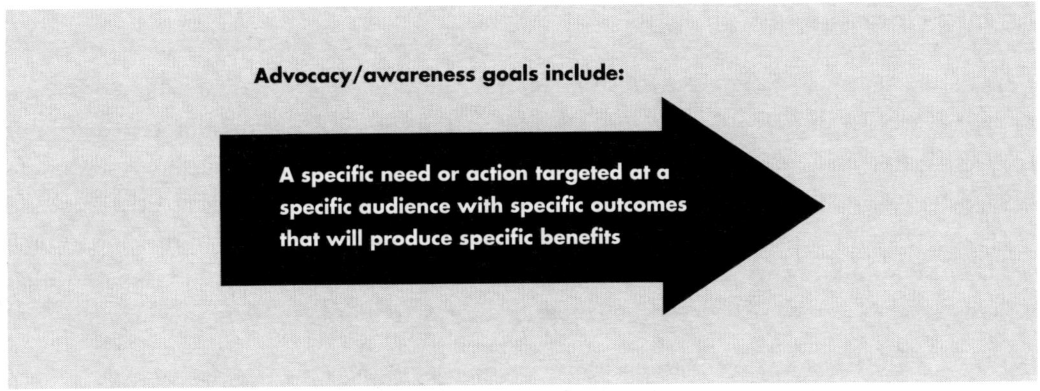


**FIGURE 7.** Components of Advocacy/Awareness Goals

**Source:** David W. Carmicheal and Kathleen D. Roe, "Advocacy and Awareness for Archivists Workshop," 2008, reproduced by permission of the author and David W. Carmicheal.

to expand its collections relating to the Asian-Pacific Islander community may want to include a component to raise awareness among potential donors of both the institution and the kinds of records it is seeking.

In the context of planning for such efforts in an archival setting, the goal(s) identified should address a specific need or action that is targeted at a specific audience with specific outcomes that will produce specific results and/or benefits. (The repeated use of the word *specific* as shown in Figure 7 is intentional.) There is a real tendency to rely on vague phrases like "the general public" or "to gain better understanding" that can seriously hamper the success of advocacy and awareness efforts.

When asked to define their goals for advocacy and awareness, archivists too often respond with suggestions such as those shown in Table 3. These statements are drawn from comments made by participants in the "Archives, Advocacy and Archivists Workshops" offered over several years by the Society of American Archivists. They are characteristic of the way in which many archivists conceptualize their goals. This is not unique; many professionals portray their goals similarly. But these statements address only the processes or resources needed to accomplish the purpose. Instead, the goal statement should be drawn out of the "what" and "how" that mask these initial statements.

**Table 3. Archivists' Typical Responses to "What Are Your Goals for Advocacy and Awareness?"**

| Goals for Individual Institutions | Goals for the Archives Profession |
|---|---|
| We need to digitize our records and put them online.<br>We need to clear up our processing backlog.<br>We need to collect records representing under-documented communities.<br>We need more staff.<br>We need more money. | More people need to make use of archives.<br>There needs to be better understanding of the importance of the work of archivists.<br>Employing organizations should provide better salaries for archivists.<br>There needs to be more federal funding for archives. |

## Setting an institutional goal

Consider the statement "We need to clean up our processing backlog." Lurking behind this is the implied belief that there is a research value in and need for timely access to unprocessed archival records. To accomplish that, there will most likely be a need for additional staff ("We need more staff.") and for supplies and equipment ("We need more money."). So the specific need is for the target audience (the manager and/or institutional resource allocator) to believe that the institutional mission will be better supported if resources are directed to processing and making backlog records available for users. An archivist might state the goal for this in the following manner:

> I will demonstrate to my library administrator the research and public relations value of the archives with specific examples of how research in our holdings had real outcomes for individual users. I will further demonstrate the amount of information not available to address user needs because of our processing backlog.

To better define the outcome or goal you actually want to achieve, it can be useful to reflect on broader questions like "What do I want to change, and why?" and "What outcomes am I seeking?" Think about the "hard questions" that might be posed by someone who was skeptical of the need to address the goals stated above and how they could be answered. For example, for the statement "We need to digitize our records and put them online," how might you answer questions in the chart below:

| The "Hard" Questions | Your Answer |
|---|---|
| What needs to be digitized—everything? Some things? | |
| Who would actually use this stuff?<br>How do you know that? | |
| Why does it have to be put online? | |
| What will they do with it that makes it worth our using funding for this? | |

Once you have your answers, craft your goal statement using the following points to help you get specific:

- Need or action
- Audience
- Outcomes
- Benefits

Following are two scenarios, each with possible responses and goal statements; each involves advocating for resources to digitize records for two institution types. The resulting goal statements reflect the difference in institutional mission.

**Scenario 1:** A city archives wants to "pitch" the idea to its budget office of digitizing records for online access.

| The "Hard" Questions | Your Answer |
|---|---|
| What needs to be digitized—everything? Some things? | We need to digitize our military service records (Civil War, Spanish-American War, World War I). |
| Who would actually use this stuff?<br>How do you know that? | Genealogists/family historians, military history avocationists. We keep statistics on our email, phone, social media, and onsite requests that show the extent of these requests. |
| Why does it have to be put online? | We receive more than 10,000 requests a year for searches and copies of individual service records by people who cannot travel to our facility and more than 4,000 onsite requests. If we put materials online, people can do their own research. |
| What will they do with it that makes it worth our using funding for this? | By people doing their own research, we would save 30 percent of the time of an archivist to do the searches and 20 percent of the time of a clerk to do the copying/mailing. That will allow staff to do other work to address requests from city agencies and our direct constituents. It will also increase the amount of usage for these records—other municipal archives who have put military service records online report an increase in usage of 55 percent. |

The components of the goal statement might look like this:

| The Specific | Your Answer |
|---|---|
| Need or Action | Digitize military service records |
| Audience | For use by family historians, military history reenactors, and avocationists |
| Outcomes | Users can do their research on their own. |
| Benefits | It will save and redirect staff time and expand the amount of use. |

The actual goal/purpose for an advocacy effort for this scenario might look like this:

> We will demonstrate to the Budget Office that we can make more efficient use of staff time and expand the use of our military service records by family historians and military history buffs by digitizing those records and making them available online.

**Scenario 2:** A women's college archives wants to obtain support from its library manager to digitize its records.

| The "Hard" Questions | Your Answer |
|---|---|
| What needs to be digitized—everything? Some things? | Records of the board of trustees from the college's founding in 1880 through 1980, departmental curriculum files and course catalogs from 1880–1980, and students' personal paper collections from 1880–1980 |
| Who would actually use this stuff?<br>How do you know that? | Professors teaching the required U.S. history course and the four elective history courses in women's history assign research projects and papers that use these collections.<br>We do presentations at faculty meetings for key departments and have had an increase in the number of professors who indicate they would use this kind of tool. |
| Why does it have to be put online? | The college archives is only open from 9 a.m. to 5 p.m., and students are often in class during this time. Students do their coursework at all hours and both need and expect access to resources required for their classes for a broad range of time. |
| What will they do with it that makes it worth our using funding for this? | Professors in the history department feel use of primary resources is essential to students developing critical thinking skills and the ability to assess and analyze the trustworthiness of sources. This supports the pedagogical goals of the college and is more cost efficient than providing additional (but still not 24/7) open hours over a period of years. |

The components of the goal statement for this scenario might look like this:

| The Specific | Your Answer |
|---|---|
| | Digitize key college records collections |
| Audience | For use by students in required U.S. and elective women's history courses |
| Outcomes | To ensure students have reliable, timely access to the resources they need for meeting course requirements |
| Benefits | This supports history professors' pedagogical goals of educating students in critical thinking and analysis skills. |

The actual goal/purpose for an advocacy effort for this might be:

> I will demonstrate to my library director that we will support the educational and informational goals of the college and make more efficient use of resources by digitizing and making available online key collections in the college archives that are required for use by professors teaching U.S. history and elective women's history courses.

In a real-world example, the Documenting Ferguson Project provides an excellent example of a well-constructed and focused goal statement. As project staff members note, "This document is integral to our efforts of making the Documenting Ferguson Project a robust and lasting effort. The statement, along with the project outline, also provides valuable guidance as the project is publicized and discussed more broadly."[3]

> Documenting Ferguson is a digital repository that seeks to preserve and make accessible community- and media-generated, original content that was captured and created following the killing of 18-year-old, Michael Brown by police officer Darren Wilson in Ferguson, Missouri on August 9, 2014. A freely available resource for students, scholars, teachers, and the greater community, Documenting Ferguson has the ultimate goal of providing diverse perspectives of the events surrounding the conflicts in Ferguson.
>
> —*Documenting Ferguson, 2015*

## Setting professional goals

Archival professionals often express their concern regarding the perception and understanding of archives and the work of archivists. The SAA Committee on Public Awareness has been working to address this issue and provide motivation, examples, and resources through its *ArchivesAWARE!* blog. A series of posts on this blog under "Asserting the Archivist" draw attention to the work of archivists. Another series of posts, "There's an Archivist for That," shares examples of the range of organizations with archivists from Yellowstone National Park to the Hallmark Company and the Irish Distillers Pernod Record.[4] Other posts address particular tools and techniques such as using video, Facebook Live, and social media for awareness. Efforts such as these aimed at developing advocacy and awareness goals relating to understanding the work of archivists often involve long-term efforts. To make the needed changes in perception and understanding, developing a clear focus and specificity of goals remains essential to achieving a broader awareness and support of archivists and the archival function.

As a goal, "Need for better understanding of the importance of the work of archivists," while real, is extremely broad. To address this, we need to raise awareness of the "general public." Yet the general public is an inherently ill-defined, amorphous audience that is nearly impossible to address in a truly effective way. It is daunting, if not futile, to attempt with one approach to reach a wide range of ages, genders, racial and ethnic groups, education levels, and occupational groups. There is in truth no "general" public, but an amalgam of different though intersecting designations. Attempting to design a message that will meet many of the ways we characterize ourselves will be so diluted that it will have minimal interest to any one person. The impact and real effectiveness of any attempt is likely to be inconsequential—and we are not a profession with the luxury of time and resources to waste. It is necessary to identify audiences with some cohesiveness that can be cultivated or expanded, learn enough about them to understand what approaches will best address their interests, and determine how to deliver a message that will appeal to them. No one will raise the visibility and understanding of archives and the work of archivists by trying to communicate a message that engages most people of most ages, most races/ethnicities, most regions, and most personal, professional, social, economic, and political interests. It sounds silly to even say that—yet that is what constitutes the "general public."

American Archives Month is often seen as an opportunity for the staff members of an organization to raise awareness about both their own institution and of archives and the archival profession generally. To produce effective results, there still needs to be a well-articulated goal with a clear focus, even if it targets a wide audience. For example, the Council of State Archivists (CoSA) developed an ongoing initiative to raise awareness about the value and contributions of state government archives by focusing on its role in addressing the management of electronic records. Since 2010, CoSA has sponsored an annual Electronic Records Day during American Archives Month to draw attention to the considerable existing guidance available through state archives regarding regulations, laws, and best practices for managing electronic information in legal, effective ways.[5] CoSA began by sharing that information with state government records officials and has each year expanded the groups that it encourages to read and redistribute its information and tip sheets as well as those participating in webinars or events on that day.[6] That message now reaches more than 10,000 chief information officers, state officials, and local government officials annually to raise awareness about issues as well as opportunities to work with their state archives. This effort has increased understanding of archives and archivists by identifying a substantial but focused group at which efforts are targeted.

It is possible for a group or institution to make the Archives Month activities have more impact by focusing on a specific goal in the larger national effort. Following is an example of how to address that using the process suggested earlier for crafting a goal statement for advocacy and awareness:

| The "Hard" Questions | Sample Answers |
|---|---|
| What issues or concerns do you have that could be addressed, at least in part, by support from external groups, including those who may never actually use archives? | People have misconceptions about archivists and think we deal with "treasures" or that we work in attics and mess about with old papers. |
| What group(s) can influence or affect those issues/concerns? | News media, particularly journalists, and more specifically regional/local journalists |
| What would you want them to do relating to your issues/concerns? | Write accurate articles periodically sharing information about archives; use the archives as a resource for expert opinions and information as evidence for articles on contemporary issues, news, and events |
| How would their actions or understanding help you? | More accurate representation of the work of archivists and more opportunities for their constituents to be exposed to information that helps them understand the role and value of archives and archivists. |

One goal that results from this analysis might be to develop and invite members of local news media to an Archives Month program on electronic records and email that will expand their understanding of the role of archivists in electronic records management and preservation and lead them to contact archivists for information for writing about electronic records issues.

Use the chart in Figure 8 to identify other groups in the "public" that may be influential for your own organization and to determine how you might answer the questions posed. Or consider what you might like to see your regional archival organization or SAA do to address this issue. Some options for groups to consider who can influence or affect issues/concerns might be local government leaders; state government leaders; members of communities that are underrepresented in archival collections; the leaders of the university alumni association; heritage or genealogical groups; and professional groups such as teachers, actors, surveyors, or environmentalists.

Defining a clear goal for your advocacy or awareness initiative is essential to its success. Your goal may be an individual effort focusing on your own institution or it may be one that addresses goals for the archival profession. Knowing the goal you want to achieve will help define the audience to which you will "pitch" your effort, as well as identify key stakeholders and supporters. Your goal will also help focus your message and affect the delivery of that message. Having a well-defined goal provides a firm foundation for subsequent steps in planning and carrying out your effort. Taking time to think through and clarify goals is a worthwhile investment.

| The "Hard" Questions | Answer |
|---|---|
| What issues or concerns do you have that could be addressed, at least in part, by support from external groups, including those who may never actually use archives? | *Sample:* People have misconceptions about archivists and think we deal with "treasures" or that we work in attics and mess about with old papers. |
| What group(s) can influence or affect those issues/ concerns? | |
| What would you want them to do about your issues/ concerns? | |
| How would their actions or understanding help you? | |

Now, draft a goal statement to address the issues or concerns you have addressed above:

________________________________________

________________________________________

________________________________________

________________________________________

**FIGURE 8.** Crafting a Goal Statement for Advocacy and Awareness

To create an effective goal statement for advocacy and awareness, you need to start by answering the hard questions that will be asked of you.

## NOTES

1 Julia Hendry, "Primary Sources in K–12 Education: Opportunities for Archivists," *American Archivist* 70 (Spring/Summer 2007): 114–129.

2 Michele A. Christian and Tanya Zanish-Belcher, "Broadcast Yourself: Putting Iowa State University's History on YouTube," in *A Different Kind of Web: New Connections Between Archives and Our Users*, ed. Kate Theimer (Chicago: Society of American Archivists, 2011).

3 Jennifer Kirmer and Sonya Rooney, "Documenting Ferguson: Capturing History as It Happens," *Archival Outlook* (November/December 2014): 3, 24–25.

4 For example, see "Asserting the Archivist, No. 3," *ArchivesAWARE!* (blog), Society of American Archivists, Committee on Public Awareness, May 16, 2018, https://archivesaware.archivists.org/2018/05/16/asserting-the-archivist-no-3/, captured at https://perma.cc/N8XG-9JS8; and, as another example, see "There's an Archivist for That! Interview with Meredith Torre, Archivist, Atlanta Housing," ArchivesAWARE! (blog), Society of American Archivists, Committee on Public Awareness, September 13, 2018, https://archivesaware.archivists.org/2018/09/13/theres-an-archivist-for-that-interview-with-meredith-torre-archivist-atlanta-housing/, captured at https://perma.cc/E2D5-Q9JL.

5 Council of State Archivists, "Electronic Records Day," www.statearchivists.org/programs/state-electronic-records-initiative/electronic-records-day/, captured at https://perma.cc/LW47-C9EY.

6 Council of State Archivists, "Electronic Records Day Promotional Materials," www.statearchivists.org/programs/state-electronic-records-initiative/electronic-records-day/electronic-records-day-promotional-materials/, captured at https://perma.cc/EH7E-U6MD.

# 4

# Understanding Audiences, Key Stakeholders, and Supporters

A critical element of effective planning for advocacy and awareness initiatives is to identify and understand the interests and needs of your audience(s), key stakeholders, and supporters. Assuming that you are undertaking advocacy and awareness efforts to accomplish some change, ask yourself: "Who holds the power to make or break the desired change?" Those who hold that power generally fall into three groups:

- *The audience(s):* The person(s) whose opinions, behaviors, or actions you want to influence. Presumably they will benefit from the outcomes of your effort.
- *Key stakeholders:* The individuals or groups who have some influence in whether or how you are able to accomplish your goals
- *Supporters:* Individuals or groups who can and will support your efforts to accomplish your goals. They may be closely involved or may be those you can call on for support when a need arises.

The more you understand the motivations, concerns, and proclivities of any person or group, the more effectively you can plan an advocacy or awareness initiative, including your "message," the methods to be used, who will be involved in conveying that message, and the actions you will take to accomplish your goal.

## Who Are You Talking To?

Begin by identifying those individuals or groups that will be the primary focus of your efforts—the person or persons whose opinions, behaviors, or actions you want to affect because their influence can help you accomplish your goal. When we talk about audience, we usually mean the people who we envision will be the direct recipients or those we want directly participating in or responding to our advocacy or awareness initiative. However, as noted previously, it is also important to identify the less direct audience(s): key stakeholders who may be necessary for approval or funding or supporters who can assist you in a range of ways from information to credibility to bring your efforts to fruition. It will take time to define which people or groups constitute those audiences and which among them will be your focus. Your definitions need to be as specific as possible so you can focus your efforts on real people and groups and their needs or interests. The idea of directing something at the "general public" is a common approach that is so wide and amorphous that it provides little focus or real guidance; as a result, it usually compromises any real effectiveness.

For example, perhaps you are on staff at a university archives and special collections and want to increase the holdings from a more inclusive range of faculty members. In listing potential audiences, key stakeholders, and supporters, you might consider:

- Potential audiences: What types of "inclusion" are you seeking to represent in the faculty? Ethnicity, race, gender, sexual orientation, socioeconomic status, immigrants, academic specialization, disabilities, and educational background are only a few of the options.
- Key stakeholders: Who are the individuals, as noted above, who will have a role in making it possible for you to proceed with your plans? These might include your immediate supervisor, other levels of administration, other departments like the fiscal offices who are needed to support the costs to expand your collections, or colleagues or staff whose cooperation is needed.
- Supporters: Who or what groups might help you reach out to faculty or support the value of your effort? This list might include unions representing the faculty, including national groups; department chairs; the university administration; diversity/inclusion offices or officers; the public relations office; or local chapters of national groups, such as the American Association of University Women, the National Association for the Advancement of Colored People, or many others.

Consider the range of possibilities and then identify those that will be critical to the success of your effort and that will give you real opportunities to succeed. It may be necessary to identify the best possibilities for initial success with audiences and then, based on results, expand at a later time.

It is important to clearly define the composition of that audience and then learn about their "backstory" in order to focus efforts in a way that connects with them. There are many things you may want to know about that audience. Basic biographical data *may* provide key information, including gender, race/ethnicity, religious affiliation, age, educational background, personal roles and affiliations, or relevant geographical locations. If the target audience is an individual, such as the leader of an organization, a government official, a respected elder, or a key opinion leader, then specific personal information may be more useful. With both individuals and groups, learning about and being respectful and aware of the cultural context in which they function can provide guidance in more effectively addressing them.

In addition to gathering personal information, remain aware of the social, political, economic, and cultural trends and other concerns that affect or are important to the audience. Again, this information may be more easily gathered with individuals than with groups, but in either instance it is important to not make stereotypical assumptions. Real information obtained from reliable sources on a person or group can provide essential guidance in more effectively communicating with that audience. The more you understand and are aware of the audience's context, the more equipped you will be to develop a coherent, compelling message. This kind of contextual research underpins much of our appraisal and description work, so those skills can be readily redirected to researching potential audiences.

## Who are key stakeholders?

In addition to the direct audience, it is useful to identify key stakeholders. These are the individuals or groups who have some influence on whether or how you are able to accomplish your goals. They may not be the direct beneficiaries of your effort but may be affected by your organization's actions and activities. Key stakeholders are often the managers and resource allocators in an institution whose permission will be necessary to proceed or who may determine whether initiatives are consistent with the institutional mission, or they are groups who will be affected by the actions you plan to take. As with the target audience, understanding the concerns and context in which key stakeholders are operating can help in gaining essential support and understanding for any initiative. It is not productive, either for an immediate initiative or for future relationships, if key stakeholders feel they have been "sidestepped" or do not understand the goal and value of an advocacy or awareness effort.

Most archivists recognize the importance of immediate managers in approving an initiative, but in some cases it may be important to ensure that additional levels of management, members of the organization, or related parts of the organization are also familiar with your plans. A university archives planning to create an exhibit during homecoming week to encourage alumni to donate their papers will likely find that the alumni office and alumni organizations are key stakeholders; it would be important to inform them as well as seek their support and even their assistance.

Your own colleagues, support staff, student workers, or those you supervise can be key stakeholders as well. If your initiative will involve them directly, affect their work, or involve shared work space, ensuring they are informed of and preferably supportive will be instrumental in your success. Introducing change can be challenging in any organization, and, like many archivists, at some point you may have heard that old refrain, "This is the way we've always done it." You may need to direct an advocacy effort at your own colleagues to make those changes occur, particularly when they involve a change of mind-set. In theory and practice, enlisting colleagues to undertake changes brought by developments can be particularly challenging because they require substantial reexamination of our profession's past and the practices so many have followed for much of their careers.

For example, the introduction of descriptive standards into archival practice during the 1990s was met with considerable resistance in many repositories where there had been no tradition of following standardized practice. This situation was further complicated by a reluctance to use online catalogs and computer systems to support access. Archivists who entered the profession after that time find it almost inconceivable that there would have been any concern or opposition, but those who "lived through it" recall some very difficult conversations and experiences in introducing this change.[1]

Current efforts to be proactive in documenting a wide range of racial, ethnic, or gender communities or other issues and topics concerned with ensuring inclusivity involve changing ways of thought and practice that are challenging for some current practitioners. For example, efforts with diverse communities will be compromised if potential donors, users, or interested groups are met onsite or by phone with unreceptive or uncivil interactions from staff who do not reflect cultural competency. There is a need to ensure that the institutional context supports our efforts to make needed changes by advocating with, or raising the awareness of, our professional colleagues as well as our support and technical staff.

## Who are your supporters?

For "big" advocacy efforts that involve changes in strategic directions, policy, or legislation, it is essential to identify supporters who can also play a role in accomplishing your goals. These supporters are not directly responsible for your initiative, and they may not benefit directly from it, but they understand its value and are willing to provide assistance by lending their voices. They may range from those who are closely involved to those you can call on periodically when the need arises. It is important that you give your supporters the information they need to be knowledgeable about your effort and that they are willing and able to take action on your behalf—by writing a letter of support, providing a "testimonial," speaking with the press or writing a letter to the editor, or making a phone call or personal contact. Many archives have donors or users who can provide this kind of support, yet we are often reluctant to ask for their assistance. A supporter's "outside voice," however, can bring credibility to the value of your initiative. Supporters can have a "multiplier" effect.

## What about the "opposition"?

We tend to focus planning on those who will benefit from and appreciate our efforts. But realistically it is also important to identify any groups or individuals who may impede or oppose your efforts. Opposition may come from the individual who demonstrates a general lack of support or interest by stating that "I hated history in school," or from the resource allocator who sees archives and historical records collections as "nice" antiquarian pursuits that are tangential to the mission of the organization or to the functioning of society, or from archives colleagues who do not want to take on the extra work that could result from an increase in users, or from colleagues who are not comfortable dealing with any change in "the way we do the things we do." Others who may raise difficult questions or object to archival initiatives include departments that are competing with your program for scarce resources.

There may also be initiatives that will raise concern (if not outright opposition) from those who have political, social, or financial positions that are at odds with the goal you hope to achieve, with the mission of your organization, or with the archives profession itself. For example, public university archives advocating for retention policies that support transparency and accountability encounter real challenges from the departments and officials they seek to document. In the case of religious group or institutional archives that maintain nongovernmental vital records information (such as birth, marriage, death, or membership records), leaders of the larger organization may have concerns about ensuring privacy and restricted access to information in those records or protecting the organization from potential legal challenges. Legal departments in many businesses, governments, universities, and even cultural organizations are often very conservative in their approaches to donor requests, records retention, accessibility and use, or copyright, placing emphasis on legal protections over access and use.

Potential questions, concerns, and impediments need not prevent or diminish an advocacy or awareness effort, but your planning should include a frank assessment of who might have issues and what their concerns might be. It can be useful to include them in order to take their perspectives into consideration—and, potentially, to get their buy-in. For example, if the staff of the library and archives of a major historical society that traditionally has served scholars and adult researchers wants to develop a program to bring in high school students to use primary sources, the institution's preservation staff may be very concerned about physical damage to the records because of student inexperience and age. Including the preservation staff in developing guidelines for students, and perhaps even doing an initial "how to handle archives" orientation for students, may help to allay fears while also educating students and preventing actual problems.

Be aware that audiences, key stakeholders, supporters, and even opponents do not necessarily align into discrete and rigid categories. An organization that is part of your initial target audience may become an engaged supporter. Your own boss may be your first target audience, whom you need to address in order to gain approval to move forward with an initiative. Afterward, that person becomes a key stakeholder who provides the resources that allow you to achieve your goal. Even those who start out as opponents can—with cultivation—become firm supporters over time.

As you start your planning, create a list for each of these types, ensuring that you consider all of those who hold the power to make or break your desired change. As you create your list, add to it their possible roles, as well as reasons for support or concerns. Then review your list to assess whether you are overextending your resources and capacity by including too many individuals and groups. Staff members of a corporate archives may want to raise various departments' awareness of the services and value of the archives. However, if the parent organization is large and complex, it is likely more effective to target a few key departments or begin the process with departments that are more likely to be receptive to provide some solid "wins." These early supporters and "key

In developing the Colorado Chicano Movement Archives at Colorado State University–Pueblo, a range of individuals and groups were the focus:

| | |
|---|---|
| Audience: | The Chicano community from whom the university would seek donations of personal and organizational records |
| Key stakeholders: | Grassroots organizers in the Chicano movement of the 1960s and 1970s; leading individuals from the community who served on an advisory board |
| Supporters: | The Colorado Chicano community; the Chicano Studies Program at the university that involved students in conducting oral histories; the university administration that approved application for and management of a grant to fund the initial project |

**FIGURE 9.** Example of Audience, Key Stakeholders, and Supporters

**Source:** Beverly B. Allen, "Power to the People: Building the Colorado Chicano Movement Archives," *Archival Outlook* (September/October 2014): 6–7, 32.

opinion leaders" can then influence other individuals and departments later. Although it may take more time to proceed in "small bites" given the nature of workloads and other resources, a phased approach often has a better chance of succeeding.

Identifying individuals or groups who hold the power to make or break your desired change does not have to be an arduous or exhaustive task, and you will probably be able to develop a list expeditiously. The benefit of creating a chart or list is simply that it prompts you to think through this component and focus on being prepared to meet real needs, interests, and concerns. As with much of our professional work, planning in advance whenever possible increases the likelihood of success.

## Assessing Your Audience, Key Stakeholders, and Supporters

Once you have identified key groups or individuals, you need to consider the context in which they operate, regardless of whether their ultimate role is as audience, stakeholder, supporter, or potential opponent. Fortunately, assessing context is a core capacity that archivists need at any level and with any function, so that skill set can be applied to advocacy and awareness as well.

As we undertake various archival functions, we often spend time considering the backgrounds and needs of such external groups as potential donors, researchers, teachers or professors, government officials/legislators, and even various groups in the "general public." But our own employing institutions or professional organizations also include a number of possible internal audiences, stakeholders, or supporters for which contextual and background information can be essential to our advocacy and awareness efforts.

Your assessment of individuals or groups can be aided by asking the following questions:

**Who are they?**

- What information is relevant or helpful to know about the individual's background, focus, interests, and personally identifying characteristics?
- What are the responsibilities, functions, and focus of an organization, its departments, or an individual's professional role in it?

**What matters to them?**

- What social, economic/fiscal, or cultural context issues, successes, or challenges are important?
- What are the current pressures, expectations, timelines, and parameters that affect the organization or an individual's role in it?

**What can I do for them?**

- What content in an archival collection will be useful or of interest?
- What outcomes of archival work might be useful or of interest?
- How can archives/the archives program benefit an individual or group?
- What services will best support their efforts and needs?

The following discussion looks at some of the characteristics and concerns to consider with a number of common internal and external groups with whom archivists will need to work. These groups may have multiple roles: the direct audience to which you need to appeal can later become supporters who speak on behalf of the archives or of particular initiatives. Similarly, an individual may be a stakeholder who moves from the role of opponent to supporter. Whatever the role at any given time, having a clear idea of the context and how it may change will be essential to determining how best to communicate with them to gain their support, understanding, involvement in, and response to your efforts.

## Assessing internal groups

*Institutional Management.* Virtually all archivists, even those in management and supervisory positions, are "responsible" to some manager, board, or oversight body. And nearly all will need the support of at least one or more immediate managers to proceed with our advocacy and awareness initiatives. Knowing the context in which our management operates is crucial to determining what their needs are and to gaining their support. We also need to consider how to effectively (and ethically!) address their priorities while advocating for our programs.

> You should be "a constant ambassador" to your boss and other resource allocators.
>
> —*Mark A. Greene, 2015*

For many who work in organizations of any size, whether a business, a religious institution, a historical society, a university/college, a government, or a museum or library, somewhere in the hierarchy the archival program reports to a person who is not an archivist (by profession or even proclivity). Consider some of the following questions in assessing your institutional management:

- While the archival program reports to them, do they see it as a priority? What *do* they see as program priorities?
- What interests do they have, either personally or professionally, that connect to your goals?
- Do they understand the value that the archives program brings to the organization and its mission? (A manager may have an "interest" in history or see the archives or special collections as a "jewel in the crown," but that does not equate to having a firm understanding of how it contributes to the organization and its mission.)
- What opportunities do you have to advocate for the overall archives program? When can you share information on program progress and achievements that gives a supervisor or manager concrete evidence of what the archives contributes?[2]
- Are they held accountable for any goals/priorities to which you might connect your archival advocacy/awareness goals?
- Will they respond better to data and statistics or to anecdotes/stories or qualitative but demonstrable outcomes?

In addition to immediate managers, consider including the next level (or more) of institutional managers and resource allocators in your regular program awareness or advocacy efforts. Their understanding of the archives program's value is important as well, and they need to be sufficiently informed to support it. As Larry Hackman has pointed out, we need to make it both easier for upper-level managers to support the archives and harder for them to say "no" to our requests.[3] Reaching out to raise awareness about additional levels in the hierarchy should, of course, be done with the knowledge and support of your direct manager—unless you encounter an immediate and unplanned situation like an "elevator" speech opportunity.

> When you are talking with a resource allocator—particularly one who has no past experience with archives—lofty ideals and notions of identity building or remembrances of past events aren't going to cut it when they want to know why they should give you a sliver of the money pot (particularly when it's shrinking).
>
> —*Erin Lawrimore, "The Big Picture: Effective Advocacy through Institutional Alignment," 2013*

Managers should be given clear statistics as well as anecdotal and quantitative data on users and the research conducted in your records. In addition, sharing staff achievements or notes of recognition provides "ready-made" information that can support a manager's need to demonstrate overall program progress and success to a governing board, budget office, or manager. Traditionally, archivists have collected data on our collections and functions but have been less sanguine about how useful this information may be or how to demonstrate its value to our managers. (Chapter 5 discusses options for providing quantitative and qualitative information of different types.) Remember that any manager is likely to find it useful to discuss what data they need for reporting and information purposes, and that conversation will provide insight into the context in which they may view your advocacy or awareness initiative. However, with any manager, it useful to discuss what data they need for reporting and information purposes in order to understand their context and to support future communications and program awareness.

> At the time its archival program was being established, the New York Philharmonic had three power centers: the Board management, the music director, and the orchestra musicians. Each needed to be addressed with a message and approach that spoke to their particular interests.
>
> *Barbara Haws, 2011*

*Institutional Groups That Affect the Archives Program Operation.* Other internal groups in the larger organization may have a role or an interest in your advocacy or awareness effort. Some will be departments or individuals who can contribute to the success of your efforts, others may be those who can benefit from your plans, and some will pose the "hard questions" or the obstacles that you must overcome for your initiatives to succeed. Each organization will have individuals and offices who have influence on decision-making. That may not always be the upper level of a hierarchy, and it can be important to become familiar with those who operate as key opinion leaders (that is, the people to whom decision-makers and other colleagues listen).

Consider some of the following questions when assessing other institutional groups:

- What are their programmatic goals and responsibilities?
- What are their priorities and pressures?
- Will they be competing with the archives for resources?
- What do they already know about the archives?

- What is their current relationship to the archives—Do they provide services to the archives or rely on services from the archives?—and how do they perceive that relationship?
- What effect can their work have on the archives?

Sometimes our advocacy or awareness efforts will address groups whose work affects ours operationally. For example, human resources departments may need to have an understanding of the differences among credentials for archivists, librarians, historians, and museum curators in order to post job openings and appropriately screen applicants. They may also have limited understanding of the professional competencies necessary for archival work. In more than one instance, human resources staff members have equated archival functions with clerical functions. Given that archival positions are often at lower pay or lower grade levels than other professions with lower educational requirements, it is important to ensure that human resource professionals are better informed about the required skills and complexity of responsibilities for archivists.

Budget office staff members focus on the fiscal health of the organization, and the reason for costs associated with archival work may not be evident to them. Many archivists have been asked why all the records are not simply digitized and put online and the originals destroyed to save the costs of storage, maintenance, and access. Finance staff members are not intuitively aware of the challenges of digitizing records given the variety of ages and formats held in archives or of the less obvious costs related to creating metadata or migrating and managing digital images over time. Don't be offended by their lack of understanding; take the opportunity to educate them about how the archives program is cost effective and supports accountability.

You may also need to familiarize legal departments or organizational lawyer(s) with how the archives' issues may differ from those of other parts of the institution. Lawyers typically wish to restrict access to information to protect an organization and its assets. But that proclivity can often be at direct odds with archivists' commitment to ensuring open access within the parameters of existing laws. In one instance, lawyers who were unfamiliar with archival practices wanted a government archives to require each patron to file a Freedom of Information request every time they wanted to use records, including those already entirely open to the public. Although that might be a viable requirement from a legal standpoint, it is clearly unproductive and contradictory to government transparency and open access. That approach reflects the lawyers' lack of understanding of the basic functions and purposes of archival programs in providing access and supporting research. On the other hand, institutional lawyers can be key allies and supporters in developing effective donor agreements, managing copyright and privacy issues, or dealing with the demands stemming from legal claims and litigation that are increasingly an issue for government and university archivists; therefore, ensuring their understanding and support of your archival program can be essential.

Information technology (IT) staff are another internal group that can positively or negatively affect the archives program. When IT resources are managed centrally, the staff can be instrumental in ensuring that archives staff members have access to effective resources and support. IT departments often are staffed by individuals whose focus is on current operational systems and who don't "look back." Information technology typically requires that professionals adopt a flexible, project-based mind-set. A specific need is identified, tasks are laid out, deadlines are set, and progress toward the stated goal is monitored. Speed and adaptability—not longevity—are favored because it is understood that a tool created today may be considered out of date in the very near future.[4]

You may need to help IT staff become aware of how a function that they see as being about "the past" in fact requires contemporary approaches to provide essential services and how those services can be made more efficient and effective through the use of technology. Although many archivists have technical skills, they often need IT professionals' knowledge and competency in emerging approaches. Working with skilled IT staff can significantly expand the ability to accomplish archival functions, but archivists need to find ways to understand IT professionals' vocabulary and working processes to enlist their support and assistance. In addition, opportunities and needs for managing electronic records and systems have become increasingly essential for archivists. Enlisting the assistance and support of informed and supportive IT programs and staff will be critical to ensuring effective management of electronic records. Their understanding of the vicissitudes of technology may, in fact, make them one of the most effective supporters of electronic records management.

> Bill Jackson of the Harley-Davidson archives has written a useful blog post about the way in which he created and emailed a 4-minute video to inspire H-D employees and inform them of what capacity and resources are available in the archives. The Society of American Archivists Business Archives Section's "BAS Advocacy Success Stories" contains this contribution, as well as many other helpful examples of advocacy work.

*Institutional Groups That Can Benefit from/Use the Archives Program.* Some archivists focus on external researchers and miss important opportunities to develop user relationships in the organization itself. Public relations departments, college/university alumni offices, and legal departments are among the types of institutional groups whose own functions can benefit from a relationship with the archives. Corporate archivists often are specifically tasked with supporting the direct needs of their own organization, so their work provides very positive examples for other archivists in how to advocate for the archives program with internal entities. The SAA Business Archives Section's microsite provides a range of helpful examples of activities and approaches for reaching out to other departments that can contribute to the program's success and benefit from its services.[5]

Consider some of the following questions when assessing institutional groups that may use the archives to support their own work:

- What are the priorities and goals for the institutional program that might be served by a connection with the archives?
- What reporting or information dissemination do other departments do?
- What do they know about the archives already? How do they perceive your services?
- How much help will they need, and how much help can you provide them? Are you willing to do their searching for them or provide copies or other materials?

## Assessing external groups

Archivists direct many of their advocacy and awareness initiatives at external groups and often think that their experience in working with a range of users, donors, and supporters has given them an understanding of those groups. Advocacy and awareness are critical components of reaching existing and potential donors, users, and supporters and ensuring that efforts correlate with their needs, concerns, and interests. So what are some of the key external groups with whom archivists do interact or should consider interacting, and what should be considered when reaching out to them? Following are some examples of concerns and considerations when assessing and working with those groups.

*Records Creators/Donors.* Although archivists take an active role in acquiring records of significance from individuals and organizations, they often overlook the advocacy and awareness component of the records management and acquisition process. In some cases, individuals or organizations have not even considered the potential value their records may have for current and future research by a range of users. Others may view permanent retention of records as an unpleasant requirement that is best avoided or left to languish until a "convenient time" arises. In still other cases, concerns about potential problems or embarrassments in records can derail the transfer to an archives. And for some donors, particularly individuals who inherit ownership of a person's papers, complications may accrue from grief and a sense of loss, from concerns about personal privacy or how information might be used, or from the belief that the records have significant monetary value. As a result, too many records that should be placed in an archives are never transferred or donated, resulting in incomplete and spotty documentation. In some cases, donors may need to be informed about what their own role is in making a donation or transfer, or they may need reassurance that it will not be taxing or demanding of their time. They may need information about how the archives will handle their records to reassure them before making a donation or transfer. Raising potential donors' and records creators' awareness of the value of archives and, in some cases, advocating to ensure that they are managed and appropriately retained is essential to moving toward a more comprehensive and balanced documentation of our communities and country.

> The University of Nevada, Las Vegas, Special Collections created a 3-minute video, entitled *What We Do with Your Donations* (2015), directed at donors to provide information on how their records will be managed, preserved, and made accessible for research. The video is available on YouTube.

Consider the following questions when assessing records creators and potential donors:

- What is the relationship of the person/group to the archival records? Are personal, emotional, or financial concerns likely to affect the relationship?
- What do they know about archives already? Do their current perceptions about archives need to be changed?
- What value for the records they hold/manage might make sense to them as a reason for being part of an archives?
- What can you do to make the process of donation/transfer less daunting or complicated for them?

*Underrepresented/Diverse Communities.* For decades many archivists and archival institutions functioned in a relatively passive mode with external groups. That meant acquiring records offered by organizations and individuals but not proactively seeking them out as part of a comprehensive or carefully conceived acquisition plan. Documentation collected in archives also has largely reflected people and groups of privilege and power. In the 1960s and 1970s the "new social history" movement emerged, stressing the need for a more comprehensive history and for an archival record to support it. Urged on by F. Gerald Ham in his seminal article, "The Archival Edge," archivists have pursued efforts to expand the archival record and the relationship of archives with a wider community.[6] Initial efforts included those to establish labor and women's archives as well as collections focusing on African Americans, Latinos, Native Americans, LGBTQ+ individuals, and the many voices and experiences not documented in traditional archival collections. Today there is increasing emphasis on the need for archivists to develop cultural competency skills in order to address the lack of inclusiveness in the historical record. This is critically important to effective advocacy and awareness and, in fact, will have significant impact on the success of any effort.[7]

In advocacy and awareness initiatives, it is essential that archivists learn and then *employ* cultural diversity competency skills in order to develop respectful and responsive approaches to individuals and groups. The archivist's role must adapt to each community so that they can provide the type of assistance or information needed for the cultural context. For example, some groups or communities will not feel comfortable placing records in a university archives or special collections that is part of an institution associated with white privilege and that, therefore, is not a place that a particular community's members would find amenable or inclusive. Instead, the archivist's role may be as advisor on the development and operation of a community archives or assisting in ways defined by the community members.[8] Other communities may rely more on oral traditions, so documentation may take forms other than the traditional "paper records" of letters, diaries, or organizational files. As Natalia Fernández noted in a 2017 SAA Annual Meeting presentation, oral history is often a more effective method for engagement with communities of color and the LGBTQ+ community.[9] Assessing the varying community contexts and communicating openly and respectfully is essential to effective advocacy and awareness efforts in these communities.

> How are we to expand the archival record and share the importance of archives as essential evidence of society especially to traditionally underrepresented communities . . . if we are unable to effectively work and communicate with a diversity of cultures?
>
> —*Helen Wong Smith, 2015*

Consider some of the following questions when assessing underrepresented/diverse groups:

- Have you and your staff been trained in or developed skills in cultural competency?
- Are the community, its leaders, and key individuals interested in working with you/your institution?
- What kind of relationship does the community/group want to have with you/your institution? What do they want and need from you? What roles are you willing/able to take?
- What does the community/group see as the value of archives to them?
- Are you and your institution willing and able to work collaboratively and change approaches and procedures as necessary?

***Historical Researchers/Users.*** Individuals undertake historical research for a wide range of purposes. The common perception is that archives are the locus for historical research conducted by academics/scholars whose expected product will be a written volume on history, biography, or politics. There are, indeed, archival users with those purposes to be served. However, researchers are also doing considerable research in the sciences, environmental studies, medicine, anthropology, and law that involves information from the "past." In addition, senior high school students are increasingly becoming an important user group.[10] Comparably, college professors and their students are a key potential audience for archives programs. And there are many researchers who may be encouraged to use archives for research in such areas as genealogy, military reenactment, cooking, historic homes, railroads, or car restoration. To advocate effectively with any of these groups, archivists should become familiar with the parameters of research work being done in those areas, the information-seeking approaches used, the organizations in which such researchers may "congregate," and the communications routes by which they can be reached. In the archives profession as a whole, there are limited (and erratically collected) data about the external groups that archives serve, how they "find" archival collections, what additional groups archivists could work with, or users' thoughts on how to best serve them.[11]

> Archival institutions require a greater knowledge of the needs of their users and potential users as well as a better understanding of how users interact with archival institutions' services and systems.
>
> —*Wendy Duff et al., 2008*

In 1986 Paul Conway put forward a framework for user studies in archives, and a number of studies have followed.[12] Archivists who have subsequently pursued developing a stronger profile of users have employed several approaches to gathering this information.[13] Exit interviews with current researchers have been used, as have citation studies, and some archives have conducted focus groups with users. A range of possible approaches can be pursued, but each requires some careful time and attention to developing the questions or approach so that useful information can be obtained. In addition to reviewing the archival literature on user studies, archivists need to learn the techniques and approaches for information gathering from other professions that have best practices and processes for this, or they can contract with or employ an individual with experience in conducting focus groups, surveys, or other information-gathering methods to obtain reliable, useful data. These are skill sets that may not have been part of an archivist's education and cannot necessarily be developed by simply reading a few articles, books, or websites.

> The Northwest Digital Alliance consortium (now ArchivesWest) interviewed core researchers to gather information on their needs and preferences regarding the selection of materials to be included and how it is presented in order to better serve users and support the value of presenting archival materials online in a cooperative website/catalog.
>
> —*Jody Allison-Bunnell, Elizabeth Yakel, and Janet Hauck, 2011*

Before launching an advocacy or awareness effort aimed at researchers, consider some of the following questions for individuals or groups with whom you work:

- What do you know and where can you learn about the trends and approaches in a particular area of research?
- Are there commonalities in research methods and approaches that will help define their needs?
- How do researchers find information about archival collections that might be of interest?

- How do they search for materials in collections (known item searches, browse searches, etc.)?
- What access tools (finding aids, online catalogs, digital collections) do they actually use and prefer?
- What routes can you use to communicate with researchers (websites, listservs, professional organizations, university programs, etc.)?
- What services do they value?
- How do they want to interact with archives?
- What have they done or will they do with the results of their research?

*Supporters/Friends.* Many archivists find it useful to have formal groups that can provide input and support for the archives program. The roles these groups assume can vary. Some groups assist with fundraising, ranging from selling products (publications, t-shirts, memorabilia, or reproduction copies) to seeking grants for major projects (such as digitization or conservation) that the archives could not otherwise undertake.[14] Some groups sponsor or assist with public programming, including lectures, conferences, workshops, exhibits, and publications. Others focus on providing advice from key constituencies to assist the archives program in better meeting the needs of its constituencies or developing new programs and services.

In other cases, particular individuals may be called on to provide support. Although such individual contacts generally should be used carefully and at only key times, they can provide introductions to other individuals and groups. They may have standing in a community, in a profession, or nationally that draws the attention of others and lends credibility. Individuals can support your program by providing quotes or testimonials, writing letters to the editor of an influential local newspaper, or speaking about the value of an archives program. Some individuals can serve as a key contact to potential donors, arrange an introduction to a legislator, or provide an introduction to a funding agency or foundation.

To enlist either individuals or groups to assist an archives program, they will likely need to be the subject of a less obvious advocacy or awareness effort themselves. Unlike researchers or other constituents, they may be unlikely to benefit directly from the archives program, so it is important to understand their interests, personal and professional directions, and the impetus that motivates them to take the time and effort to provide their "name" and assistance. Consider some of the following questions regarding individuals or groups to whom you may want to appeal for assistance and support:

- What do they know about archives already? What do they see as the value or benefit of your archives program?
- How much time and effort are you going to ask them to expend? Do they understand and agree to the involvement you are hoping for or expecting?
- How long are you anticipating they will remain involved with your organization?
- Are you anticipating a financial commitment from them? (Many boards expect regular donations from their members. Be sure to make any financial expectations clear from the beginning!)
- What kind of support or assistance will your organization provide (staff support, drafting documents, technical assistance, etc.)?
- How will their involvement benefit *them* as well as your organization?

Once goals are established for an archival advocacy or awareness initiative, developing an understanding of the target audience, key stakeholders, and supporters is essential. Too often, archivists defer performing a thorough assessment of these groups. It is easy to assume based on experience or previous conversations that one knows what researchers, managers, colleagues, resource allocators, and the "general public" want, what motivates them, or what will speak to their interests. But reliance on such assumptions can seriously limit success in planning and carrying out any initiative.

> We often make up our minds about people based on a few familiar terms they use. If someone says they support the Second Amendment, we often believe we know all we need to about them.
>
> —*Celeste Headlee, 2017*

Investing time in getting to know more about the individuals in these groups will have positive and productive results. No business would introduce a new product without solid market analysis and testing to determine the potential for success. To be successful in our efforts, we need to promote an understanding of our profession, obtain resources for our work, and have the support of our organizations. The more we know about our audience, our key stakeholders, and our supporters, the more effectively we can undertake other functions in addition to advocacy and awareness. The investment of time and effort to do this assessment will have considerable benefits for archives and archivists.

## NOTES

1 Steven L. Hensen, William E. Landis, Kathleen D. Roe, Michael Rush, William Stockting, and Victoria Irons Walch, "Thirty Years On: SAA and Descriptive Standards," *American Archivist* 74, Supplement 1 (2011): 706: 1–36.

2 Mark A. Greene, "Putting Archives on the Agenda," *Archival Outlook* (July/August 2015): 29.

3 Larry J. Hackman, "Love is Not Enough: Advocacy, Influence and the Development of Archives," *Journal of the Society of Archivists* 33, no. 1 (2012): 9–21.

4 Erin Lawrimore, "Collaboration for a 21st Century Archives: Connecting University Archives with the Library's Information Technology Professionals," *Collaborative Librarianship* 5, no. 3 (2013): 189–196, http://libres.uncg.edu/ir/uncg/listing.aspx?id=15271, captured at https://perma.cc/B65F-VWZY.

5 Society of American Archivists, Business Archives Section, "BAS Advocacy Success Stories," www2.archivists.org/groups/business-archives-section/bas-advocacy-success-stories, captured at https://perma.cc/XB9Y-F4FE.

6 Gerald F. Ham, "The Archival Edge," *American Archivist* 38 (Winter 1975): 5–13.

7 See SAA's online workshop on cultural diversity competency at www.pathlms.com/saa/courses/48.

8 Jeannette A. Bastian and Ben Alexander, *Community Archives: The Shaping of Memory* (London: Facet Publishing, 2009).

9 Natalia Fernández, "Oregon's LGBTQ+ and Communities of Color: Community-Based Oral History Projects" (presentation, SAA Annual Meeting, Portland, OR, July 28, 2017).

10 See, for example, Kaitlin Holt and Jen Hoyer, "The Way for Student Success: Lessons in Education Outreach," *Archival Outlook* (January/February 2018): 8, 29.

11 Dennis Meissner, "Leadership Plenary," SAA Annual Meeting, Cleveland, OH, August 21, 2015.

12 Paul Conway, "Facts and Frameworks: An Approach to Studying the Users of Archives," *American Archivist* 49 (Fall 1986): 393–407.

13 For a summary of user studies in the United States and Canada, see Hea Lim Rhee, "Reflections on Archival User Studies," *Reference and User Services Quarterly,* 54, no. 4 (June 2015): 29–42, www.researchgate.net/publication/279183209_Reflections_on_Archival_User_Studies, captured at https://perma.cc/9SQK-SJJL.

14 Examples include the National Archives Trust Fund Board, www.archives.gov/about/laws/nara-trust-fund-board.html, captured at https://perma.cc/4TPC-T8LE; the New York State Archives Partnership Trust, www.nysarchivestrust.org/, captured at https://perma.cc/QR5A-7TFL; and the Society of American Archivists Foundation, www2.archivists.org/foundation, captured at https://perma.cc/6R26-E3T3.

5

# Developing a Compelling Message

> In developing your message, think first about your audience. What do you want them to think? Feel? Feelings are what motivate people to act. That feeling may be compassion, concern, anger or joy. One of your goals in delivering your message should be to spark a feeling, whether it's pride, frustration or outrage.
>
> —*American Library Association Advocacy Institute, 2009*

Every advocacy or awareness effort needs a core statement that clearly and succinctly conveys the concept and purpose on which it is based. This is essentially a statement that you can repeat over and over again, something that you can say in a conversation, in an interview, in presentations. The American Library Association's *Advocacy Action Plan Workbook* stresses that this statement must be easy to say and remember; in fact, ALA recommends that this core statement should not be more than fifteen words. It also suggests that the statement meet the "SPIT test." That is, to be effective, the statement should be:

- Specific
- Personal
- Informative
- Trustworthy

(By "trustworthy," they mean you should be a trustworthy source who will check back with your contact, follow up, and do what you say you are going to do.)[1]

You need to convey your goal to your intended audience(s) and do so in a way that is approachable. One single statement serves as the core, but you should also be able to adjust the language in consideration of the audience's familiarity with or understanding of archives. Providing your core statement may be the first and most critical opportunity to engage and interest your audience, whether that audience is a manager, user, community member, or resource allocator. Those "first impressions," as old adages note, really do matter. Investing time to develop a powerful core statement is important for explaining your initiative but also in providing a solid foundation for further messaging to promote your efforts.

## Conveying Your Message Through Stories

Storytelling is perhaps the oldest form used by human beings to convey information and traditions. Its appeal has provided the basis for literature, theater, music, and folk traditions, and it is the substance of many family histories. StoryCorps and the Moth Radio Hour are good examples of efforts based on storytelling that currently have substantial popularity and impact.[2] Research has revealed the actual neurological effects of storytelling in conveying information and having an impact on the individual.[3] Our colleagues in the museum and library professions often share stories as a valuable method of conveying information about their work and issues.[4] Fundraisers also use stories successfully to interest donors and supporters.

> Researchers at Washington University have shown that we respond to stories with far more of our brain than we use for most tasks. Bullet-point facts activate only one part of our brain: the language-decoding center. A story lights up areas all over the brain.
>
> —*PGAV Destinations, 2014*

Because archives hold an incredible array of "stories" and narratives that can pique the interest of a range of audiences, we possess a great opportunity to draw on this approach as we undertake advocacy and awareness initiatives. We can relate information *about* the records we have in our holdings by sharing stories that reflect the individuals and events in them. We can also demonstrate the impact and outcomes that result from a user's research in our collections. Both can be very effective ways to demonstrate the value of archives to a range of audiences.

### Sharing information about archival records

As archivists, we often seek to engage others by sharing information from our records that will be interesting, surprising, or useful. This can be a productive approach *if* we carefully match the informational content with the interests of the audience(s). Often we tend to select items or information that was created by a "famous" person or that has national significance. Those people or events may have immediate name recognition for

> Exhibits of our treasures, at Archives Week events or other occasions, are fine, but people must understand the personal utility of those treasures before they will ever become our advocates.
>
> —*John J. Grabowski, 1992*

others, but it also directs their understanding of archives to iconic events (the American Revolution, World War II) or to individuals who represent past traditions of power and influence (Thomas Jefferson, Albert Einstein, Ernest Hemingway). But relying on the impact of recognizable names and events actually confines people's understanding of archives to being a place and profession of "treasures" that are valuable but useful only to vaunted researchers, scholarly publications, and exhibits. On other occasions, we share "curiosities" that may engage or be exciting to our audiences, such as a childhood letter penned by a famous actress, a photograph of a renowned scientist riding a bicycle, or a lock of hair from a former president. Again, unless such items relate to a specific focus of interest for the person or directly support the point that you are trying to make, it reduces archives to being entertaining but not for serious and purposeful use.

When you share archival holdings with others, match the records to your purpose. For example:

- Show a parchment map or daguerreotype portrait to a group of individuals or a foundation from whom you are seeking preservation fund donations to demonstrate the fragile and challenging types of media that archivists manage.
- Teachers will respond to documents that reflect current curriculum requirements, that will pique the interest of students, and that are visually appealing. Although iconic documents like a letter from Thomas Jefferson may have high value for traditional historical reasons, a one-page letter from a local soldier who served in Vietnam (which students consider ancient history!), in which he describes his experiences in handwriting that they can read, is more likely to engage their interest—and therefore be better used in a classroom to promote students' critical thinking skills.
- Share records with your manager that reflect their professional or personal interests. That might be historic photographs of the community in which they live, administrative records of their predecessor, or letters from people with the same ethnicity/race/gender or personal interests, like music, sports, or family history.
- When seeking collaboration with underrepresented communities, share the kinds of records you *do* have relating to the group. The limited information encompassed in existing records, as well as the gaps and the perspectives they reflect, may underscore the need for a more comprehensive, community-based documentation. If you have records from another community or know of another archives or project that shows a fuller representation, sharing those can demonstrate what should and could exist for other groups as well.
- A legislator who represents a district with heavy industry may be interested in records of working people, broadsides and advertisements from local businesses, or historical photographs of those industries.
- IT staff may become more interested in electronic records issues such as digital preservation when you share with them computer printouts, McBee keysort cards, or various floppy disk and other outdated machine-readable formats that have become part of your holdings.

The point of sharing archival records with any audience is to engage their interest initially by telling them "stories" that provide a touchstone to their own interests and experiences. Once that is accomplished, we can use that connection to move on to discussions of the value of archival records, of a planned project or initiative, and of the importance of ensuring access to, use, and preservation of the historical record.

## Sharing information about the impact of using archival records

One of the most powerful ways to demonstrate the value of archives can be sharing information and stories about outcomes that have resulted from the use of archival records. This information may be more complicated because it generally involves gathering information from users after they have completed their work. However, in many cases the uses they intend may be sufficiently obvious at the time of their research or we can let them know of our interest in hearing about the outcomes of their work. If the user is willing to share that information, it can provide powerful stories that indicate both the range of uses and the impact of archives.

There are so many compelling stories about the use of archives that we can share with our audiences to gain their support and understanding. Here are a few examples:

- *Creating new knowledge:* United States Geological Survey research geologist Bruce Molnia is part of an international effort to study changes in glaciers. Drawing from historic images and data from archives like the National Snow and Ice Data Center's Barry Archives, Molnia's research goal is to provide "unequivocal, unambiguous, visual documentation of the effects of changing climate and to share this information as broadly as possible."[5] His research in archives has done just that: It resulted in the published study *Glaciers of Alaska*. One pair of the archival images he located has been reproduced more than five hundred times and even appears on refrigerator magnets and postcards; another dozen are the basis of a National Center for Atmospheric Research game designed to raise public awareness about climate change. Furthermore, he has served as a senior legislative fellow in the U.S. Senate with a focus on policy issues. The knowledge resulting from his archival research is influencing public awareness and policy.
- *Protecting individual rights:* A widow in Pennsylvania needed documentation of her husband's military service to obtain veterans' burial benefits. The Pennsylvania State Archives provided a copy of his World War II compensation application to fulfill this request.[6]
- *Ensuring accountability:* The Canadian Defence Department instituted a review of military personnel files in the National Archives of Canada regarding individuals who were forced out of the military because they were gay or lesbian. The research was intended to identify the number of individuals discriminated against and determine whether a redress package should be provided by the federal government.[7]
- *Educating and improving student skills:* In his research for a History Day project on changes to victims' rights laws resulting from local murders, a Tallahassee high school student used records relating to the investigation of serial killer Ted Bundy and murders at Florida State University. The project won at the state level and went on to compete at National History Day. The student, who had previously been uninterested in school, credited his research experience with igniting his interest in education. He went on to complete law school, passed the Florida Bar, and is now practicing law in Florida.[8]

- *Ensuring historical accuracy:* A designer working in National Historic Site properties uses archives to view historic photos, postcards, menus, and other documents that establish the original designers' intent. These records provide a context and a road map for design work.[9]
- *Protecting cultural heritage for the public:* During the resolution of Detroit's 2013 bankruptcy filing, creditors asked for the sale of collections from the Detroit Institute of Art, which were owned by the city at that time. During the bankruptcy proceedings, DIA records maintained by the Research Library and Archives demonstrated that the majority of the holdings were purchased without city support. That information was used extensively in the final financial agreement and saved these important public art collections from sale and dispersal.[10]

Establishing and maintaining communication with users can assist archivists in identifying impacts and outcomes. Reference exit interviews are a good opportunity to determine users who are likely and willing to provide this kind of input. Social media also can serve as a resource for eliciting information from users, especially if you provide examples from either your repository or one with similar focus. Enlisting colleagues in regularly capturing these stories and creating a file for current and future use can have substantial benefit for advocacy and awareness.

> We know too little about whom we serve, how much they gain from interaction with our holdings, and the real, practical impact of our work to make an effective case about resource needs, return on investment, or "value." Our previous attempts at data gathering, while distinctly valuable in many ways, have nevertheless been too self-referential to answer these questions. And our previous strategies for making the case for resources—basing our arguments primarily on who we are, how many collections we hold, or how many tasks we perform—have not been effective.
>
> *Dennis Meissner, 2017*

# Using Data to Demonstrate the Value of Archives

Anecdotal information conveyed in stories provides one path for demonstrating the value of archives. However, it is critical to have demonstrable and credible data to explain and make a convincing case for archival needs, practices, and outcomes. As former SAA President Dennis Meissner has pointed out, such information has not been a focus for many individual archives or the archives profession. Colleagues in both the library and museum communities have established research arms to provide essential data for their professions.[11]

Simply citing numbers will not make a strong case, especially for audiences that take a strong interest in hard data. When

> **For More Information**
>
> Included in the public services standard are metrics and measures for:
>
> - User demographics
> - Reference transactions
> - Reading room visits
> - Collection use
> - Events
> - Instruction
> - Online interactions

advocating for both our profession and our institutions, archivists need to carefully identify the type of data that will, in fact, be useful in advocacy efforts. This often means gathering both quantitative and qualitative data. Some recent archival research has focused on assessment options for compiling a range of data types.[12] A number of toolkits are available from Archival Metrics.[13] Attention has also been focused on standardizing public services measures. SAA and the Rare Books and Manuscripts Section of the Association of College and Research Libraries (SAA-ACRL/RBMS) have worked cooperatively through a Joint Task Force on Public Services Metrics to develop a set of standardized measures and metrics for public services.[14] These could provide useful resources for future messaging efforts.

## Quantitative data

Quantitative data is statistical information that can be quantified and verified. For archives, those data may result from a survey of a constituency or from onsite user statistics, website analytics, search patterns in online finding aids, size and extent of collections, or financial benefits from management or use of archives. When using quantitative data in advocacy or awareness, it is important to understand the source of the data, including when and how it was created and what the data actually "mean." If you do not have training in statistical analysis, seeking assistance from someone with verifiable experience can be instrumental to ensuring both the accuracy of data collection and your interpretation of it.

Some of the data that archives have traditionally collected is necessary for managing archival work and functions. For advocacy or awareness purposes, those data may not be useful in demonstrating the outcomes and impact of archives. For example, archivists often cite the number of users who make requests onsite or via mail, email, or telephone. Although they may feel that a thousand onsite research visits demonstrates considerable use to the library administrator, the administrator may be accustomed to seeing circulation statistics in the tens or hundreds of thousands and therefore may find the archives use data to be insignificant in comparison. A useful variation on user statistics in a college setting suggested by Erin Lawrimore is collecting the number of research hours spent by undergraduates on class assignments in the archives. This can better demonstrate to an administrator the extent and intensity of student use and therefore the archives' connection to the university's research and education mission.[15]

Museums have compiled data on their economic impact for a number of years and have put those data to good use in advocacy efforts.[16] Approaching this for archives, researchers at the University of Michigan and the University of Toronto collaborated on a study to assess the indirect benefits to local economies resulting from patron visits. They conducted a survey in government archives to gather information from onsite users regarding their expenditures on hotels, food, and entertainment during their stay; over the course of a year, more than $2.64 million was spent by visitors in the subject institutions.[17] In an institution-specific study to demonstrate economic impact, staff of the Butte-Silver Bow Public Archives conducted a user survey focusing on the impact of out-of-state researchers. They determined that 59 percent of users were from out of state and 25 percent were accompanied by another person. The average minimum stay was 3 days, with some stays as long as 6 months. These data were used to demonstrate the Archives' contribution to the local tourist economy.[18]

Sharing data on costs, savings, and cost benefits is another approach that has been effective. In Alaska, the State Archives' holdings of email and electronic records from fifty-five state government executives led to a $250 million settlement in a pipeline corrosion case.[19] At the Procter & Gamble Company, archivist Ed Rider found more than 300 unique videotape copies of international commercials that were seriously deteriorated. After he shared information on the number of staff requests for this resource with the Advertising Development Department, that department funded the digitization and indexing of this information by the archives.[20]

Data resulting from the use of social media and web resources have been used by some archivists to assess use and user statistics, and this type of analysis may also produce useful information for advocacy and awareness purposes. In a study assessing web analytics at the University of Illinois, Christopher Prom emphasizes the need for careful analysis and a systematic understanding of how the data are developed and interpreted.[21] Sam Houston State University Special Collections conducted a useful study for collecting data on the effectiveness of social media for marketing finding aids.[22] Of ten social media options, they determined that blogs, Facebook, and Twitter were the most effective in raising awareness about special access tools.

With any approach using "hard data," it is important to ensure that the information used for advocacy or awareness will be perceived by the target audience as meaningful and substantive. Finding ways to present those statistics to demonstrate why the number is significant is an essential part of making the message compelling.

## Qualitative data

Qualitative data, information that describes conditions or characteristics, can also be useful in archival advocacy and awareness. These types of data may be collected through focus groups, observation, or interviews—methods that assist in characterizing needs, conditions, uses, or audiences. There is a considerable body of literature on conducting focus groups that can be retrieved from various management and university websites.[23] Archival research and experiences with focus groups have also been presented at conferences and discussed in the archival literature.[24] A number of researchers have conducted usability studies aimed at assessing online access to archives. Although not specifically oriented toward advocacy or awareness goals, these studies provide some insight into gathering qualitative data for archives, especially in online venues.[25]

Efforts to collect qualitative data for raising awareness about documentation needs were undertaken by the New York State Archives. The organization worked with a consultant to gather information to support development of documentation plans in three critically underdocumented areas for that state: Latino communities, mental health, and environmental affairs. A series of focus groups and individual interviews were held with representatives from state and local government, nonprofit organizations, activist groups, business, education, social services, religion, the arts, and journalism. The participants provided advice on identifying the major topics, issues, events, and trends and on establishing priorities for documentation. The results from those focus groups were used to raise awareness in those communities of the types of collections that were most important to identify and preserve. They also provided useful information about groups and organizations that they perceived to be truly significant to the community and therefore in need of documentation. In a number of cases, the focus group participants offered to serve as liaisons or to take the lead in talking with these groups.[26]

Benchmarking can be an effective method for evaluation or comparison of similar institutions or issues as part of an advocacy/awareness effort. It can be useful to provide information to internal audiences (such as managers or resource allocators) on a comparable institution with which they may be familiar or that they think provides a standard or is a worthy competitor. At the University of Wyoming's American Heritage Center, Mark Greene reported to the administration on how the Center compared with national norms in areas such as the number of undergraduate students conducting research there.[27]

For some audiences, it can be productive to get insight from an expert. They can provide quantitative and/or qualitative data and recommendations that may often be seen as more impartial. For example, the board and staff of the New York Philharmonic had differing opinions regarding whether a performing arts organization needed to have its own archives, so the board commissioned a study that resulted in a firm statement of the value of having and supporting its own archival program.[28]

## Make the message compelling

As noted throughout this chapter, there are many options for developing the content of an advocacy or awareness message. Depending on the target audience and what you think is most likely to move that audience to understand your message, you may choose to tell a story about how an individual's life was affected by information found in archival records. Or you may choose to present quantitative or qualitative data to support your core statement. The important thing to remember is that you should craft both your message and the way in which it is packaged to what is most likely to resonate with your target group. How does your message (the story you tell or the data you present) "speak" to the interest or needs of the person or group that is your focus? To state the obvious, different things appeal to different people. Archivists have so many potentially compelling ways to reach out and demonstrate the impact and value of archives. Understanding the key audience and then finding effective ways to convey a compelling message to that audience takes some work, but the payoff can be great in moving toward achievement of advocacy and awareness goals. Developing a strong, focused message or set of messages will provide a firm foundation for putting advocacy and awareness initiatives into practice.

## NOTES

1 American Library Association Advocacy Institute, *The Advocacy Action Plan Workbook* (Chicago: American Library Association, 2009), www.ala.org/advocacy/sites/ala.org.advocacy/files/content/advleg/advocacyuniversity/advclearinghouse/Advocacy%20Action%20Plan%20-%20revised%2001-09.pdf, captured at https://perma.cc/Q5W3-TJWK.

2 StoryCorps, https://storycorps.org/; https://themoth.org/radio-hour.

3 For discussion of research on the brain, see "Storytelling: It Can Change Your Mind" (St. Louis, MO: PGAV Destinations), 21–24; Richard Restak, MD, *The Naked Brain: How the Emerging Neurosociety Is Changing How We Live, Work, and Love* (New York: Harmony, 2006), 121–136; and Simon Sinek, *Start with Why*, 56–64.

4 For examples, see Paul Vandecarr, "History museums and social-change storytelling," 2014, http://workingnarratives.org/museums-and-storytelling/, captured at https://perma.cc/4SXR-JS3V; and Network for Good, "Storytelling for Nonprofits: How to Present Stories That Attract Donors, Win Support, and Raise Money," www.fundraising123.org/files/NFG-Storytelling-Guide.pdf, captured at https://perma.cc/CPE4-6SU3.

5 John F. Shroder Jr., "2009 GSA Public Service Award," Geological Society of America, 2009, www.geosociety.org/awards/09speeches/psa.htm, captured at https://perma.cc/6CBT-JEKX.

6 Council of State Archivists, *Importance of State Archives*.

7 Jim Bronskill, "Military Faces Archival Search to Pinpoint Number of People Forced Out for Being Gay," *The Canadian Press/The Globe and Mail*, June 4, 2017, www.theglobeandmail.com/news/national/military-faces-archival-search-to-pinpoint-number-of-people-forced-out-for-being-gay/article35198686/, captured at https://perma.cc/YT4Z-GP3R.

8 Elisabeth Golding, email to author, March 3, 2014.

9 Edward McCann, email to Joseph Coen, Archdiocese of Brooklyn, March 4, 2015.

10 Danae Dracht, "Federal Funding Impact Story #4: Project: Detroit Institute of Arts Archives Assessment," *ArchivesAWARE!* (blog), Society of American Archivists, Committee on Public Awareness, May 23, 2017, https://archivesaware.archivists.org/2017/-5/23/federal-funding-impact-story-4, captured at https://perma.cc/M9L9-7RMR.

11 Dennis Meissner, "Bare Necessities," *American Archivist* 80 (Spring/Summer 2017): 6–18.

12 Elizabeth Yakel and Helen Tibbo, "Standardized Survey Tools for Assessment in Archives and Special Collections," *Performance Measurement and Metrics* 11, no. 2 (2010): 211–222, https://doi.org/10.1108/14678041011064115.

13 Archival Metrics, https://sites.google.com/a/umich.edu/archival-metrics, captured at https://perma.cc/A5XC-8WHZ.

14 Society of American Archivists, SAA-ACRL/RBMS Joint Task Force on Public Services Metrics, "Standardized Statistical Measures and Metrics for Public Services in Archival Repositories and Special Collections Libraries," updated June 26, 2018, www2.archivists.org/standards/standardized-statistical-measures-and-metrics-for-public-services-in-archival-repositories, captured at https://perma.cc/CP4Y-S32A.

15 Erin Lawrimore, "The Big Picture: Effective Advocacy through Institutional Alignment," *Archival Outlook* (July/August 2013): 3, 25.

16 American Alliance of Museums, "Center for the Future of Museums," www.aam-us.org/programs/center-for-the-future-of-museums, captured at https://perma.cc/55FQ-BMG7.

17 Elizabeth Yakel, Wendy Duff, Helen Tibbo, Adam Kriesberg, and Amber Cushing, "The Economic Impact of Archives: Surveys of Users of Government Archives in Canada and the United States," *American Archivist* 75 (Fall/Winter 2012): 318.

18 Ellen Crain and Donna E. McCrea, "Building an Archives for Butte, America," in Hackman, *Many Happy Returns*, 123–137.

19 Council of State Archivists, *Importance of State Archives*, 4.

20 Adkins and Benedict, "Archival Advocacy," 52.

21 Christopher Prom, "Using Web Analytics to Improve Online Access to Archival Resources," *American Archivist* 74 (Spring/Summer 2011): 158–184.

22 Felicia Williamson, Scott Vieira, and James Williamson, "Marketing Finding Aids on Social Media: What Worked and What Didn't Work," *American Archivist* 78 (Fall/Winter 2015): 488–513.

23 See, for example, the Center for Innovation in Research and Teaching, https://cirt.gcu.edu/research/developmentresources/research_ready/focus_groups/effective_questions; Duke University, https://assessment.trinity.duke.edu/documents/How_to_Conduct_a_Focus_Group.pdf; and the Free Management Library, http://managementhelp.org/businessresearch/focus-groups.htm.

24 For example, see Adam Kriesberg, "Focus Groups in Archival Institutions: A Pilot Study" (presentation, 2011 SAA Research Forum, Chicago, IL, August 23, 2010), and Ciaran Trace, "Focus Groups" (presentation, MAC 2010 Symposium Archival User Studies, Dayton, OH, October 11–13, 2010).

25 Burt Altman and John Nemmers, "The Usability of Online Archival Resources: The Polaris Project Finding Aid," *American Archivist* 64 (Spring/Summer): 121–131. This case study examines how the Florida State University Libraries' Claude Pepper Library planned the first phase of the Pepper OnLine Archival Retrieval and Information System (POLARIS) Project—the development of an online finding aid and search engine. Rachel Walton, "Looking for Answers: A Usability Study of Online Finding Aid Navigation," *American Archivist* 80 (Spring/Summer 2017): 30–52.

26 New York State Archives, *A Manual for Documentation Planning in New York State* (Albany: New York State Archives and State Education Department, 2002, revised 2010), www.archives.nysed.gov/publications/manual-documentation-planning-new-york-state, captured at https://perma.cc/T3UB-4YUW.

27 Greene, "Putting Archives on the Agenda," 12.

28 Barbara Haws, "Advocating with the Institution: Twenty-five Years for the New York Philharmonic," in Hackman, *Many Happy Returns*, 189.

6

# Putting Advocacy and Awareness into Practice

Preparation is key to successful advocacy and awareness. As noted in previous chapters, planning should involve defining a clear, achievable goal that may include both short- and long-term objectives. You should undertake careful contextual research on the individuals and groups you plan to involve as your audience or supporters. You should formulate a clear and compelling message that explains your goal and can be modified to "resonate" with a variety of individuals in different situations. And you need to gather the stories, quantitative and qualitative data, and other information that illustrate your message and make it memorable.

Once that background and planning is done, it is time for the final steps in launching your effort. As in every phase of your planning, there are several considerations:

- Knowing the current landscape. Consider the timing and conditions that may influence and support your effort.
- Determining who will deliver your message to the primary audience.
- Identifying the approaches and techniques for carrying out and communicating about your advocacy or awareness effort.
- Assessing progress and adjusting your approach, if necessary, along the way.

# Knowing the Landscape

## Timing is everything

Whether you are undertaking an awareness effort with the professors at your university related to the acquisition of a new collection, working with your regional archival organization to raise the visibility of the archives profession, or participating in a national effort to influence federal legislation on privacy and access, it's important to time your effort in a way that supports and enhances your chances of success. There are a number of time-based cycles or opportunities that are useful to consider as you carry out your effort.

## Budget cycles

Your initiative may require or benefit from funding in your institutional budget. There are few "no cost" efforts—unless you take resources away from something else or pay for them yourself (the latter of which is not a good idea). For example, you may need special supplies, computer software, or consulting services. You need to know when requests for that funding should be submitted, to whom, and with what process. Archivists are sometimes reluctant to ask for additional funds, but well-justified, worthy projects can get support more readily if the needs are expressed in time to coincide with the budget planning process. If you are not familiar with the process, work with your immediate manager or with the financial officer so that your request meets all requirements and is timed appropriately.

If your project involves state or federal funding, it is important to learn about the budget development cycle and approval process. State government websites generally provide this information. If you need advice or insight from archival colleagues, contact your state archivist. If you are not already connected to that person, current information appears on the website of the Council of State Archivists.[1] The federal budget year begins in October, but preparation and negotiation typically begins more than a year in advance. This process is complicated, as it involves the White House, federal agencies, and both houses of Congress, so it is very helpful to be aware of the various roles, actions, and procedures involved.[2] Although there is a projected timetable for the federal budget process, the schedule can change from year to year. Be sure that you don't make assumptions and that you do your homework each year.[3]

## Knowing the schedule

For any meetings, events, or actions you plan, it is important to determine how they fit in or conflict with the schedules of your audience, your key stakeholders, or the supporters whose help you want to enlist. For example, if your audience is legislators or public officials, it is essential to know when they will be in their central offices (those on Capitol Hill) and when they are likely to be in their regional/district offices. With other audiences, it is important to determine what time of the year or the month is best for meetings or events and even what time of day is most likely to be productive. In a college setting, for example, when is it best to engage professors, students, alumni, or administrative staff? As we have all experienced, some people are very responsive early in the day when they are fresh from that first cup of caffeine, while others are best approached later in the day. The days that work for us as individuals may not be amenable for a given group, and professional obligations, religious observances, or even season of the year may have to be taken into account.

> The Northwestern University Archives developed an innovative marketing plan to make its blog known to students. It focused efforts on reaching them during the first few weeks of school when they were likely to be more curious about the resources available.
>
> —*Kevin B. Leonard, "Blogs and Blog Marketing: Bringing New Users to the Northwestern University Archives," 2009*

Depending on the focus of your efforts, look for opportunities that may be important times for your target audience and deliver them in a way that addresses their interests or preferred approaches. If your institution has a public relations officer or department, it may be a good source of dates or events that offer opportunities for drawing attention to advocacy or awareness efforts. Planning for events in advance will help draw attention to your efforts and can provide an easy way to keep your work in the minds of your audience, your management, and your supporters.

## Who Will Deliver Your Message?

Many archivists assume they will have most of the responsibility for advocacy and awareness efforts, including conveying the message to their audience. But in many cases other people or groups can and should be involved in moving initiatives forward. (If you have not had previous experience or are concerned about how to "pitch" your efforts, see Chapter 8 for a discussion of "finding your own voice.") Managers and institutional leadership may want to take a role as well. In addition, it is important to consider the opportunities for "grassroots" and "grasstops" support to deliver your message in a variety of ways.

### "Grassroots" support

Grassroots advocacy involves enlisting the support of individuals and organizations that value and are willing to speak on behalf of archives. They bring numbers, energy, and a wealth of stories and perspectives in support of advocacy and awareness efforts. Our archival associations and colleagues in all sizes and types of archival repositories can be effective advocates. Other advocates may include members of a community or group that uses archives, from genealogists and historians to land surveyors, scientists, or the local business community.

> When the Georgia Archives was threatened with closure, various groups and individuals came together to fight this move, including the Society of Georgia Archivists, the Georgia Genealogical Society, African-American genealogists, historians, and local legislators, among others.
>
> —*Kaye Lanning Minchew, 2013*

Advocates may be related professionals who rely on archives to undertake their work, such as teachers, museum curators, public relations departments, or historic preservationists. Many archives have friends groups that include both of the previous groups as well as individuals who are energetic about history and historical resources, even if they are not immediate or active users. Depending on the type of advocacy needed, a range of potential grassroots supporters can be identified and involved effectively.

## "Grasstops" support

"Grasstops" advocacy involves enlisting the support of key opinion leaders, well-known authorities, or influential individuals with connections to public officials or your audience. Although the numbers produced by grassroots efforts can have a major impact, having a "name" support your issue has benefits as well. A surprising number of actors, musicians, sports figures, authors, and business leaders have a passion for history that can be drawn on to gain their support. Such well-known individuals as historian Doris Kearns Goodwin, composer/playwright Lin-Manuel Miranda, actor Tom Hanks, writer bell hooks, and civil rights icon Fred Shuttlesworth have all spoken about the importance of the historical record. Don't assume that only those with a national reputation have this cachet, however. Depending on the audience(s), influential individuals who can provide support may be the president of the university they attended, a leader in their professional field, a community activist, or a family member or person of influence in their lives.

> In addition to the many voices, a few prominent voices are essential.
>
> —*Richard Pearce-Moses, 2013*

Sometimes people of influence can be reached through our managers and their contacts or through governing boards or friends groups. Another often productive route is researchers. Exit interviews provide an excellent opportunity to engage with users and enlist their assistance now or in the future. At the very least, we can solicit "testimonials" or quotes to use in demonstrating the value of our records or our work. Although it can be intimidating to ask for their support, many are extremely generous in providing it. Often, we simply need to ask.

> Gail Lang, an employee of the Open Book, an LGBTQI (lesbian, gay, bisexual, transgender, queer, intersex) bookstore, recognized the lack of institutional archives that were collecting and providing access to records of the Sacramento queer community. She was instrumental in the creation of a resource center, the Lavender Library, Archives and Cultural Exchange of Sacramento, Inc. Lang and others involved used their personal connections to encourage individuals to donate collections as well as encouraging them to donate funds to support the Center.
>
> —*Diane Wakimoto, Debra Hansen, and Christine Bruce, 2013*

# Communicating About Your Efforts

As an advocacy or awareness initiative moves forward, you will be communicating about your project with your audience, key stakeholders, supporters, and others, whether the press or the "public" who may become interested in your effort. Each situation or opportunity may involve written, online, or in-person communication. It is important to plan and prepare for how you will share information about your effort. Have a range of options ready, and prepare information in a way that can be adapted to a particular person or group, a situation, or a particular form of communication. In many cases, you will have one chance to convey your core message in a compelling, convincing way. Make sure you are ready to take full advantage of every opportunity.

## Writing about it

Preparing written statements that support your advocacy and awareness can serve a range of purposes. Writing down your message, explaining the quantitative and qualitative data, and capturing compelling stories will help you clarify how you convey the information. Your writing can form the basis for a case statement, for briefing materials or handouts to use with in-person meetings, for shorter pieces that can be used on social media, and for communicating with the news media. It also provides you with an opportunity to think about the language choices that will best convey your message and how to adapt them for different situations or audiences.

Many of the basic guidelines for effective communication apply here—and they should be used in any written materials relating to archival advocacy or awareness. Some reminders:

- Write to the specific audience and their interest. This is not usually an academic piece, so write in a way that will engage their interest and that shows your passion for the subject. Test your materials on a willing audience member, if possible, to see how they react and whether they "get" your message. Don't let them get away with saying that it sounds fine or is well written.
- Tell your audience what they need to know to be involved with your effort. Our tendency as archivists is to provide much more background, explanation, and contextual information than is often necessary. As an example, avoid details about how we do what we do ("Archivists acquire, assess, organize, manage, preserve, and maintain control of . . .") when writing for an audience that is interested in *using* records.
- Use *compelling* examples, stories, or data. Graphics, charts, and images help convey your intent, but they must be easy to understand and appeal to the audience.
- Make it clear at the outset whether you are asking for action or support. Say it as you begin, and say it again at the end.

If you have access to a public relations department, its staff can provide assistance in writing to specific audiences.

Most of all, make the time to create a well-crafted, interesting written piece. Learning to adjust writing to different audiences for a range of purposes requires real skill and can be invaluable for advocacy and awareness.

*Case Statements.* A number of organizations have developed case statements in their efforts to promote awareness or to serve as a basis for fundraising. Many organizations use case statements to explain a need or issue, describe how it has or will be addressing that need or issue, and tell the reader what they can do to support the effort. The American Association for State and Local History has developed a leaflet, "The Gift of History," for its members' use in introducing the value of local and state historical societies, historical museums, historic houses, and related cultural institutions.[4] History Associates created a case statement to introduce businesses to the value of a corporate archives as an asset that provides a "favorable return on investment."[5] A case statement can be useful as a basic tool for introducing and providing context for your initiative and/or your institution to individuals who may not be familiar with archives or archival functions. The use of case statements is best focused on audiences or key stakeholders who need to have a deeper understanding of your effort so that you can gain their involvement or financial support. Case statements tend to include:

> History Associates' case study provides an explanation of the values to businesses of a corporate archives: Properly managed, archives are assets that can help you:
>
> - Reduce operating costs through efficient information retrieval
> - Contribute to a sound risk management program
> - Communicate stability in times of change
> - Get the most out of your brand image
> - Generate added value for marketing and public relations activities
> - Produce revenue through licensing programs with third parties
> - Strengthen consumer loyalty through showcasing company achievements
>
> —*History Associates, Inc., 2013*

- A strong opening statement that draws attention to the value of your effort/institution.
- Mission and goals for your effort, your institution, or for the archives profession, as relevant.
- Brief background to provide context for your effort.
- Statistics, stories, outcomes, and proof of impact that demonstrates why what you are doing is going to be of benefit and to whom.
- The ask: What can readers do for you? (Provide financial support? Assist with advocacy or lobbying? Provide feedback?)

A case statement is *not* the basic brochure that many archival institutions have developed for their programs. It is more focused and should be used to provide the foundational information that supports your advocacy or awareness effort.

*Peripherals.* Whether you are meeting with an individual or group in your target audience, a legislator or public official, a journalist, or a group that is already interested in your advocacy or awareness effort, you will probably want a "leave behind" as a reminder of your key points and what you want them to do. If you choose to provide that as hard copy, follow a simple format: Tell them your goal or what you want from them; provide brief backup information or illustrative points; and tell them what you want them to do next. It should be a very succinct document, three to five bulleted points, preferably with some attractive graphics, charts, and lots of white space. Limit yourself to one page—literally, one page with 12-point type and normal margins. You are providing either an introduction or a reminder, not an in-depth explanation. (See the examples in Appendix A.)

## Talking about it

There will be many opportunities to speak directly about your advocacy or awareness effort from the time you first conceive of it through its various stages of development. And there will be a range of individuals with whom to talk, in both informal and formal settings. In every case, however formal or informal the setting, it is important to be prepared with core points and to focus them in a way that "speaks" to your audience. The reminders provided above for written communication also apply in face-to-face meetings:

- Match your presentation or discussion to the audience and address their interests.
- Use engaging examples, stories, or data that will speak to the individual or group. Watch the reactions you are getting, and be prepared with additional or different examples based on that response.
- Listen to your audience. Give them time to interject, ask questions, and make comments. These will help you gauge their responses and get clues on what directions you might take in the discussion to support your message.
- If you are not comfortable speaking, consider working with another person who might deliver the message. Consider joining groups like Toastmasters,[6] taking a public speaking course, or working with a mentor to develop your skills.

*The Elevator Speech.* Archivists, like many in the nonprofit, fundraising, and business communities, have become interested in the idea of elevator speeches.[7] The idea is to be prepared to give a quick summary of your work or project that can be delivered in the time it takes to travel several floors on an elevator, about 30 to 60 seconds. Recent research indicates that the average adult attention span is 8 seconds.[8] This is not an effort to try to provide a complete picture and summary. Instead, you should use an elevator speech to engage listeners' interest and lead them to seek further information.[9]

Many archivists have tried to explain our profession in simple terms, so we know how challenging it can be. Saying less can often be much more difficult, so you need to develop a core statement in advance that you can adjust to each listener. Here are the basic elements to include:

- Your name, your profession, your organization/affiliation (as useful)
- The advocacy or awareness goal/effort you are pursuing
- An example that might interest/connect with the listener
- What you hope to achieve that will engage the listener to care about your effort

Here is an example of a succinct elevator speech:

> Hi, I'm Kate Valdez with the Fremont County Historical Society. We are working to ensure that the voices of all the people in this county are made available in the historical records we keep. One group that is not well represented in the records is the Korean American community here. There are so many of its members' contributions and experiences that are important for people to know about. We've been working with the Korean Small Business Center and the Korean Methodist Church to connect with groups and individuals who might be interested in our effort. These records would be so valuable for teachers in our county schools, for people doing local history, for journalists, and for family research. Do you have any suggestions for other groups or people who might have family items like letters, photographs, or personal papers that would help us tell the story of Korean Americans in Fremont County?

Remember that this is just a first foray; use simple concepts that can convey your message without being confusing. Be prepared with a core message, but really try to adjust your elevator speech to each person or situation. If you are not confident about what you plan to say, try it out on colleagues, friends, and family. Then give your elevator speech at every opportunity. The more you do it, the easier it will become. This is a critical first opportunity to connect, and when you are successful, you will have more opportunities to expand and make more detailed points.

*Face-to-face Meetings.* In-person meetings with your audience or potential supporters can be an opportunity for meaningful communication about your advocacy or awareness effort. Although time pressure can complicate scheduling, an in-person meeting can provide benefits. In the business community and other communities, with their increasing reliance on technology, there has been much discussion about the value of meetings. Research in a number of universities indicates that face-to-face contact is most effective for establishing trust, building relationships, and inspiring positive emotion/response from your audience.[10] Whether the meeting is with your boss as part of gaining their support, with a key individual in an underrepresented community you seek to document, or with a group from whom you are seeking grassroots advocacy, look for opportunities to make the "human connection" to promote your work.

> The archivist at the National Realtors Association is part of their library's liaison program, communicating directly with those departments deemed most likely to benefit from and use their services. The archivist connects with them to learn about their needs and how the archives might help them. Opportunities have included press releases for media and communications staff to oral history projects or other long-term needs.
>
> *—Heather Hathaway, 2017*

*Moving the Message with Video.* Archivists in the United States and around the world have pursued efforts to deliver a variety of advocacy and awareness messages to audiences by posting videos on YouTube. This channel has real benefits as a means of bringing to life the stories and visual components of archives and the work of archivists in engaging ways. The SAA Committee on Public Awareness has provided useful guidance on producing successful videos for awareness efforts.[11] Major points include the following:

- Clearly define your goals and your audience; be sure you know *why* making a video is the best option for delivering your message.
- Content should be compelling and demonstrate a passion for archives or archival work. Tell fascinating stories or engaging collection highlights.
- Visual or audio appeal is essential. Production values matter in producing a video that will be effective. Not everyone is a video/audio producer; real skills are involved to develop a high-quality product with, for example, consistent sound quality and seamless edits. For advocacy or awareness purposes, "good enough" rarely is.
- Promoting the audio/video product is key. Simply posting it to a website, YouTube, Facebook, or Twitter is not a promotion plan. You need to determine how and where to get the word out to your audience regarding your production.

Professional archival organizations are using video for a range of purposes relating to advocacy and awareness. SAA worked with a professional service to develop *Archives Change Lives,* a video created to encourage archivists to become involved in advocating for and raising awareness about archives and the work of archivists. It focuses on archival value and demonstrates how other archivists can also accomplish the same goal.[12] The International Council on Archives Section on Professional Associations held a film festival in 2016 and plans to continue the event to share approaches for using video in raising awareness about archives. The entries provide some examples internationally with ideas that may be useful for other archivists.[13]

Archivists seeking examples of the use of video may also find a range of approaches and options from both the U.S. National Archives and the National Archives UK. The U.S. National Archives provides a range of videos that address how to use the Archives onsite as well as its online tools, along with specific types of records (e.g., military history and genealogy) and how to research them.[14] The National Archives UK has created an *Explore Your Archive* video series focusing on topics such as "What is an archive?," "What impact have archives had on your life?," and "What would the world look like without archives?"[15]

Archival institutions are using video productions to raise awareness about their holdings and services. Staff members at Brigham Young University's L. Tom Perry Special Collections have pursued two different approaches to providing a general introduction to their institution. First, they developed a promotional video using the approach of theatrical trailers for adventure movies, with rousing music and images and a message that underscores that the archives is a place where "anyone can come" and where "the past has a way of catching up with you."[16] They later created a standard introduction with more specific information and practical details for potential users.[17]

Video and audio have also been used to raise awareness about specific holdings in a repository, either for illustrative purposes or to encourage use. Although more focused on library collections, videos in the University of Iowa's Special Collections' "Staxpeditions" series have an energetic, lighter tone. One video features manuscript collections in "Exploring Mystery Boxes: Manuscripts Edition."[18] The Kansas State Historical Society created podcasts to draw the attention and interest of teachers to its Kansas Memory Project.[19]

Other archival institutions have sought to explain the work of archives and archivists as part of their effort to raise awareness about both their collections and the processes that are involved in the collections' care and access. As part of American Archives Month, the Lowell Observatory created the video "What Is an Archivist?" to give an overview of what archivists do and the Observatory's collections.[20] The Freer Gallery of Art and Arthur M. Sackler Archives produced "A Day in the Life of An Archivist," addressing basic information on the role of the archivist.[21]

Locating examples of video and audio implementations can be challenging because there is no consistent approach to sharing information about videos, podcasts, or other productions. The only current source for suggesting video and audio resources is the *ArchivesAWARE!* blog from SAA's Committee on Public Awareness. In addition to challenges in locating examples, there have been very few attempts to share assessments of successes, failures, and the lessons learned when archivists use audio and video either to raise awareness or to support an advocacy campaign. The extensive efforts that have been undertaken to create video and audio programs imply that archivists and their organizations believe that these likely constitute valuable approaches. The profession still must undertake additional research, discussion, and structured evaluations. Given the potential and some of the exciting efforts to date, this is research that is much needed to support effective use of video and audio for advocacy and awareness.

*Blog, Post, Tweet, Snap, Flick, Tumble, or Pin About It.* Many archives are making use of websites and social media to raise awareness of their institutions and collections. Whether using websites, blogs, Twitter, Facebook, Pinterest, Instagram, or other opportunities, you should use social media sites as tools when they support your goals and are effective in reaching your target audience and in conveying your message. When using the web and social media specifically for advocacy and awareness, it is helpful to consider several things:

> One common misconception of archives often leans toward old, musty, and out of touch. Social media can help archives to change this view by offering an opportunity to communicate effectively through the channels people already use every day, providing a new way to research and teaching the online community about the relevance of archives.
>
> *—Lauren Oostveen, 2011*

- What tools are your audience members most likely to use regularly for other purposes?
- How will they find out about your use of those tools?
- How will they know that the information comes from your organization/institution, and will they need or have the option to seek further information?
- Does your content reflect interesting and compelling stories or information for the audience?
- What results are you hoping for or expecting?
- How will you assess the implementation? What kinds of use or engagement numbers will make it worth continuing?
- How much time and what resources are necessary to manage your web and social media presence—and do they provide outcomes that justify your work?

It is important to match the medium to the message. That is, ask yourself what forms of social media will best deliver your message to your target audience and help you get to your goal. It can seem easier to take a tool with which you or colleagues are comfortable and try to adapt it to your goals, but that may in fact limit the impact. Archivists are using a range of web and social media alternatives that are worth exploring. There is no one central or comprehensive resource for doing so, and the range of uses is both wide and constantly growing, so published literature can fall behind developments quickly. There are online and published resources that provide ideas and information on using various forms of social media.[22] Colleagues can also provide helpful insights on options, challenges, and successes.

When considering alternatives for using social media or the web to support and facilitate the goals of an advocacy or awareness effort, it is important to maintain a focus on those goals and ensure that the medium supports the message and audience. With that caveat, social media and the web provide many exciting and sometimes unexpected opportunities for archivists and archival institutions to further their advocacy and awareness initiatives. Following are a few examples of how advocacy or awareness goals have been pursued using the web and various social media tools.

One of the goals for many professional archival organizations as well as individual institutions is to achieve some "name recognition" or raise interest in archival records or the work of archivists generally. Twitter and Facebook, in particular, have been used to raise awareness in both the general public and in targeted groups, like younger audiences or members of diverse communities. For example, since 2014, SAA and its Committee on Public Awareness have hosted an annual #AskAnArchivist Day on Twitter as a general awareness effort that reaches 3,000+ individuals in an unstructured situation.[23] Popular hashtags like #ThrowbackThursday and #TBT have put archival collections in the company of pictures of 1980s hairstyles or Matthew McConaughey's under-21 driver's license. Social media bring archives to the attention of many nontraditional audiences. It can also be very effective for sharing notices of events relating to annual celebrations, such as American Archives Month or exhibits, talks, or activities at individual repositories.

Many archival repositories have created Facebook pages based on the perceived expectation of existing and potential audiences that this is now a standard tool for public institutions.[24] Other repositories have reached general audiences with Facebook Live to share exhibits with those unable to come to the facility. The University of Iowa Special Collections livestreamed a tour of its display from Gene Wilder's papers that had been assembled in recognition of the public response to his death.[25]

Another approach worth noting engages users directly in interacting with online collections and developing in them a sense of "ownership" and involvement. The National Library of Ireland's Photographic Archive shared images on Flickr Commons for which information was limited or unknown and sought input from the public to identify places, names, or events. During the past 6 years, more than 34,000 individual "photo detectives" in Ireland and worldwide have provided some 40,000 comments, thus helping to increase the images' usefulness.[26]

Another awareness goal for many repositories is to draw attention, interest, and potential users to specific collections. Facebook, Twitter, or photo-sharing media like Flickr can be used as a very broad indicator of potential collections of interest. Twitter has been used to share entries from journals or letters to raise interest, such as the 1877 diary of James Redford, a homesteader in Sandy, Texas.[27] The University of Iowa Women's Archives uses Tumblr to share images ranging from a script for a women's seder to physical education class photos with captions that ask questions or invite readers to respond. Other efforts to interest and encourage users are often provided through media that support more information sharing, including blogs and podcasts. The University of North Carolina created a blog, *A View to Hugh,* to provide known and potential users with information on the Hugh Morton Photographs and Films, high-demand acquisitions that would require 2 to 3 years to process.[28] It shares information of potential interest on how archivists work with a collection of this type, highlights significant discoveries, and encourages dialogue among visitors and potential users.[29] In yet another approach directed at a specific community, the University of South Florida provides bilingual podcasts to raise awareness with diverse communities and promote collections that match users' needs.[30]

By the time this volume has been published, there can and should be many, many more approaches of interest that have real potential for archivists and archival organizations to engage and energize users, stakeholders, and supporters. Thoughtfully planned and designed social media and web implementations can be strong tools for raising awareness and supporting advocacy efforts.

*Using the Press and Media.* Engaging with the press and media can be an excellent way to spark public awareness and public education. Local newspapers, newsletters, and the Internet are useful media outlets. Knowing what issues are current or what topics are of current or seasonal interest is the best way to plan strategic communications involving the press and media. If you plan to use media to advocate for a specific issue with government officials, staying up to date also allows you to keep up with the official position of your legislators on the issues that are important to you. Think about how to use articles or news events as an opportunity to draw attention to your work and how that work connects to or provides additional information on an issue.

*Letters to the Editor and Op-Ed Pieces.* Letters to the editor are good tools for responding to recent articles by expounding on them or providing rebuttals. Articles that explicitly address an archival issue are fairly rare, but there are opportunities. You may find a news story that can be connected to your efforts, even if it is not explicitly focused on archives and records. For example, articles that raise concerns about email provide an opportunity for a letter to the editor that addresses the need to appropriately manage electronic records for long-term or permanent preservation. You might use the celebration of a holiday or event such as the 100th anniversary of World War I to draw attention to the resources in your repository/locality. Or when an article has one of those jaw-clenching references to archives as "dusty" or records as "lost," there is a perfect opportunity to speak out about the actual conditions and skills existing in professionally managed archives.

Don't confine yourself to the major national or large-city newspapers. Regional and local newspapers often cover the same news topics or rely on news services like the Associated Press. If the AP picks up your story, it may then get national distribution. The chances of having your letter published will be better with regional/local press and you can tailor your remarks to a more specific audience and region. In addition, if you are able to use your institutional attribution, chances are it will be recognized by a state/local audience.

Look on the website of the newspaper/media outlet for rules for submitting letters to the editor. Follow those rules carefully to improve your chances of publication (some newspapers, like the *New York Times,* publish a limited number of letters in the print version but a much-expanded number of letters online).[31] When writing a letter to the editor, keep in mind the following basic points:

- Write your letter directly in response to breaking news. Submit your letter within one to two days of the article.
- Observe the word count limits, usually 150 to 400 words. These are taken seriously and are generally inflexible—really.
- Focus on one point in the article that you feel is most critical and will be of interest to readers. This will help with clarity and length. You simply cannot respond to every point

of concern raised in the article. Go with your best and most compelling argument/statement.

- If you cite any facts, be sure to check the original source and ensure that they are accurate. Don't cite facts from a source citing another source. It rarely ends well!
- Avoid jargon or acronyms. Consider whether your audience will even understand the terms that archivists think of as obvious, like "digital preservation," "records schedules," or "finding aids."

Another way to get your issue into the public view, to educate, and to raise awareness is via an op-ed piece. Regional, state, and local newspapers generally provide a more viable opportunity for op-eds than do national media. As with letters to the editor, news media outlets have guidelines for op-ed pieces that should be followed explicitly. This is another situation in which your "grasstops" supporters may be particularly helpful, as having an article by a person with a reputation or a position readers will recognize can increase the chances of being published. You may want to offer to draft the op-ed piece for your supporter to make it easier for them. Look online for sources that provide advice and tips for guidance in preparing a brief but effective piece.[32]

## Reaching out to the press

At a number of points in your awareness/advocacy efforts, press coverage may help you achieve your goals. Although there are no guarantees of interest, you are best served by issuing a press release or making direct personal contact with a journalist to set up an interview. If your organization has a press or public relations officer or department, working with them is usually both required and the best option. If you don't have a professional PR staff to advise you, more detailed advice is available in SAA's *Public Relations and Marketing for Archives*.[33]

To set up interviews with the press, call your local news organizations. Ask to speak with a reporter who covers your issue of interest. This is a good way to report your own involvement. In preparing for your interview:

- Thoroughly prepare your thoughts.
- Be prepared to explain the same thing in a few different ways.
- Highlight your key points first, in an understandable manner.
- Keep your statements concise and quotable.
- If you don't know an answer, don't try to answer the question. Instead, offer to research the question and then provide the answer.

SAA's website for American Archives Month provides useful information that can be applied in many media situations, such as "Tips for Media Interviews," "Creating and Maintaining Good Media Relations," "How to Know If Something Is Newsworthy," and other media guidance.[34]

Although some archivists have experience with press releases, creating them in a way that will engage interest can be challenging. Many of the approaches suggested for elevator speeches can be productive here as well because you are similarly trying to spark interest in someone who may have little knowledge of archives and, perhaps, a limited affinity for history and may not have sought you out with serious interest in engaging on your subject. In the SAA Committee on Public Awareness's

*ArchivesAWARE!* blog, Erin Lawrimore provides the following useful tips for archivists on getting the attention of a busy journalist:

- Be sure that what you have to say is *really* newsworthy. Don't flood your new reporter friend's inbox with notes about every event, activity, or acquisition. Focus on the really important things that have a strong, and potentially lasting, community impact.
- Create an informative, jargon- and acronym-free headline that would allow a reasonably intelligent person to understand the importance of your message.
- Write in a clear and concise manner. Think Strunk and White (or read *The Elements of Style*, if you haven't already). Avoid passive voice. ("The archives hosts…" instead of "The archives has been hosting…").
- Keep your release short, factual, and to the point. Aim for 500 words or fewer (definitely keep it to one page!), and include links to your website for additional information.
- Focus on your opening sentence. This is your sales pitch. It needs to contain all of your critical information (who, what, when, and where), and it needs to convince the busy reporter to read on.
- Don't forget to include contact information (name, email, and telephone number)![35]

## Facsimiles and bookmarks and games

A range of other types of "reminders" may be useful in advocacy and awareness initiatives. The options for materials are nearly unlimited, and many colleagues have found creative routes to drawing attention to their advocacy and awareness efforts. Digital copies of documents can be helpful to share in meetings with legislators, journalists, and many others, but they should be compelling, of high quality, and readable by the audience with whom you are communicating. Bookmarks that summarize your key points are another relatively easy item to create, but they should be professionally produced—as should any other "marketing" items that you may develop, like buttons, posters, or notecards.

> The escape room was part of a campus wide welcome event for new and returning students at the University of Nebraska-Lincoln for Fall semester 2017 [to familiarize them with the resources available]. . . . The storyline we created was a time machine that would take the players back in the history of the campus to events that did or could have occurred on the campus. Players would then need to use library resources strategically placed in the room to help them solve the puzzles and return to the present time.
>
> *—Laura Weakly, interviewed in "Escape the Room . . . with Archives," 2018*

There are many exciting, even alluring, opportunities to develop support materials for your advocacy or awareness initiative. Think carefully about what you use and ask yourself a few questions before launching into production:

- Does it speak to the interests of the audience that matters most?
- Does it present information in a way that will be easy for that audience to use?
- What outcomes will it help to achieve?

- Is it flexible and relatively easy to adjust to speaking to different situations, components of your audience, or particular individuals?
- How much work and time will it take to develop and how much to manage and maintain?
- What are the costs? Include costs such as the time you, other professionals, support staff, technical staff, or others will invest; printing (even if on local color printers); mailing; food/refreshments for meetings/receptions; software; and online costs.
- Can you create and manage peripherals with the quality of production and appearance that will represent your work, your institution, and you as highly professional and competent?

## Assessing Progress and Adjusting Your Approach

As you undertake an advocacy or awareness effort, be conscious of your progress. That may involve developing or adapting a more formal assessment methodology, if it seems appropriate and you can do so.[36] Holding periodic focus groups with your primary audience, conducting a survey, doing web analytics, or gathering data on the activity of supporters are among the ways to assess whether an advocacy/awareness initiative is achieving the intended goal and impact. This information will be helpful in determining whether and how to adjust your goal, your audience, supporters, the message, and how you carry out your initiative.

> While the assessment of any digital program is essential to developing a sustainable media relationship with an audience, in many archives, the actual implementation of that assessment is often an afterthought to program development.
>
> *—Michael Church, 2009*

The Kansas State Historical Society developed podcasts to raise awareness among K–12 teachers and students of the primary sources available for their use. As part of that effort, KSHS staff recognized the need to have an assessment tool in place from the outset to justify the continuation of their program.[37] As a result, they learned that in 2008 there were 34,654 downloads for 35 programs. Further, production of each podcast cost $200 and required 8 hours of staff time. This kind of information can help determine whether an approach is worth pursuing, needs adjustment, or should be discontinued because it is not productive.

Some efforts, such as an Archives Month public program to raise awareness about your institution, have a short time frame. In that case, basic evaluation of attendance, audience response, and, perhaps, the number who joined a friend group afterward may be the extent of assessment needed. Other efforts that involve legislation or changing knowledge and attitudes about archives may require a longer time frame and more in-depth overall assessment. Even with long-term efforts, interim steps can be evaluated, such as audience reaction to a blog, sharing of social media posts, or the number of grassroots supporters who assist in your effort. Because advocacy and awareness are aimed at informing, changing attitudes or behaviors, or accomplishing some purposeful change, it is important to remain aware of how your effort is being received. That may change over time or in different situations, so flexibility is fundamental to your success.

## NOTES

[1] Council of State Archivists, *Directory of State Archives,* www.statearchivists.org/connect/resources-state/.

[2] Congressional Research Service, "Introduction to the Federal Budget Process," December 3, 2012, https://fas.org/sgp/crs/misc/98-721.pdf, captured at https://perma.cc/79VF-ZJ96.

[3] Information on the projected schedule each year may appear on the websites of the House Committee on the Budget and Senate Committee on the Budget: https://budget.house.gov and https://www.budget.senate.gov.

[4] Dennis A. O'Toole, "The Gift of History," *AASLH Technical Leaflet #252, History News*, 65, no. 4 (Autumn 2010): 1–4, www2.archivists.org/sites/all/files/AASLH_Tech+Leaf+252.pdf, captured at https://perma.cc/JV2H-TESE.

[5] History Associates, *Business Case.*

[6] Toastmasters International clubs around the country work with members to develop speaking skills. See www.toastmasters.org/ for more information.

[7] Society of American Archivists, Committee on Public Awareness, "Crafting Your Elevator Speech."

[8] Kevin McSpadden, "You Now Have a Shorter Attention Span Than a Goldfish," *Time Magazine*, May 14, 2015, http://time.com/3858309/attention-spans-goldfish/, captured at https://perma.cc/HBH7-F9E5.

[9] Nora Murphy, "Your Perfect Pitch: Elevator Speeches from the Field," *Archival Outlook* (January/February 2014): 6, 25.

[10] Susan Adams, "Why We Need to Meet in Person," *Forbes Magazine*, February 11, 2011, www.forbes.com/sites/susanadams/2011/02/11/why-we-need-to-meet-in-person/#705211c92626, captured at https://perma.cc/7NJN-7UYF.

[11] Chris Burns, "Sound and Vision: Using Video to Tell the Tales of Archives and Archivists," *ArchivesAWARE!* (blog), Society of American Archivists, Committee on Public Awareness, July 12, 2016, https://archivesaware.archivists.org/2016/07/12/sound-and-vision-using-video-to-tell-the-tales-of-archives-and-archivists/, captured at https://perma.cc/M955-53Z6.

[12] Society of American Archivists, *Archives Change Lives*, updated March 28, 2016, www2.archivists.org/advocacy/archiveschangelives, captured at https://perma.cc/F4WZ-9EAJ.

[13] International Council on Archives, Section on Professional Associations, "Film Festival 2016," www.ica.org/en/film-festival-2016, captured at https://perma.cc/Z8FN-F6KQ.

[14] A range of relevant videos can be viewed on the U.S. National Archives YouTube site at www.youtube.com/user/usnationalarchives.

[15] The National Archives UK offers a number of videos online at www.youtube.com/playlist?list=PLddhSH7bW0pW97staCfFGDFgLF6zI0aMI.

[16] Brigham Young University Library, *Special Collections Theatrical Trailer,* March 14, 2011, www.youtube.com/watch?v=GIUiH3PNOAE, captured at https://perma.cc/RMY5-7HTJ.

[17] Brigham Young University, L. Tom Perry Special Collections, *Introduction to the L. Tom Perry Special Collections,* March 1, 2013, www.youtube.com/watch?v=tZ_VGEzwvDw, captured at https://perma.cc/93Y8-9AKD.

[18] University of Iowa Special Collections, *Staxpeditions 6: Exploring Mystery Boxes: Manuscripts Edition!,* November 6, 2013, www.youtube.com/watch?v=xbhDIerW2u4, captured at https://perma.cc/54CZ-HRRG.

[19] Michael A. Church, "Archives to Earbuds: Podcasting Collections at the Kansas State Historical Society," in *The Interactive Archivist: Case Studies in Utilizing Web 2.0 to Improve the Archival Experience*, ed. J. Gordon Daines III and Cory L. Nimer (Chicago: Society of American Archivists, 2009), http://interactivearchivist.archivists.org/case-studies/podcasting-at-kshs/, captured at https://perma.cc/A4W6-BT49.

[20] Lowell Observatory, *What Is an Archivist?,* October 10, 2016, www.youtube.com/watch?v=tg54sP3bXaI, captured at https://perma.cc/MN2H-2FB5.

[21] Freer Gallery of Art Archives, *A Day in the Life of an Archivist,* August 13, 2010, captured at https://perma.cc/GMP5-CQ6G.

[22] Lauren Oostveen's "Social Media," in *Public Relations and Marketing for Archives,* ed. Russell D. James and Peter Wosh (New York: Neal-Schuman Publishers and Society of American Archivists, 2011), provides useful basic information on "how to" get started and examples of uses for Twitter, Facebook, Flickr, YouTube, and Pinterest. In addition, the SAA Committee on Public Awareness's blog *ArchivesAWARE!* (https://archivesaware.archivists.org/) includes a number of posts that reflect ways archives have used tools like Facebook Live and Twitter for public awareness. Articles in both of SAA's publications, *American Archivist* and *Archival Outlook,* have provided ideas for and analysis of using social media.

[23] Peter Gottlieb, "#AskAnArchivist Day: A Tweet Success," *Archival Outlook* (November/December 2014): 21.

[24] Joshua D. Hager, "To Like or Not to Like: Understanding and Maximizing the Utility of Archival Outreach on Facebook," *American Archivist* 78 (Spring/Summer 2015): 18–37, http://americanarchivist.org/doi/pdf/10.17723/0360-9081.78.1.18.

[25] Jennifer Koerber, "Live from the Library," *Library Journal*, April 10, 2017, https://lj.libraryjournal.com/2017/04/marketing/live-from-the-library/, captured at https://perma.cc/GJ6Q-JWMB.

[26] Vittoria Traverso, "How 'Photo Detectives' Have Helped Reveal Irish History," *Atlas Obscura*, November 2, 2017, www.atlasobscura.com/articles/photo-detectives-ireland-irish-history-archives-exhibition-crowdsource, captured at https://perma.cc/LPV6-9LVV.

[27] The University of Texas at San Antonio's Twitter account that shares information on James Redford is @RedfordDiaries.

[28] Hugh Morton was a prominent North Carolina entrepreneur, tourism booster, environmental activist, and sports fan whose 500,000-item collection was donated to UNC in 2007.

[29] Stephen Fletcher, "A Priceless Gem for Only Ten Bucks," *A View to Hugh: Processing the Hugh Morton Photographs and Films* (blog), University of North Carolina, University Libraries, October 27, 2018, http://blogs.lib.unc.edu/morton/, captured at https://perma.cc/K7AX-T5QZ.

[30] Tomaro I. Taylor, "Connecting to Marginalized Groups through Web 2.0," *University of South Florida Scholar Commons*, January 2010, http://scholarcommons.usf.edu/tlas_pub/67/.

[31] For an example, see Kathleen D. Roe, "A Recent Opportunity to Raise Awareness of Archives," *Off the Record* (blog), September 5, 2014, https://offtherecord.archivists.org/2014/09/05/a-recent-opportunity-to-raise-awareness-of-archives-4/, captured at https://perma.cc/L93N-X4Z8.

[32] See, for example, "Op-Ed Writing Tips and Tricks, The Op-Ed Project," www.theopedproject.org/oped-basics/, captured at https://perma.cc/QMW6-MMT5, or Harvard's Kennedy School of Government's "How to Write an Op-Ed or Column," https://www.shorensteincenter.org/wp-content/uploads/2012/07/HO_NEW_HOW-TO-WRITE-AN-OPED-OR-COLUMN.pdf, captured at https://perma.cc/9MCN-WDJF. See also "Sample Op-Ed Piece on Presidential Records Act Amendments of 2007 and Executive Order 13233" at www2.archivists.org/sites/all/files/Op-EdonPRA-EO.pdf, captured at https://perma.cc/Z6UN-AK3L.

[33] Russell James and Peter Wosh, eds., *Public Relations and Marketing for Archives* (New York: Neal-Schuman Publishers and Society of American Archivists, 2011), 9–71.

[34] Society of American Archivists, "American Archives Month: The Power of Collaboration," www2.archivists.org/initiatives/american-archives-month-the-power-of-collaboration, captured at https://perma.cc/4A62-CPGX.

[35] Erin Lawrimore, "Effective Media Relations for Your Archives," *ArchivesAWARE!* (blog), Society of American Archivists, Committee on Public Awareness, June 13, 2016, https://archivesaware.archivists.org/2016/06/13/effective-media-relations-for-your-archives/, captured at https://perma.cc/3YH6-XMKE.

[36] Online resources demonstrate various approaches. For a few examples, see M+R Strategic Services, "Assessing Effectiveness of Advocacy Efforts Process Indicators," www.powerprism.org/AssessingEffectivenessEfforts.pdf, captured at https://perma.cc/A386-PPWR; and Julia Coffman, Ehren Reed, and Innovation Network, "Unique Methods in Advocacy Education," www.pointk.org/resources/files/Unique_Methods_Brief.pdf, captured at https://perma.cc/57RG-5ERG.

[37] Church, "Archives to Earbuds."

7

# Advocating with Government Officials

Advocacy is an effective tool for influencing policy and increasing general understanding of archives by elected and appointed officials at all levels of government. It follows the same core practices and approaches discussed previously. Most archival advocacy efforts with groups such as members of the U.S. Congress or state legislatures and officials require a coordinated effort led by a professional association or an advocacy group. However, individual archivists have a critical role to play, either as leaders or supporters in these initiatives.

This chapter departs from the more generalized discussion of principles and practices provided in previous chapters. Instead, it focuses on specific guidance regarding approaches and considerations in applying those general principles and practices when advocating in a government setting. Public and legislative advocacy has specific and defined practices, approaches, and sometimes rules of conduct and operation for those advocating with or lobbying government officials. Archivists should be aware of these when advocating with federal officials, in particular, but also at other levels of government. The discussion here will primarily reflect the national level, addressing approaches to use when dealing with the U.S. Congress, federal agencies, and the White House.

## Archivists' Role in Advocating with Government

Advocacy can and should be done at all levels of government, of course. For example, the challenges of managing email as a public record is just as applicable to a city mayor as it is to a governor or the president of the United States. Educating government officials at more "local" levels can be a good long-term investment that will pay off in the future. A result of the recent "Archives on the Hill" effort by four archival organizations—SAA, CoSA, RAAC, and NAGARA—the *Archives,*

*Public Policy & You: Advocacy Guide* is a useful resource for guidance in federal, state, and regional advocacy efforts.[1]

Advocacy at federal, state, and local levels may be needed to address a range of issues that affect the archives profession as well as research communities and those groups, topics, and events archivists seek to document. Federal granting agencies, such as the National Historical Publications and Records Commission, the Institute of Museum and Library Services, and the National Endowment for the Humanities, are an important source of funding for many archives. Federal privacy and Freedom of Information laws can affect many archives and special collections, such as universities with student records, nongovernment archives programs that manage the records of former members of Congress, institutions that manage medical information, and records of individuals and groups that have been involved in protests or challenges to government or institutions. Other archives may encounter issues with copyright and intellectual property laws affecting audio and visual material collections or unpublished works. For many years archives often operated without having to be particularly concerned about legal issues because information was known to a few and the chances of discovery of breaches were limited. The revolutionary access offered by the Internet means that archival catalogs, finding aids, digital collections, and social media options have put many archival records in the public eye. Today, it is essential that every archivist ensure that federal, state, and even local laws support archival goals and protect archival subjects appropriately.

The following sections address how to focus the tools, information, and approaches needed to undertake effective public advocacy. They will help you advance the issues that are important to you—whether open access to such government records as vital statistics, appropriate management of electronic records of government from Twitter to body cameras, funding for archival projects and institutions, copyright law, or other immediate or systemic issues relating to archives and records.

The most powerful tool available to you in advocating for archives is the realization that *you can make a difference.* Whether you are leading or participating in an effort coordinated by SAA, your regional association, or some other group with a particular concern, with some effort and the appropriate know-how your actions can have direct political implications. The following guidelines outline the most effective methods of communicating with your elected officials, but it is up to you to engage actively in public advocacy.

## Preparing to Advocate with Government Officials and Legislators

Changes in attitude and practice that involve archival issues need to be accomplished at all levels and with a range of officials, not just those who are publicly elected or most visible. Archivists can take two kinds of actions with government officials:

- Seek their support through votes on legislation pertaining to immediate issues.
- Develop a relationship and knowledge base to inform future actions that will support archives and archival issues.

Take time to plan your advocacy effort so that you have the necessary foundation to carry it out and feel comfortable with the information you will provide and your approach. For many archivists, this is not a function for which they are trained or have prior experience. Being prepared is important in both reducing personal stress and maximizing the opportunity to make your case effectively. Returning to practices discussed in Chapter 3, this begins with having a clear goal, identifying the target audience, and developing a clear message.

## State your goal clearly—and often

Be prepared to state your purpose or goal as a clear, succinct request in the form of a specific action. Be ready to state it at the beginning, repeat it at the end, and support it throughout any communication. Make sure the officials and their staff are very clear on what you are asking them to do. Be prepared to repeat your request at other times, perhaps in different ways or by enlisting others to deliver the same message. As a voter/citizen/community member, it is your role and your right to ask elected officials to take action.

A succinct request for action to a government official might include a brief problem/issue statement followed by the specific action you seek, such as:

- City council members are using Facebook, Twitter, and Instagram to conduct and comment on city business. These communications may be public records subject to the records retention laws of this municipality and state. The city council should adopt and follow policies and practices to ensure that the public records it creates on social media are being kept in accordance with the law in order to ensure government accountability and transparency.
- The governor's records are not currently defined as public records in our state law. Because the governor is the highest elected official charged with doing the business of this state, the law should be changed to include the records of the governor and the governor's office. Please introduce (or vote on) legislation to achieve this.
- The National Historical Publications and Records Commission, a program of the National Archives, provides competitive grants to archival institutions around the country. Funding is not included in the presidential budget for this year. Please contact the House Appropriations Subcommittee on Financial Services and General Government and ask that funding be restored at $10 million for this fiscal year.

## Identify your audience

Whether your write, call, or visit, consider with whom you will be communicating. Make sure you know the roles and responsibilities of the person's office so you know you are talking to the right person(s) or that they can convey your message to the appropriate person. It is important to remember that for virtually all legislators at any level, as well as elected officials at any level of government, being elected and reelected is a primary motivating force.[2] They and, in particular, their staff members know that listening to constituents is an essential element of their role.

Learn what you can about the person's background and interests so you can focus your message in a way that will draw their attention more effectively. Members of Congress as well as most state legislators have websites where you can find the following kinds of useful information:

- Basic biographical data, such as family relationships, schools/colleges attended, professional affiliations, social organization memberships, or personal activities from family history to the arts or sports.
- Issues of particular concern and legislation sponsored that can help you prepare for potential questions you might receive, particularly if the member may not automatically be receptive to your request.
- The institutions, businesses, or groups with interest and influence on issues in the legislator's district or state, which may be those that support as well as those who are possible sources of opposition. In particular it can be helpful to identify the number (even if approximate) of institutions that hold archival collections in the district/state.

## Target your message

You will, as noted, want to present your request as the initial part of your message. Once you convey that, if the person with whom you are communicating is receptive (or at least willing to listen), follow with some concise and compelling reasons for why you believe they should support your request. It is useful to incorporate a few focused examples of data or compelling stories that demonstrate why you are making the request. Whenever possible, those examples should be directed to the interests you have identified for that person. In most cases you will have a very short time to present your request, so be prepared to provide brief but compelling information.

As noted in Chapter 2, in fall 2012 the Georgia Secretary of State announced that the Georgia Archives would be closed to public access as the result of a 3-percent budget reduction required of all state agencies. A group of concerned archivists, researchers, and citizens formed the Coalition to Preserve the Georgia Archives to advocate with Governor Nathan Deal and the Georgia Assembly to prevent the closure. They compiled an impressive array of data demonstrating key points. Fiscal data included graphic information (see Figure 10), benchmarking data (see Figure 11), and significant uses of information from the Archives (see Figure 12).

Examples can incorporate a range of types of data, but it is essential to ensure they address the concerns and interests of the key audience(s). It is important to adjust and try different approaches, if necessary as your efforts proceed, until you find what "works."

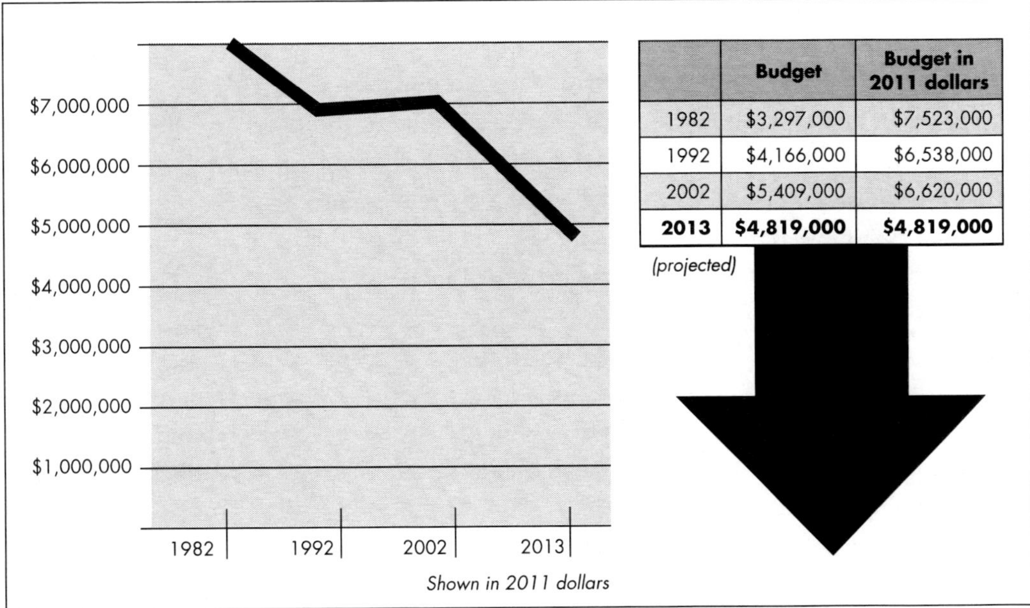


| | Budget | Budget in 2011 dollars |
|---|---|---|
| 1982 | $3,297,000 | $7,523,000 |
| 1992 | $4,166,000 | $6,538,000 |
| 2002 | $5,409,000 | $6,620,000 |
| **2013** | **$4,819,000** | **$4,819,000** |

**FIGURE 10.** Budget for the Georgia Archives 1982–projected 2013

**Source:** Coalition to Preserve the Georgia Archives

**The Georgia Archives will be the ONLY state archives in the nation with NO PUBLIC HOURS beginning November 2, 2012.** In contrast to Georgia, the Mississippi and Virginia Archives are open 6 days a week, the South Carolina Archives is open 5 days a week, and the Alabama Archives is open 4 days a week plus every second Saturday.

**FIGURE 11.** Benchmarking Data Comparing Research Hours Among State Archives

**Source:** Coalition to Preserve the Georgia Archives

Secretary of State Brian Kemp recently negotiated a dispute about the Bibb-Monroe county line.

When no records of a survey could be found, it cost $1.5 million in litigation. Kemp notes, *"Settling disputes can be very expensive if you don't have the documents."*

Savannah River boundary dispute with South Carolina settled using records of a 1787 agreement that gave Georgia the right to certain lands south and southwest of the river, as well as all islands in the river.

Cobb County used GDOT maps to establish right-of-way for utility property interest.

Georgia Pacific used environmental records to determine the type of air filter that was placed in the burner smokestacks at its plant in Warm Springs.

Physicians and researchers used public health records to compile data about epidemics.

City and county officials regularly request copies of their charters and founding documents.

**FIGURE 12.** Examples of Recent Projects Supported by the Archives

**Source:** Coalition to Preserve the Georgia Archives

## Deliver your advocacy message

Once you've developed a well-focused message, the next concern is how to effectively deliver it. You want maximum impact from communications. Personalizing that message will also demonstrate your interest and commitment. If you are asking others to make similar contact, strongly encourage them to create their own personalized version of the communication.

Many offices will not track or respond to communication from outside their constituency. They feel their responsibility is to represent the citizens of the state/district that they were elected to serve. If a legislator is in the leadership of a committee responsible for addressing your issue, however, you can reach out to them in that capacity. In the U.S. Congress, the contact information for the chair and ranking member of a committee is *not* the same as the contact information for the member's congressional office. The committee's website will have the contact information you need to use in addressing the member in their committee leadership role. (See Appendix B for information on key congressional committees.)

Opinion among advocacy groups differs on the efficacy of using templated letters or email messages, pre-scripted phone calls, postcard campaigns, and online petitions. In addition, some officials/offices prefer one form of communication over others. Many people have ideas about what is most effective, but the "best way" to convey your message may change even in a few months or years. Seeking input from others who have demonstrable and current experience with effective advocacy can be very helpful. If you work for an institution with a formal government relations office or one that works with a lobbyist, seek advice from that office or lobbyist on what is currently the most effective route for contacting a particular member of Congress or public official. You have a core message; the method(s) for communicating should be flexible and may change over the months or years of your advocacy work.

*Written Communication.* Write a personal letter to your elected public official, if possible. Formal letters have long been the most popular form of communication with congressional offices, but because mail delivery is often delayed due to anthrax screening, you may need to send your letter via email or fax. The Internet and email are powerful tools for communicating with elected officials. Most federal legislators have websites that include a general office email address. Offices keep count of the email messages they receive on each issue.

Following are some tips for writing effective letters or email messages to your legislators or public officials at any level of government (see the sample letter in Figure 13):

- State your credentials. Be sure to include your institution (if you are permitted to do so) and voting address if you use email so that the offices know you are a constituent.
- Make it clear that you are a constituent.
- Cover only one issue per letter/email.
- Avoid jargon.
- Keep your comments to *one page.*
- State your reason for writing in the first paragraph of the letter.
- When writing about specific legislation, identify the bill number and the sponsor, if available.

- Ask your legislator or public official to take a specific action.
- Explain how the issue affects you, your repository, and/or your patrons. Personal anecdotes are particularly effective.

Look for addresses and contact information for all of the members of the U.S. House of Representatives and Senate at www.house.gov and www.senate.gov.

Dear [Representative Name],

As a constituent of the 96th district of New York and an archivist at the Energetic Historical Society, I am writing to express my concern that the president's proposed budget for FY 2018 has eliminated funding for the National Historical Publications and Records Commission. I believe this will have serious consequences for our community, and I ask you to support the restoration of $10 million in funding for the NHPRC.

The NHPRC is a grant program of the National Archives that provides competitive grant funds to state and local organizations to develop archival programs, promote the preservation and use of historical records, and promote regional and national coordination in addressing major archival issues. When Congress created the NHPRC, it recognized that the history of this country does not take place solely in federal offices in Washington, D.C., and that significant evidence of national issues exists in the states, regions, and lives of individuals around the country.

My institution, the Energetic Historical Society, received an NHPRC grant to preserve and digitize records relating to the building of the Erie Canal. We are now able to provide wide access to essential evidence of the impact of the canal on our community, reflecting on our role in the beginning of westward migration as well as documenting the first major public works project in the United States.

The NHPRC has clear financial benefits in addition to preserving our heritage. Historical records projects are "jobs-heavy." On average, *75 percent of funds for such projects are used to pay staff.* In our project, 85 percent of funding supported staff salaries. Our board was able to raise funding to continue employing our project archivist after the grant. NHPRC requires cost-shared funds of 50 percent from all its grantees—so it stimulates expenditure of local dollars to match the federal investment.

I would like to invite you and your staff to visit the Energetic Historical Society so that we can share with you the collections and the many ways in which they are used by historians, land surveyors, transportation agencies, teachers and students, and family historians.

To provide essential opportunities for us to expand the ways in which we serve your constituents as well as researchers nationally, I urge you to support the restoration of $10 million in funding for the NHPRC. Please contact Representative XYZ, chair of the House Appropriations Subcommittee on Financial Services and General Government, to express your support for NHPRC.

Thank you.

Sincerely,

Grace Allen<br>
Archivist, Energetic Historical Society<br>
111 Main Street<br>
Port Energy, New York<br>
96th District

**FIGURE 13.** Sample Letter to Congress

*Place a Phone Call.* Place an issue-oriented phone call to your elected official's office. Phone calls are a convenient way to discuss urgent issues that do not allow time for letter writing or visits. If you have a personal relationship with your elected official, ask to set up a call with them. Otherwise, expect to speak with a staff member. Offices keep track of how many calls they receive on each issue. Even if your call does not make it past the receptionist, you have still accomplished something. You can find elected officials' telephone numbers on their office websites. In addition, the U.S. Capitol switchboard (202-224-3121) provides the phone numbers of federal legislators. See Figure 14 for details on making such calls.

- Telephone calls typically are taken by a staff member, not the member of Congress.
- Ask to speak to the aide who specializes in your issue.
- Identify yourself as a constituent and give your credentials and phone number so that the office may call you back, if necessary.
- Briefly state your reason for calling. Be focused, as you will have limited time.
- If appropriate, explain the reasons for your support or opposition to an issue. Present facts, not just opinion.
- Whenever possible, use local examples to bolster your case.
- Ask for your legislator's position on the issue. If the staff member is not aware of the legislator's position, ask for a written response to your call.
- Thank the staff member and offer to answer any questions in the future.
- If your call is directed to voicemail, leave a message and request a call back. Try your call again at another time of day and continue to do so until you talk "live" to a person.

**FIGURE 14.** Phone Call "How-Tos"

*Schedule an Appointment.* Schedule an appointment to visit your elected official's office. A face-to-face meeting with your legislator and their staff makes you and your issue more memorable. It also provides the opportunity for you to better assess the kinds of questions or concerns that may result and gauge the response. Below are some tips on scheduling visits to your elected official.

***Scheduling a Meeting with Federal Legislators***

- Federal legislators are generally in Washington, D.C., from Tuesday through Thursday. If you wish to meet with a legislator on Capitol Hill, call the Washington office and ask to speak to the scheduler. If you wish to meet with your legislator in a home district office (and there are usually several), contact them at that office. Again, ask to speak to the scheduler.
- Briefly explain to the scheduler the issue you wish to discuss. Try to limit yourself to one issue per phone call and meeting request.
- Keep in mind that you may meet with a staff member, because most legislators have extremely busy schedules. Do not take this as a drawback in communication. Usually staff members specialize in specific issue areas and advise the legislator on how to vote. In fact, staff members often know more details about an issue than the legislator does. They have "the ear" of the member, and if you convince them of the importance of your issue/request, they can be influential in gaining the member's support.

### *Preparing for the Meeting*

- Determine whether your legislator has taken an official position on your issue of concern. A good place to start is by locating your member's website at www.congress.gov.
- Determine whether your legislator serves on any relevant committees. Appendix B contains a list of key committees frequently contacted on archival issues. These can change in name, function, and membership. Current committee structures and members can be found on the Senate (www.senate.gov) and House websites (www.house.gov).
- Know your issue well and prepare examples in advance.
- Leave a "paper trail."[3] Take a fact sheet or outline of your issue that you can leave with the legislator or staff person. Again, keep this to one page, concise, with bulleted points. Try to keep to three to five bullet points, and do not make them text-heavy. Never use smaller than 12-point type and don't skimp on the margins—really. Make sure the piece is focused on that legislator and their state/district.
- Know ahead of time with whom you are meeting and how to get to the meeting place. Get there early.

### *At the Meeting*

- Plan to spend no more than 15 minutes in your meeting; be brief.
- Bring your business card, and exchange cards with the relevant staff member, if possible. Their contact information will give you the opportunity to follow up in the future.
- Explain why the issue is important to the district or state. Then explain why the issue is important to you. Be ready with examples, compelling stories, or hard data.
- Take brief notes during the meeting, or bring along a colleague who can do so. You want to be clear on what the member/staff person says and the response to your request. The pressure of making your "pitch" can make it hard to recall everything later.
- Know your facts. If you do not have an answer, do not guess. Instead, promise to follow up after the meeting.
- Offer yourself as a resource and let the legislator know that they can call on you for advice or input.
- Thank each meeting participant for their time.

### *After the Meeting*

- Send a thank-you note to the people who participated in your meeting. Also send a thank-you letter to the legislator, and mention the name(s) of the staff person(s) with whom you met. Staff are more likely to share a thank-you letter that points out the positive response they/their colleagues are getting from constituents and that increases the opportunity for your message to get before the legislator.
- In the note, briefly restate your position on the issue and again offer yourself as a resource.
- Stay in touch with your legislator's office to maintain the relationship.
- If appropriate, invite your legislator and their staff on a tour of your repository or institution.

*Maintain the Relationship.* Develop a personal relationship with your elected officials and their staffs. Officials may be more receptive when they have had regular contact with a constituent rather than hearing only when there is a problem. In addition, archives and archival issues often require some explanation. If you have to begin each communication by explaining what an archives is, it takes time away from the actual issue at hand. Building on a base of understanding and familiarity with you or your institution can be extremely helpful in gaining future support. Following are tips for cultivating a relationship with your elected officials. Once a relationship has been established, you can become a trusted advisor on archives issues. And perhaps your legislator will even become a "champion" for archives.

> For advocacy, the big picture for the future is that relationships still matter. Whatever the tactics are, relationships remain the core of good advocacy.
>
> —*Campaign Workshop, 2015*

*Invite Your Elected Official on a Repository Tour.* Use a tour to educate your legislator and their staff about your repository and how it has an impact on the district and state. If you receive federal grant money, highlight this fact and show them how you are using the money. Also use this opportunity for media attention. Work with your legislator's press secretary to give the legislator favorable media coverage.

*Present an Award to Your Elected Official.* You may have a connection to your legislator through a local professional organization, a religious or social group, or a high school/college relationship. Use these ties to strengthen your relationship. Invite your legislator to speak to the group and present an award to them for good service or strong leadership. Legislators appreciate positive feedback from their constituents.

## Enlist outside support

Archivists should not assume sole responsibility for addressing archival issues and goals with government officials. Outside supporters can be particularly effective. An archivist asking for support from a federal grants program has a direct professional stake in and will benefit from that funding. When civic or organizational leaders, influential individuals, or community members speak up on behalf of archives, their support may be particularly well received. To obtain such assistance, it is critical to communicate effectively, provide clear requests for action, and supply the core message and materials to make it possible for supporters to act quickly and with reasonable effort. Building active and effective bases of support may take some time, so it is important to begin identifying potential opportunities well in advance. Experts in advocacy and lobbying estimate that around 5 percent of those who could be supporters can actually be counted on to take action.[4] So preparing and facilitating their participation is essential to success.

## "Grassroots" support

Grassroots advocacy efforts involving the support of individuals and organizations that value and are willing to speak up for archives offer several advantages with government officials. To most legislators, receiving input from five to ten constituents makes an issue worthy of note. Archival supporters such as genealogists or community groups can often exceed those numbers by several orders of magnitude. In addition, grassroots advocates can be very passionate and convey individual stories about why archives matter to them. These supporters give archivists both numbers and passion for their causes.

When seeking grassroots advocacy support from government officials, keep the following in mind:

- Ask for support when there is a specific action to be taken or issue to be addressed. People are more likely to respond to an urgent need ("If funding is not restored to the archives budget this fiscal year, research room hours will be reduced to one day a week.") than a general request for support ("The archives is important to my research and deserves more funding.").
- Provide clear directions on what you want your advocates to do—make a call, write a letter or email message, or make a visit.
- Provide sample language that they can adapt and personalize. Encourage them to individualize their request so it will have more impact.
- Ask for help when you really need it. Not everyone will respond each time you ask for action. Some supporters will take action only once. Use your requests effectively; don't wear out your welcome.
- Ask your supporters to share their letters or email messages or the results of their phone calls or visits. It will help you know how much response you are getting and may provide you with good stories or data that you can share later. Just be sure to ask for permission to cite them.
- Report back to them on progress or responses to your advocacy effort.
- Thank them sincerely for their assistance.

## "Grasstops" support

It can be particularly effective to enlist key opinion leaders, well-known authorities, or influential individuals who may have cachet with public officials. They need not always be "nationally known" individuals. There are many people with considerable reputations in a state or region whose names and opinions will matter to your government officials. This is when your background research may be particularly helpful in identifying individuals who might have influence with a particular government official; it may be the president of the university they attended, a leader in their professional field, or a family member or person of influence in their life.

When seeking the support of key leaders or public figures, keep the following in mind:

- Indicate the specific action you are requesting and be sure it is something they can reasonably do. Although they may not be willing to make a personal visit, perhaps a phone call or letter/email message will be viable.
- Make their involvement as easy as possible. Offer to prepare a draft letter/email message for them to edit and use. Perhaps a photograph and a quick quotation from them is an option. If you plan to quote/cite it later or use it in social media, have them approve how it will be used.
- Make sure your manager or the staff of your public relations office are aware of, and approve of, your making this request.
- You may need to work through your manager, a board member, a colleague, or another supporter to ask for the support. If so, make sure you have provided that person with clear information about what you are seeking. They may be willing and able to include you in the "ask" so that you can help guide the request. Thank this person and ask to be apprised of any response received.

## Make the commitment

Legislative advocacy is essential to the archives profession. It helps address the need for effective legal foundations for the creation and management of archival records. It is also necessary for ensuring federal funding for archives that is comparable to resources devoted to other information and heritage professions, such as libraries and museums. To date, advocacy at the national level has focused on specific issues or actions ranging from establishing the National Archives, supporting such legislation as the Presidential Records Act, or seeking federal funding for the National Historical Publications and Records Commission, the Institute of Museum and Library Services, or the National Endowment for the Humanities.

In the past decade archivists have begun to focus more intensively on legislative advocacy as part of ongoing professional activity. The Society of American Archivists has developed an advocacy agenda.[5] Other organizations, including the Council of State Archivists, the National Association of Government Archives and Records Administrators, and the Regional Archival Associations Consortium and many of the regional archival associations it represents, have also identified advocacy priorities. Several national and regional archival organizations participate in the National Coalition for History to pursue national legislative initiatives.

These efforts are a positive development for the profession but are in the very early stages of creating a productive and continuing presence at the federal level. In most cases, the same is true at the state and local levels. Government officials and legislators still lack essential awareness of the value of archives and the benefits that archives bring to government itself and to the communities and individuals it serves. Some archivists have not had experience in legislative advocacy; others believe they do not need to participate in advocacy efforts that don't have immediate impact on their individual repository or job. But the archives profession must focus on advocacy with government officials and leaders to ensure that there is a better understanding of the purpose and contributions of archives and to garner support for essential legislation and funding. To achieve this, advocacy must be taken on as a professional responsibility by all members of the archives profession.

## NOTES

1 Society of American Archivists, Council of State Archivists, Regional Archival Associations Consortium, and National Association of Government Archives and Records Administrators, *Archives, Public Policy & You: Advocacy Guide,* 2018, http://files.archivists.org/advocacy/SAA-Advocacy-Guide-2018.pdf, captured at https://perma.cc/P227-LEH3.

2 Nancy Amidei, *So You Want to Make a Difference: Advocacy Is the Key,* 16th ed. (Washington, DC: OMB Watch, 2010).

3 Amidei, *So You Want to Make a Difference.*

4 Amidei, *So You Want to Make a Difference.*

5 Society of American Archivists, "Advocacy Agenda," 2015.

# 8

# Advocacy and Awareness: Taking the Next Steps

Advocacy and awareness rarely (if ever) appear on a list of core archival functions. In the professional literature, in archival education, and in their day-to-day work, archivists focus on the theory and practice of appraisal, acquisition, arrangement and description, preservation, reference, and access. Nonetheless, advocacy and awareness are important—indeed essential—to the health of institutions with archival holdings and for the archives profession itself. To move forward, archivists must focus on embedding advocacy and awareness more clearly and effectively into ongoing activities and practice. This final chapter considers the steps archivists must take to prepare for effective advocacy and awareness on behalf of and in concert with archival institutions, the archives profession, and the many individuals, groups, and organizations that will benefit in both small and large ways from a strong understanding and use of archives.

## A "To Do" List for Advocacy and Awareness

Advocacy and awareness initiatives are not simple or formulaic acts. Following are the things that we need "to do" in order to create the context and conditions for effective advocacy and awareness. They are not in a linear order; some may be more readily addressed, while others may take time, resources, or the cooperation of others to achieve. Some can be accomplished by specific actions, others require developing a mind-set or focusing on approaches that will support advocacy and awareness. Review the following list and consider where you are, where you need to be, and how you might proceed "to do" the things suggested.

### *1. Make time for advocacy and awareness.*

Given that most archival institutions have too few staff members and too much work to do, advocacy and awareness initiatives are often delayed or put aside in favor of "immediate needs." Yet archivists continue to be concerned about the lack of understanding of the value of archives and the lack of respect for archival practice. Archives are all too often associated with words and phrases like *dusty, old, curiosities, treasures,* or *lost records* by everyone from immediate employers to users and stakeholders, the press, legislators, and society in general. It is important to take the time to overcome these perceptions and raise positive awareness for archives and archivists. The time investment does not have to be extraordinary or extensive; as archivists gain experience in doing advocacy and awareness, greater facility for the work will develop. You may want to actually schedule a few hours a week to think about opportunities you can incorporate into your work and to do background research or stay in touch with ongoing records issues. Make time for advocacy and awareness—your institution and your profession need the benefits your participation will bring.

### *2. Plan your efforts.*

In every profession, there are people who enjoy planning—and those who do not. Planning for advocacy and awareness does not have to be onerous or elaborate, though it should be thoughtful. In fact, it can be a useful change from daily activities in that it may provide an opportunity to think about what you do in a larger framework. As archivists, we understand the value of our work and are passionate about its importance. Planning provides the opportunity to think that through and devise ways to convey that value to an audience. Appendix D provides a checklist for planning your advocacy or awareness initiative.

As noted previously in this volume, a well-articulated goal connected to institutional or organizational goals is essential. Planning that addresses those goals will have more impact and help keep activities focused and purposeful. It can be so easy to get derailed by ideas that sound good at the time but don't really support your goal or take up far too much time for the resulting impact. A well-considered plan will save time in the long run and help increase the impact your efforts can have.

### *3. Listen to your audience and your supporters.*

Archivists are passionate about the archival record and the work we do. But to be effective in reaching others, we need to focus on learning what speaks to them and what will engage them rather than drawing from our own sources of enthusiasm and interest. There is a difference between sharing information about archival records in a way that makes them appear as interesting "curiosities" or treasures to be revered (and maybe ignored) and conveying the very real impact and importance that archives can have for a wide range of audiences.

Listening to your audience and supporters involves finding ways to get to know them. Engage in conversations with key opinion leaders and seek advice from members of your audiences, whether informally, through a focus group or using an advisory group. Include them in your planning efforts, if possible and practical. People are generally quite good at telling you what matters to them, what interests them, what kinds of activities they are willing and able to participate in, and what they will (or will not) support.

To understand what will interest people and how to reach or work with them effectively, *listening is absolutely essential.* We make assumptions, based on our own experience and cultural context, about what will interest or appeal to a person or a group. This is particularly damaging when we work with just about anyone who is not from our ethnic, racial, gender, age, professional, or socioeconomic group. Developing our cultural competency skills is essential for archival advocacy and awareness just as it is for other efforts. The knowledge you gain from listening will benefit more than an immediate advocacy or awareness effort; it will inform your work in the future and help immeasurably in establishing productive relationships that will continue over time. There is so much to be gained by respectful, engaged listening.

### *4. Be aware of the context in which your organization operates.*

Most archives and historical records collections are part of a larger organization—a library, a university, a business, a religious group, or a government. Each of those bodies has its own mission, goals, policies, and organizational structure. Each has its own cultural context and business practices. And each also has social, political, and economic forces that influence how an organization operates.

You must be able to demonstrate how your efforts fit within and support the larger goals of your organization or your professional association(s). Connecting to existing goals can enhance your chance of gaining support and furthering the impact of what you plan to do. Participating in institution-wide committees, attending meetings that may not be directly germane to the archives, and connecting with other parts of an organization will provide critical information that you can use to help guide and gain support for your efforts. As archivists, we know that context is essential to understanding records; the same is true for understanding how to work in our employing institutions. For advocacy and awareness efforts, it is important to the health of an archival program to gain as much knowledge and experience as possible in working within the context of an organization, both to identify positive opportunities and to be aware of forces or issues that may hamper your efforts.

### *5. Be aware of the context in which our profession operates.*

Compared to the number of librarians, university professors, teachers, lawyers, journalists, business owners, land surveyors, or government officials in the world today, there are relatively few archivists, so we must be aware of the range of issues and concerns that our archival colleagues deal with in order to provide advocacy and support at critical times. Most archivists now deal with issues of managing electronic information, such as email and creating digital collections for wider access. But we all need to be aware of the challenges faced by colleagues in different types of archival settings. Those working in government archives deal with issues related to presidential and gubernatorial records or Freedom of Information and privacy laws. Those working in religious archives may face issues regarding access to records with personal information or those relating to clergy sexual abuse. Business archivists face challenges in managing records of mergers and reorganizations, as well as responding to public interest in the records of a private corporation. University archivists struggle with convincing departments that they have a responsibility to manage their records and turn them over for permanent care and access.

Staying in touch with the range of challenges we all face is an essential professional responsibility. Professional associations provide many opportunities to do so through their meetings, conferences, websites and social media, and publications. To advocate effectively for the archives profession and to raise awareness about its value, we should all be aware of the context and challenges that our colleagues face.

### *6. Be aware of issues and developments in your community and in our society.*

The archives profession does not "set the agenda" for legislation, policies, or political, financial, or social developments, but archivists are responsible for preserving and making accessible the essential evidence of society, its organizations, and its populations. That responsibility provides many opportunities for advocacy and awareness initiatives connecting to the current and often urgent issues in our communities, government, and society. If archivists want to be seen as having a role beyond that of gatekeeper to history (or the unhappier version of "managers of dusty attics of lost treasures"), we must relate our work to ongoing situations, information needs, and issues that capture the attention of the public.

As citizens, we should pay attention to current media with an eye on identifying the archival implications. There is a wide array of topics for which an archives or records "angle" exists. Archivists can draw on collections and on archival expertise to connect with contemporary issues and interests. Those may include connecting people with their family and community heritage, contextualizing and documenting social action, providing perspective on local issues and events, responding to natural disasters, or providing expertise on electronic records. There are many awareness opportunities to connect with the present by drawing from insights and resources in archives.

### *7. Watch for unanticipated opportunities and take advantage of them.*

Careful planning and preparation for advocacy or awareness activities is critical. However, as archivists, we should be flexible and prepared to take advantage of unexpected opportunities to draw attention to the value and importance of archives and archivists. Some of those we can "plan" for in advance by enlisting staff and users in identifying "finds." Processing staff should be on the alert for items that might connect with current concerns or provide interesting stories. Researchers may similarly be asked to share information or documents that we can use for immediate press opportunities, whether with formal media outlets or our own use via social media.

Other opportunities may come with little warning. Public relations staff, an alumni office, the office of a university president, a legislator, or even an organization's webmaster may present the archivist with a "Do you have something?" request. Those requests are fertile ground for just-in-time awareness that not only underscores the value of your holdings but also positions the archivist and the archives in the mind of the requestor as a cooperative and useful resource. Although you may be tempted to see these requests as diversions from the work that needs to be done, they can be an effective route to establishing a positive mind-set in the requestor of the value of the archives and archivist. That status can be extremely beneficial for future efforts or when you need supporters for your program.

### *8. Continue to hone your advocacy and awareness skills.*

Archivists often claim that our profession is dominated by introverts, so speaking publicly or interacting with people is seen as an area in which we do not (and, by implication, cannot) excel. Few people are by nature effective advocates. As with many other skill sets, regardless of personality characteristics, practice and repeated application is key. If you are motivated to learn, educational opportunities are available. The Society of American Archivists offers regular online and onsite educational options.[1] Regional and state archival organizations periodically provide both workshops and program sessions that address advocacy and awareness. The American Library Association has online offerings that provide advocacy resources based on topics such as privatization, value of libraries, and Internet safety; challenges such as knowing what to say and getting decision-makers to listen; and advocating for specific groups, such as young adults, academic libraries, and rural libraries, among others.[2]

Many adult learners benefit from seeing real-world examples of advocacy and awareness materials produced by others, particularly in related professions. The Society of American Archivists' Issues and Advocacy Section and the Business Archives Section have developed advocacy and awareness toolkits that provide a range of useful examples and links to other resources.[3] Many other groups provide online training and resources, ranging from youth advocacy groups to disability advocates, trial lawyers, and teachers. Perusing these resources can provide tips or insights that can be helpful as well.

Probably the most productive route to honing advocacy and awareness skills is simply to do it. Elevator-style speeches benefit from repeated efforts to "try it out" on different people and gauge their reactions and then refine and try again. Encounters with reporters become easier (at least you learn what to expect will be likely misinterpretations of your words) with practice. Sharing information via social media is a less intensive way to practice honing an awareness or advocacy message. When an action alert comes out asking you to contact Congress or local officials on an issue, taking the time to make that contact will give you an opportunity to develop your skills in summarizing and demonstrating the value of archives and the work of archivists. Take advantage of more informal opportunities to try out language and approaches to enhance your own skills.

### *9. Assess your progress, including both successes and challenges.*

Not only do we need to do advocacy and awareness work; we must also evaluate our efforts to determine the effectiveness of that work. None of us has the resources or time to waste on minimally worthwhile efforts that are "full of sound and fury, signifying nothing."[4] Particularly when undertaking an advocacy or awareness initiative for which you've spent time planning and invested resources to implement, your plan should include an assessment component. The range of assessment techniques and the methods for implementing them are beyond the scope of this volume. However, many archivists work in organizations that give them access to individuals with skills in program evaluation and assessment who may provide assistance or advice. Here are some questions you may want to consider in assessing the impact of your efforts:

- Did changes take place in policy or approach?
- Are there statistics that demonstrate impact, such as an increase in users and the types of uses they made of the information?
- Did the effort result in media coverage? If yes, what kind and quality?
- What information can be gathered from our use of social media, such as retweets, likes, or web statistics?
- What feedback can we gather from key stakeholders, users, or other audiences on whom the effort was focused? How can we draw out responses that give us qualitative data on

their reactions or uses rather than just finding out whether they "liked" or were "satisfied" with the experience?

- What do staff and leadership perceive as the benefits and challenges, and what suggestions do they have for future activities?

If an advocacy or awareness activity is worth pursuing, it is also worth assessing for its effectiveness and impact. The more we learn about what works, what challenges were involved, and what makes an effort successful, the more we can improve future advocacy and awareness efforts.

### *10. Persevere. What you do will make a difference.*

Advocacy and awareness initiatives are a long-term investment. Many efforts may have an immediate or short-term goal that can be accomplished. But others, particularly those involving legislative change, take more time because of the need to work with existing systems and structures that are not amenable to rapid movement. Underlying all of our advocacy and awareness efforts is the very real need to demonstrate the role and value of archives and archivists, and that will require systemic shifts in both actions and attitudes.

Our collective past provides many examples of archival perseverance. Perhaps the most prominent example of that is J. Franklin Jameson's 30-year campaign to establish a National Archives. The Council of State Archivists has worked for more than 10 years to engage with a key stakeholder group, state chief information officers, and now collaborates with them regularly through the National Association of State Chief Information Officers (NASCIO) on education offerings and support for electronic records grant projects.[5] American Archives Month, which began in 1984 as a single week in New York City, has been taken up by archivists around the country who have been willing to direct their energy to raising awareness of the importance of archives. To accomplish real change, archivists must make a commitment to advocacy and awareness over the long run.

## Finding Your Own Voice

As noted previously, archivists sometimes express reluctance about involvement in advocacy or awareness initiatives. Some have concerns, particularly when it involves direct contact or meetings with government officials and their staff or with the president of a university, the leaders of a business or religious organization, or vaunted scholars and journalists. Few archives, library, or history training programs addressed the skills and methods for undertaking this kind of work. And internships focus on operational work; these rarely, if ever, involve practical experience with advocacy or awareness. Some archivists think this is work solely for managers and leaders of an organization.

Advocacy and awareness initiatives are essential to the health and future of our work and our profession. All archivists have a role, but there is not one job description for what that entails or a simple course on how to do this work. Each of us needs to find our own voice and determine how we can best contribute to advocacy and awareness efforts in our institutions and our profession. Some considerations for how to do that follow.

## Take stock of your skills

Each of us brings different strengths and weaknesses to our work. For advocacy and awareness, some of the skills you may need to draw from or develop include:

- *Communicating verbally:* Are you able to talk about archival and historical concepts in ways that a given audience will find both comprehensible and approachable? The concepts do not have to be simple, but they should be stated clearly and without archival jargon or technicalities.
- *Communicating in writing:* Similar to verbal communication, can you write succinctly and clearly about archives and archival records? Can you make a compelling case for your efforts? Can you adjust your writing to the delivery media, from articles to web pages to Twitter?
- *Being flexible:* Can you adjust your speaking or writing style to the needs of different audiences? You may need to try different approaches until you find the one that works best with a particular audience or in a particular situation. And you may need to make those adjustments on the spot as you are talking with a person or group.
- *Being organized:* Any advocacy or awareness initiative needs to be organized and planned in advance. This is an area where archival skills certainly overlap with advocacy and awareness.

## Collaborate and work with others

Many archivists assume they have to take the lead role or do the majority of the public-facing work. If that's not your strength, or even if it is, collaborating with others can be really productive. For example, if you need to approach your organization's leadership to ask for additional funding, the best appeal may not come from you or even your manager. After all, you will want more for your program because . . . it's your program. Having a researcher with name recognition, a key faculty member, or the leader of a community organization who will speak about the value of your work is likely to be more compelling because they will not be the immediate beneficiary. They are speaking on behalf of something they value, and that can make their argument more credible and stronger.

In other cases, you may find that making your argument through key opinion leaders will again be stronger. If you want to work with an underrepresented group in your community, you might develop relationships first with a person or a few members who can in turn make the case for documentation. Many groups have good reason not to trust the requests from people who have not developed a relationship with them in the past.

You may simply find that your skills do not match certain roles, so enlisting colleagues, managers, or others who do have those capacities is more productive. The best approach is to define the roles that need to be undertaken and find the people who can do them best.

## Be prepared

Most of us are more comfortable sharing information if (1) we are comfortable with the message, (2) we know to whom we are talking or writing, and (3) we are confident in our knowledge of the material. We need to do the background research so that we are familiar with the stakeholders, audiences, and context for our advocacy and awareness work. Having command of the information that you want to share makes it easier to be flexible and change approaches, if needed. If you are planning to talk about particular records that may be of interest or tell a story about the outcomes of using records, it can be helpful to have more than one example prepared so that you have options. Practicing a presentation of the information can increase your comfort level. With statistical or quantitative data, be prepared for questions about what the data mean, how they were compiled, and who compiled them. It can be helpful to practice presenting the data to a colleague or friend who can ask questions about it so that you can view it from a different perspective.

Finally, it's important to remember that not everyone responds to the same style of interactions. The high-powered, energetic "sales" approach may not be appealing to everyone. Sometimes a more quiet, relaxed approach will be more productive. In truth, it is less a matter of style and more the genuineness of your interest and delivery that will appeal to others. Each of us must find our advocacy voice and develop the confidence to convey a message in a way that is comfortable and conveys our message and commitment.

## Sources for More Information, Ideas, and Issues

There are many resources available through national and international archival organizations, the museum and library community, and national groups with specific advocacy mandates. These groups provide information on current issues of concern, call for specific actions, and share resources that provide useful background and context for the challenges and opportunities in archives and related professions.

### Resources from archival organizations

*Society of American Archivists (SAA).* SAA is the oldest and largest organization in North America devoted to the professional needs and interests of archivists. Since its founding in 1936, it has been involved in a range of advocacy and awareness efforts, many of which are noted in Chapter 2 of this volume. SAA currently has a public policy agenda outlining the issues on which it focuses attention. It also makes available a series of position papers and statements that reflect issues of which archivists should be aware.[6] A few examples include:

- U.S. Presidential Records Act
- U.S. Freedom of Information Act
- U.S. Health Insurance Portability and Accountability Act
- Copyright
- Federal funding for archives
- Diversity and inclusion
- Hurricane relief

SAA also issues action alerts and coordinates activities to advocate with the U.S. Congress and White House, with state governments, and on other issues affecting archival institutions. (For a complete list of SAA's issue briefs and position statements, see Appendix C.)

The SAA Committee on Public Awareness's blog, *ArchivesAWARE!*, provides guidance and ideas for public awareness. SAA also provides a range of resources in support of American Archives Month.[7]

*Council of State Archivists (CoSA).* CoSA serves the needs of the fifty-six state and territorial archives in the United States, including conducting research on conditions and issues, developing best practices, and advancing their advocacy concerns. Like SAA, CoSA supports a range of issue briefs and position statements focusing on issues that affect government records, some of which it creates in cooperation with other archival organizations. Examples of those include:

- Developing strong state archives
- Digital access partnerships
- Sale of public records
- Use of nongovernment email for government business

Like SAA, and often in conjunction with it, CoSA pursues advocacy relating to archival issues; it has been particularly active regarding funding for the National Historical Publications and Records Commission, as well as leading the national effort to obtain increased federal funding for archives nationwide.[8]

*National Association of Government Archives and Records Administrators (NAGARA).* NAGARA serves as an association for government records administrators and archivists at the county, municipal, state, and federal levels, as well as public universities and provincial governments. Because many members, as government employees, have constraints on lobbying or advocacy, NAGARA collaborates with SAA and CoSA on issue and position statements relevant to its mission and circulates action alerts.[9]

*Regional Archival Associations Consortium (RAAC) and Regional Archival Organizations.* RAAC is a formal consortium of the regional archival associations around the United States and coordinates and communicates between those groups and between the regionals and SAA. Advocacy and public awareness are among its priorities for this type of coordination to ensure the awareness and involvement of the wider archival community. Some regional archival organizations have specifically identified advocacy and/or awareness in their mission statements or strategic plans as well and have advocacy committees or projects. Many of the regional organizations that emphasize advocacy have recently experienced major challenges in the state archives or archives in their region and have been involved in concerted advocacy efforts. A wide range of regional organizations are involved, as demonstrated by examples such as the Arizona Archives Alliance, the Metropolitan Archivists Roundtable of New York City, the New England Archivists, and the Society of Georgia Archivists.

*International Council on Archives (ICA).* The ICA was created in 1948 as an international organization to advocate for archival management and protection of recorded heritage. It currently has more than 1,800 members in 199 countries. It includes an Expert Group on Advocacy and has developed a number of brochures and statements for use by its membership. In particular, the

ICA has developed a "Universal Declaration on Archives" to promote awareness and support for archives around the world.[10] This document was adopted in 2011 by the General Assembly of ICA and endorsed by the 36th session of the General Conference of UNESCO. (A complete copy of the Declaration is in Appendix E.) The ICA is working with its members to obtain 1 million signatures of individuals and institutions on the Declaration and is promoting ways to draw attention to it through such routes as signing ceremonies, seminars, and promotional materials.[11]

## Resources from related organizations

While the archives profession has its own theory and practice, archivists share and can learn from other cultural heritage professionals and their associations, including museums, libraries, historians, historical organizations, and the humanities in general. All work in comparatively small professions and ones that are frequently misunderstood or undervalued. Other professional associations provide a range of useful tools and directions for advocacy and awareness that can inform and inspire our own efforts.

*American Alliance of Museums (AAM).* Established in 1906, the AAM focuses on information sharing, development of best practices, and leading advocacy for the museum community. It represents more than 35,000 museum professionals and institutions ranging from art museums to botanical gardens, science and technology centers, and history museums.[12] The AAM focus on advocacy is very active; it sponsors an annual Museum Advocacy Day for members to advocate with Congress. It has a range of issue briefs on topics including: Institute of Museum and Library Services (IMLS), National Endowment for the Humanities (NEH), and National Endowment for the Arts (NEA); charitable giving; museums and the economy; elementary and secondary education; historic preservation; diversity, equity, accessibility and inclusion; and ethics and best practices. It also provides a number of tools to support museum advocacy, focusing on statistical and economic data to demonstrate the impact of museums.

> Archives record decisions, actions and memories. Archives are a unique and irreplaceable heritage passed from one generation to another. Archives are managed from creation to preserve their value and meaning. They are authoritative sources of information underpinning accountable and transparent administrative actions. They play an essential role in the development of societies by safeguarding and contributing to individual and community memory. Open access to archives enriches our knowledge of human society, promotes democracy, protects citizens' rights and enhances the quality of life.
>
> —*International Council on Archives, Universal Declaration on Archives, 2016*

The AAM has created the Center for the Future of Museums, which is an important resource for archivists. The Center monitors cultural, political, and economic trends that are likely to affect museums now and in the future. It publishes an annual Trendswatch report that covers topics ranging from 3D printing to crowdsourcing, trends in philanthropy, artificial intelligence, wearable technology, immigration and migration, and creative aging. It also publishes an online newsletter, "Dispatches from the Future of Museums," that disseminates information on trending topics that may affect museums and archives as well.[13]

*American Library Association (ALA).* The ALA was established in 1876 and has a membership of more than 56,000 individuals from a wide range of library types, including public libraries, school libraries, college and research libraries, and special libraries. It has a strong focus on public awareness and offers a wide range of promotional events, such as Drop Everything and Read Month, School Library Month, National Readathon Day, Banned Books Month, and Freedom of Information Day.[14]

The ALA also has an active program of advocating for libraries. As previously noted, it provides an online Advocacy University. It sponsors a National Library Legislation Day and monitors federal and state legislation and puts forth calls to action on issues such as banned books; equity, diversity, and inclusion; federal legislation; intellectual freedom; and privacy. It provides information and peripherals for librarians to use in their advocacy efforts as well.[15]

*National Coalition for History (NCH).* The National Coalition for History is the successor to the National Coordinating Committee for the Promotion of History, which was established in 1982 to serve as an advocacy voice for history on federal, state, and local legislative and regulatory issues. There are more than fifty member organizations representing historians, archivists, teachers, documentary editors, genealogists, political scientists, museum professionals, and other related organizations. The Society of American Archivists, the Council of State Archivists and several state and regional archival organizations are members. The NCH has coordinated advocacy efforts with its membership on a range of issues relating to federal grant programs (IMLS, NEH, and NHPRC), history education, the Freedom of Information Act, presidential records, and a range of other federal records issues. It has worked with members of Congress to create a History Caucus to promote awareness of history, archives, and museum-related issues. It provides regular updates through its *NCH Washington Update* newsletter.[16]

*National Humanities Alliance (NHA).* The NHA is a coalition of more than 170 museums, libraries, historical societies, research centers, universities, and state humanities councils. It was established in 1981 to advocate for humanities education, research, and public programs. It holds an annual National Humanities Advocacy Day to inform members of Congress about humanities issues of concern. It also provides a number of issue briefs on topics including the Institute of Museum and Library Services, the National Endowment for the Humanities, the National Historical Publications and Records Commission, and Title VI and the Fulbright-Hayes program.[17]

## Staying in touch with current developments

Archives and archivists do not operate in isolation. What can you promise a donor in terms of privacy for their records? Federal and state laws may affect the options. How can you prove the economic value of your archives to your boss? Work done by others may provide ideas of how to capture that information. Are you looking for ideas for raising public awareness? Some great ideas for events, posters, and campaigns are available from libraries. Are you struggling with copyright restrictions that make it difficult to share information from your collections? You can work to change the laws by supporting SAA's advocacy actions. Do you rely on grant funding to help move forward on initiatives like digitizing collections? Joining in the federal funding advocacy efforts by archives, library, museum and history organizations can help ensure those resources continue.

Archivists don't have to invent ideas and approaches—there is much to be learned by staying current with what is going on in our own profession and related professions.

## Moving Forward with Archival Advocacy and Awareness

In reality, nearly every function archivists undertake can be used as an opportunity to raise awareness. When appraising records, an archivist can talk with the records creator or donor about the records' archival value and how similar records have been used by researchers for productive purposes. While describing records, archivists can identify records or topics that will be of particular interest if shared with a supervisor, resource allocators, potential users, or with the public to raise awareness of the value of archives. The work undertaken to preserve records is an area of considerable fascination for the public and for potential financial donors. Reference activities provide a rich resource for advocacy and awareness. Researchers can provide wonderful "testimonials" on the value of archives for their work. They can be enlisted as advocates in letter/email campaigns on archival issues. And in a reference exit interview, they can be a resource for identifying unusual documents or stories embedded in archival records. As Elsie Freeman Finch so eloquently stated:

> Every time we respond to a reference question in person or on the telephone, every time we talk with a director, a university treasurer, a state legislator, board chairperson, county representative, or other resource allocator, we advocate or fail to do so. Every time we work with a donor, a county or town clerk, with a probable customer—a teacher, a film maker, novelist, scientist or medical person, for example—we advocate or we do not.[18]

We need to be involved in advocacy to ensure that the resources and laws necessary to operate effectively are available from our national, state, and local governments. We need to plan to demonstrate the value of archives and archivists to our own organization's leaders and key stakeholders. We need to expand the range of users and the uses that people can make of archival records. We need to move from being seen as a nice but antiquarian function to a recognition of the critical role that archives and archivists have in ensuring the availability of the essential evidence and cultural heritage of all parts of society. What we do is not a well-known and easily understood function in our organizations, communities, or society.

Through advocacy and awareness, we can change the prevailing conceptions (and misconceptions) about archives and archivists. As archivists, we know the value of archival records and the importance they can have for personal uses, for the operation of businesses and organizations, and for effective, responsible operation of local, state, and federal governments. Advocacy and awareness are fundamental to the effective functioning of archives and the archives profession. Each of us must develop an "advocacy frame of mind." Our institutions, our profession, and our society will benefit in real—and perhaps unimagined—ways if we take on the essential task of raising awareness about the value of archives.

## NOTES

1 For the most current offerings, see the SAA Continuing Education site at www2.archivists.org/prof-education/continuing-education.

2 See the ALA Advocacy University site for a range of online presentations and toolkits that address a range of skill sets: www.ala.org/advocacy/advocacy-university, captured at https://perma.cc/S4D5-3WXA.

3 See the Society of American Archivists' Issues and Advocacy Section's Advocacy Toolkit at https://issuesandadvocacy.wordpress.com/advocacy-toolkit/, captured at https://perma.cc/WJU5-PU94, and the Business Archives Section's Advocating Business Archives Toolkit at www2.archivists.org/groups/business-archives-section/advocating-business-archives-toolkit, captured at https://perma.cc/N867-R363.

4 From Shakespeare's play *Macbeth,* Act 5, Scene 5, lines 27–28, www.goodreads.com/work/quotes/1896522-the-tragedy-of-macbeth.

5 Council of State Archivists, "Education-Training," www.statearchivists.org/electronic-records/education-training/seri-electronic-records-institutes/seri-introductory-institute/, captured at https://perma.cc/UA79-FRTX.

6 Society of American Archivists, "SAA Public Policy Agenda (2015–2017)," updated November 7, 2017, www2.archivists.org/initiatives/saa-public-policy-agenda, captured at https://perma.cc/3DHG-24XN.

7 Society of American Archivists, "American Archives Month 2015," https://www2.archivists.org/initiatives/american-archives-month-the-power-of-collaboration/american-archives-month-2015, captured at https://perma.cc/Z7WC-GKLE.

8 Council of State Archivists, "Issue Briefs & Position Statements," https://www.statearchivists.org/programs/advocacy/issue-briefs-position-statements/, captured at https://perma.cc/BA9A-ECFX.

9 The website of the National Association of Government Archives & Records Administrators is https://www.nagara.org/.

10 International Council on Archives, "Universal Declaration on Archives," 2016, www.ica.org/en/networking/unesco/unesco-officially-endorses-uda, captured at https://perma.cc/KW7R-JM5Y.

11 Kim Eberhard and Colleen McEwan, "Spread the Word—and Support for—the Universal Declaration on Archives," *Archival Outlook* (January/February 2013).

12 American Alliance of Museums, "About Us," https://aam-us.org/programs/about-aam/, captured at https://perma.cc/AJ8G-YPN5.

13 American Alliance of Museums, "Center for the Future of Museums."

14 American Library Association, "Celebration Weeks & Promotional Events," updated June 2018, www.ala.org/conferencesevents/celebrationweeks, captured at https://perma.cc/MY8Q-E46B.

15 American Library Association, "Advocacy, Legislation & Issues."

16 For example, see Lee White, "Controversy over Proposed 'Destruction' of Interior Department Records Explained," Latest News, National Coalition for History, October 27, 2018, http://historycoalition.org/2018/10/27/controversy-over-proposed-destruction-of-interior-department-records-explained/, captured at https://perma.cc/VZ6S-6JF3.

17 National Humanities Alliance, "Advocacy Resources," www.nhalliance.org/advocacy_resources, captured at https://perma.cc/6SNX-HM46.

18 Elsie Freeman Finch, "Archival Advocacy: Reflections on Myths and Realities," *Archival Issues* 20, no. 2 (1995): 116.

## APPENDIX A

# Examples of One-page Peripherals

### EXAMPLE 1

The International Council on Archives has produced several advocacy documents for archivists to use in advocating on the value of archives and the role of archivists. The "Why Archiving?" piece below, as well as "What are archives?" and "Who is an archivist?," are available on the ICA website at https://www.ica.org/en/discover-archives.

## Why Archiving?

Archives are witnesses to the past. They provide evidence, explanation and justification both for past actions and current decisions.

Archives enable society to undertake a wide range of roles that enable civilised communities to take root and flourish, from enabling education and research, providing entertainment and leisure, to protecting human rights and confirming identity. Archives are unique, contemporaneous records and so once lost cannot be replaced. It is only through proper identification, care and wide access that the vital role that archives has can be fully realised to the benefit of humanity.

### Archives and good governance

Good archives management is not just about storing records for history and research. Archives are central to good governance.

Archives and records are the tools by which governments can make themselves accountable and demonstrate their democratic credentials. Well-managed archives and records are the means by which a country can understand the who, when, where, how and why of government actions. They enable the delivery of human rights and the ability for a government to explain and defend its actions. Good management also ensures efficient, timely government.

Archives are for life and for living. They are not about getting lost in the past but about understanding the present.

Being an archivist or record keeper is a fascinating role. There are not many jobs where it can be said that what you do today will matter hundreds of years from now. An archivist or record keeper needs a passion for history, an eye for detail and a strong commitment to service. The return is to be a custodian of society's memory.

EXAMPLE 2

The next items were developed for the SAA-CoSA-NAGARA-RAAC "Advocacy on the Hill" day held in 2018. They provide examples of how to summarize key issues for a legislative audience.

## Electronic Government Records

**. . . Touch Everyone's Lives**

From correspondence via email to the most complex geo-spatial database to vital statistics, electronic records touch all aspects of our lives. The volume and complexity of electronic government records and information continues to increase. All levels of government must work together to ensure that electronic records created today are available in the future to protect citizens' rights, document government, and preserve history.

**1,693% growth in state and territorial e-records, 2006–2016**

**. . . Ensure Government Transparency**

Government records contain public information. Government decisions and policy are being made and announced electronically. Records are key to the documentation of government policies, actions, and intent. Government data often are used at multiple levels of decision making, whether local, state, or federal. We must capture and preserve these records to be accountable to our citizens.

**1,371TB of electronic government records held by state and territorial archives**

**. . . Need Immediate Attention**

Electronic records require immediate attention to ensure that they are preserved and accessible. Preservation of electronic records is more complex than preservation of paper records. Sustained resources are needed to ensure the long-term management and accessibility of our nation's electronic records.

**445% growth in electronic over paper records in state and territorial archives**

**. . . Need Sustained Funding**

Increased investment in collaborative research is the key to finding best practices and sustainable models for the long-term preservation of electronic records. Federal grant programs from IMLS, NHPRC, and NEH play a critical role in supporting this vital research funding.

**0.007% average annual amount of total budget that states / territories spend on archives**

*Statistics provided by the Council of State Archivists.*

## Federal Funding Programs for Archives and Historical Records

Just three modestly funded federal agencies provide grants to support preservation of and access to archival materials for future generations: the National Historical Publications and Records Commission, the National Endowment for the Humanities, and the Institute of Museum and Library Services. **We urge Congress to ensure stable funding for these granting agencies in FY19 and beyond.**

### Why support NHPRC, NEH, and IMLS?

Each of these agencies has a distinguished history of supporting the work of archival repositories within academic institutions, local and state governments, museums, historical societies, and public libraries to ensure that the nation's social, cultural, economic, scientific, and political experience is available to future generations.

Grants to archives and historical records projects are a productive investment of federal funds. They:

- ***Ensure the preservation and accessibility of documentation***—especially in electronic form—to a wide array of users.
- ***Create jobs.*** Analysis of existing projects shows that at least 75% of funds are used for staff. Jobs mean purchase of goods and services in local communities.
- ***Foster tourism.*** Visitors to archives contribute to local economies via dollars spent on housing, food, and entertainment. The Council of State Archivists estimates that visitors to state archives alone contribute between $2.5 and $5 million annually to local economies.
- ***Stimulate private support.*** Grant recipients typically are required to match federal funds up to 50 percent of the overall project budget.

**Please support FY19 funding for the federal agencies that provide grants to archives and historical records programs:**

NHPRC: At least level funding of $6 million.
NEH: At least level funding of $149.8 million.
IMLS: At least level funding of $38.6 million for the Office of Museum Services and $182.7 million for the Library Services.

**And please support reauthorization of NHPRC at $10 million and IMLS at $295.1 million.**

### National Historical Publications and Records Commission

As the grant-making arm of the National Archives and Records Administration, NHPRC is the only federal program that focuses on archives and records programs and projects—and thus the only federal program that supports Americans' right and need to know both their heritage and the workings of their public offices. During the past 40 years, NHPRC has:

- Supported innovation at state and local levels that has had a major impact on federal records.

- Awarded $175 million in grants to more than 4,500 state and local government archives, colleges and universities, and other institutions and non-profit groups.
- Encouraged use of funds for various purposes—preserving historical records, digitizing collections, producing oral histories, publishing documentary editions, establishing new archives programs—all to preserve and provide access to records of national impact and importance.

*NHPRC is funded under the Financial Services and General Government Appropriations bill.*

**National Endowment for the Humanities (NEH)**

As one of the largest funders of humanities programs in the United States, NEH provides crucial support for research, education, preservation, and public programs, including vital support to archives nationwide. NEH funds research that leads to new digital tools, technologies, national standards, best practices, and other methodologies that ensure the preservation of archival and cultural resources. NEH funding reaches every state, territory, and Congressional district. And because it supports the training of archives staff, the funding helps sustain basic preservation activities at small and mid-size archives, libraries, and other historical organizations.

*NEH is funded under the Interior, Environment, and Related Agencies Appropriations bill.*

**Institute of Museum and Library Services (IMLS)**

IMLS is the primary source of federal support for the nation's 123,000 libraries and 17,500 museums, many of which maintain archives and special collections that enrich scholarly learning and civic engagement. IMLS grants:

- Foster broad public access to knowledge, heritage, and lifelong learning.
- Invest in research and development that yields long-term benefits to the public.
- Enable institutions to develop the latest technology, to digitize and share their collections, and to develop new standards and protocols for preserving and providing access to born-digital data and records.

In its role as a federal agency, IMLS provides important leadership through its support for research and policy development, as well as development of best practices to enable archives, libraries, and museums to improve their services and processes.

*IMLS is funded under the Labor, Health and Human Services, and Education Appropriations bill.*

EXAMPLE 3

The next two items are from the Partnership for the American Historical Record's (PAHR) campaign advocating for a federal grant program specifically focused on archives. The first item is a more general overview of the initiative; the second shows how the information has been adapted to present to a member of Congress whose major interest is in jobs programs.

Council of State Archivists • www.statearchivists.org
Society of American Archivists • www.archivists.org
National Association of Government Archives and Records Administrators • www.nagara.org

## What the Preserving the American Historical Record Act will Mean for Our Nation

A total of $50 million would be distributed to the states and territories each year using a formula based on population and area.

Competitive grants would be available to the nation's 87,525 local governments; more than 8,000 local archives, historical societies, and heritage organizations; 9,198 public libraries; and more than 3,650 academic institutions with library and archival holdings.

If we had this program, you might see:

- Researchers using an online digital collection of each state's historic photographs, documents, and maps
- Teachers and students using an online educational site of archival records with lessons that support the teaching of state history and a host of other academic subjects, from kindergarten through graduate school
- Family historians searching name indexes online for military service, land ownership, naturalization, and state and federal censuses
- The public attending exhibits and programs in libraries and museums—or even at interstate rest stops, shopping malls, and community centers
- Officials and researchers using databases, email files, and other digital records that have been saved in a way that they can always be read
- Government officials following a well-designed disaster plan to save essential records and resume operations after a flood or tornado

**Preserving the American Historical Record: What about jobs?**

***PAHR will stimulate job growth***

- If fully funded, PAHR will provide **$37,500,000 to support jobs** throughout the country, or over 1,000 jobs annually.
- PAHR will provide **$50 million in federal funding** to the states and territories for projects to protect and provide access to historical records.
- Historical records projects are "jobs-heavy." Existing grant programs demonstrate that (on average) **75% of funds for such projects are used to pay staff**.

***Current job statistics:***

- There are more than 11,000 professional archivists in the United States working in 8,500 government agencies, historical societies, libraries, museums, academic institutions, and other organizations in the U.S.
- These professional archivists are responsible for providing care for and public access to more than 44,000,000,000 items of paper historical records, and more than 727,000,000,000 photographs documenting the people, organizations, governments, and history of this country.
- More than 1,250 students are currently enrolled in graduate archival education programs, and they will be seeking jobs in the next two years.
- State government archives have experienced cuts in their budgets averaging 12%, including reductions in staff through retirement, attrition and layoffs, so the number of jobs is currently ***declining.***

**PAHR is a viable route for stimulating the creation and stabilization of jobs in the archival profession. The cost is small in comparison to the return on this investment!**

# APPENDIX B

# The Legislative Process

## General Information

Members of Congress are the only people who can introduce legislation. Those who introduce the bills are called "sponsors" of the bill. Often the legislation that is introduced was written or contributed to in large part by advocates and their organizations. When the bill or resolution is introduced, it is given a number. A piece of legislation in the House is labeled H.R. #### and a bill in the Senate is labeled S. ####. Legislation is divided into three categories:

- ***Authorizing Legislation:*** A bill that creates a new federal program, extends the life of an existing program, or repeals existing law. Authorizing bills usually set a limit on the amount of funds that can be spent annually by a program over a period of 3 to 5 years. An authorizing bill only establishes the framework for a federal program; it does not provide funds to operate the program.
- ***Appropriations Bill:*** A bill that allocates funding for specific federal programs. Unlike authorizing legislation, which remains in effect for 3 or more years, an appropriations bill must be enacted into law every year. Each year, in fact, Congress must pass a series of thirteen appropriations bills in order to keep federal departments and agencies running.
- ***Entitlement Legislation:*** A measure that guarantees a certain level of benefits to persons who meet eligibility requirements set by law, such as Medicare, Medicaid, and college student loan programs. Entitlement programs typically do not need to be reauthorized, nor do they require annual appropriations.

## The Committee System

Before a bill is eligible for debate on the House or Senate floor, it must first make its way through the committee system. Both the House and the Senate are made up of committees that generate legislation under specified jurisdictions. Most committees are divided into subcommittees of "specialists." For example, the House Appropriations Committee as a whole is responsible for allocating funds to all federal programs. The Appropriations Subcommittee on Financial Services and General Government makes recommendations to the full Appropriations Committee on how the money should be allocated to each of the departments for which it is responsible, including the National Archives.

Each committee and subcommittee is chaired by a member of the majority party in the House or Senate. One individual from the minority party is designated the "ranking member." There is generally a website for the committee and for each subcommittee providing information on the proceedings, actions, and issues under consideration. In many cases, there is also a website managed by the minority members of the committee and subcommittee.

Committee membership and leadership may change with each new congressional session and elections. Committee structures and jurisdiction can also change, particularly for subcommittees. When planning advocacy efforts, it is essential to check the relevant websites and target the appropriate committee and subcommittee. If it is unclear at the federal level, check with the Society of American Archivists or the National Coalition for History to confirm jurisdiction and leadership for relevant committees/subcommittees.

## Key Congressional Committees and Subcommittees

Certain committees, subcommittees, and committee members are more relevant than others to archival issues. These committees are listed below, and subcommittees are bulleted. Periodically the names of these bodies may be changed, so check the House and Senate websites.

### House Committees

#### *Appropriations Committee*

The Appropriations Committee determines funding for specific federal programs, including the National Archives and Records Administration, the Library of Congress, the Smithsonian Institution, and granting agencies that include the Institute of Museum and Library Services, the National Endowment for the Humanities, and, as part of the NARA budget, the National Historical Publications and Records Commission.[1]

- ***Financial Services and General Government Subcommittee***
  The subcommittee manages the appropriations relating to a range of fiscal and other agencies, including the Department of the Treasury, the District of Columbia, the Judiciary, the Executive Office of the President, the Federal Trade Commission, the Federal Election Commission, the National Archives and NHPRC, and the General Services Administration, along with many others.[2]

#### *Oversight and Government Reform Committee*

The Committee's mission is to "ensure the efficiency, effectiveness, and accountability of the federal government and all its agencies."[3]

- ***Government Operations Subcommittee***
  The subcommittee is charged with ensuring that "federal agencies are open and transparent in their execution of federal law."[4] This subcommittee provides oversight for the National Archives and the NHPRC.

### Senate Committees

#### *Appropriations Committee*

The committee's responsibility parallels that of the House Appropriations Committee. It develops the legislation allocating federal funding to government agencies, departments, and organizations, including those of particular interest to the archives and records community.[5]

- ***Financial Services and General Government Subcommittee***
  This subcommittee also parallels the House subcommittee with responsibility for appropriations relating to a range of fiscal and other agencies, including the Department of the Treasury, the District of Columbia, the Judiciary, the Executive Office of the President, the Federal Trade Commission, the Federal Election Commission, the National Archives and NHPRC, and the General Services Administration, along with many others.[6]

### *Committee on Homeland Security and Governmental Affairs*

This is the Senate's oversight committee with responsibility for studying the efficiency and effectiveness of government agencies, with particular emphasis on homeland security. This includes the National Archives, government information, federal civil service, government contracting, and the census and collecting of statistics.[7]

### *Subcommittee on Regulatory Affairs and Federal Management*

The subcommittee is charged with overseeing the management and efficiency of all government agencies, departments, and programs, including the National Archives and the Library of Congress.[8]

## NOTES

1. U.S. House of Representatives, Committee on Appropriations, https://appropriations.house.gov/.
2. U.S. House of Representatives, Committee on Appropriations, Subcommittees, https://appropriations.house.gov/subcommittees/subcommittee/?IssueID=34780.
3. U.S. House of Representatives, House Committee on Oversight and Reform, https://oversight.house.gov/about/.
4. U.S. House of Representatives, House Committee on Oversight and Reform, https://oversight.house.gov/.
5. United States Senate Committee on Appropriations, "Committee Jurisdiction," https://www.appropriations.senate.gov/about/jurisdiction.
6. United States Senate Committee on Appropriations, Financial Services and General Government Subcommittee, https://www.appropriations.senate.gov/subcommittees/financial-services-and-general-government.
7. U.S. Senate Committee on Homeland Security & Governmental Affairs, "Jurisdiction and Rules," https://www.hsgac.senate.gov/about/jurisdiction.
8. U.S. Senate Committee on Homeland Security & Governmental Affairs, Regulatory Affairs & Federal Management, https://www.hsgac.senate.gov/subcommittees/rafm/about.

APPENDIX C

# SAA Issue Briefs and Policy and Position Statements

## 2019

- SAA Statement on Obama Presidential Library

## 2018

- SAA Council Endorsement of Protocols for Native American Archival Materials
- Congressional Records as Public Records
- Issue Brief: Net Neutrality
- Statement on Removal of ISIS Records from Iraq by New York Times Reporter
- SAA Statement on Sexual Assault and Harassment

## 2017

- SAA Council Statement on White Supremacists' Actions in Charlottesville, Virginia
- Statement on Presidential Advisory Commission on Election Integrity Request for Voter Roll Data
- Backgrounder: Funding for the National Endowment for the Humanities
- Backgrounder: Funding for the National Historical Publications and Records Commission
- Issue Brief: Federal Grant Funding for Archives
- Issue Brief: Declassification of Federal Records
- Issue Brief: Confidentiality of Private Information Held in Records of the Federal Government's Executive Agencies
- SAA Statement on Executive Order Restricting Entry into the United States by Individuals from Seven Muslim-Majority Countries

## 2016

- SAA Statement Reaffirming Our Commitment to the Importance of Diversity and Inclusion
- Information Brief: Archives and the Environment
- SAA Statement on Draft Revision of Section 108
- Issue Brief: Archivists and the Term of Copyright

## 2015

- Issue Brief: Strengthening of Federal Records Authority
- SAA Opposes Trans-Pacific Partnership Agreement Provisions
- SAA's Criteria for Advocacy Statements
- A New Librarian of Congress: Qualities of a Successful Candidate
- Joint Statement on Conducting Public Business in Non-Government Email Accounts (June 2015)

- Issue Brief: State Freedom of Information Laws
- Statement on Use of Non-Government Email Accounts for the Conduct of Public Business

## 2014

- Issue Brief: Adequate Funding of Government Archives and Archival Programs
- Principles and Priorities for Planning Joint Meetings with Other Professional Organizations
- Issue Brief: Health Information Portability and Accountability Act
- SAA Code of Conduct
- Issue Brief: Archivists and Section 108 of the Copyright Act
- Issue Brief: Orphan Works
- Issue Brief: Freedom of Information Act
- Detailed Legislative Agenda Related to the Freedom of Information Act
- Issue Brief: Presidential Records Act of 1978

## 2013

- Principles and Priorities for Continuously Improving the SAA Annual Meeting

## 2012

- SAA's Written Testimony in Support of NHPRC
- SAA Core Values Statement and Code of Ethics

## 2011

- Statement of SAA Representative to World Intellectual Property Organization Standing Committee on Copyright and Related Rights
- Core Values of Archivists
- SAA Comments on Copyright Protection of Pre-1972 Sound Recordings

## 2010

- SAA Statement on Diversity and Inclusion

## 2009

- ALA/SAA Joint Statement on Access to Research Materials in Archives and Special Collections Libraries
- Resolution on SAA's Equal Opportunity/Non-Discrimination Policy

## 2008

- Joint Statement on "Qualities of a Successful Candidate" for Archivist of the United States
- SAA Statement on Delays by Federal Government Agencies in Responding to FOIA Requests
- ACA/SAA Joint Statement on Iraqi Records

## 2006

- Letter to U.S. Archivist Allen Weinstein Regarding Reclassification of Records

**2005**

- Joint Statement on Hurricane Relief
- Response to Statement on Orphan Works
- Statement on Orphan Works

**2004**

- Statement on the Renewal of the USA PATRIOT Act
- Statement for the Record on the Nomination of Allen Weinstein to Become Archivist of the United States
- CoSA/NAGARA/SAA Joint Statement: "Sale of Historical Public Records on eBay"
- Statement on U.S. Supreme Court Ruling Regarding Cheney Energy Task Force Case
- Joint Statement on Questions to Ask the Nominee for Archivist of the United States
- Joint Statement on Selection Criteria for the Archivist of the United States
- Statement on the Nomination of Allen Weinstein to Become Archivist of the United States

**2003**

- SAA-ARMA Statement of Joint Purpose and Cooperation
- SAA Statement on Iraqi Archives
- Statement on the Importance of Supporting State Archival Programs

**2002**

- Letter in Response to the Closing of the Teachers College Special Collections Department
- SAA Resolution on Diversity
- SAA Response to NARA Advanced Notice on Proposed Rulemaking on Electronic Records

**2001**

- SAA President Steve Hensen's editorial, "The President's Papers Are the People's Business," published in the *Washington Post,* Sunday, December 16, 2001
- SAA responds to Executive Order 13233 on Presidential Papers
- Endorsement of UNESCO Resolution on Digital Preservation
- SAA Comments on the Hague Convention on Jurisdiction and Foreign Judgments in Commercial and Civil Cases
- SAA Council's Response to Nicholson Baker's "Double Fold"

**2000**

- SAA Resolution in Support of the Organization of American Historians re: HBE/Adam's Mark
- Council Resolution Regarding Adam's Mark Hotel Chain (January 30, 2000)

**1999**

- Testimony Submitted by H. Thomas Hickerson to the Committee on Government Reform's Subcommittee on Government Management, Information, and Technology
- SAA Position Statement on Diversity

- Resolution on the Systematic Destruction of Archives in Kosovo and War-Caused Devastation of Archives Throughout Yugoslavia
- Statement on Copyright Issues for Archives in Distance Education

**1998**

- SAA Supports Petition to Open Grand Jury Testimony Related to Alger Hiss Indictments
- Letter to Senators John Warner and Daniel Patrick Moynihan re: amendment to PL104-106 to delay declassification of federal documents
- Resolution Opposing Any Extension to Copyright Term Extension Act
- Annual Business Meeting Resolution on the Digital Millennium Copyright Act
- SAA Position Statement on NARA Space Study

**1997**

- SAA Opposition to Copyright Term Extension Act
- Archival Roles for the New Millennium
- Basic Principles for Managing Intellectual Property in the Digital Environment: An Archival Perspective
- Statement on the Preservation of Digitized Reproductions
- The Preservation of Digitized Reproductions
- Copyright, Archival Institutions and the Digital Environment
- Archival Issues Raised by Litigation: Challenging General Records Schedule 20
- Response to "Criteria for the Hiring and Retention of Visual Resource Professionals"

**1996**

- SAA Response to the Draft Guidelines for Digital Images Developed by the Conference on Fair Use (June 4,1995)

**1995**

- Concerns Over the Sudden Dismissal of the Massachusetts State Archivist (June 1995)
- Critical Archival Concerns and Interests in the Development and Implementation of the National Information Infrastructure (June 1995)
- Archival Issues Raised by Information Stored in Electronic Form (March 1995)
- Resolution in Support of the National Endowment for the Humanities

**1994**

- ALA-SAA Joint Statement of Access: Guidelines for Access to Original Research Materials (August 1994)

**1990**

- Statement Concerning the Closing of Archives

**1976**

- Statement on the Reproduction of Manuscripts and Archives for Reference Service (July 1976)

*Full copies of these statements are available at www2.archivists.org/statements.*

APPENDIX D

# A Checklist for Planning Advocacy or Awareness Initiatives

1. Develop a goal statement.
   - [ ] Is your goal clearly stated?
   - [ ] Does it connect to the organizational mission?

2. Identify the audience, key stakeholders, and supporters.
   - [ ] Who is your audience? Is it clearly defined and focused?
   - [ ] Who are the key stakeholders?
   - [ ] Who are your potential supporters?
   - [ ] For each group identify:
     - [ ] What do you know about their background and interests?
     - [ ] What matters to them?
     - [ ] What can you do for them?

3. Develop the message.
   - [ ] Is your message clear, concise, and compelling?
   - [ ] How can you best convey your message?
     - [ ] What stories will support it?
     - [ ] Do you need/have quantitative data to use?
     - [ ] Do you have qualitative data to use?

4. Put your plan into action.
   - [ ] What factors need to be taken into account (timing, budget cycles, etc.)?
   - [ ] Who will deliver your message?
     - [ ] Who in your organization will be involved in the delivery?
     - [ ] Do you have/need grassroots supporters?
     - [ ] Do you have/need grasstops supporters?
   - [ ] How you will communicate about your effort?
     - [ ] What written materials do you need?
     - [ ] What oral presentations/statements do you need?
     - [ ] Do you need to have meetings with individuals or groups?
     - [ ] How will you use social media?
     - [ ] Do you need to engage with the press and other public media?

5. Assess your effort.
   - [ ] What are the ways you can measure the response to or impact of your effort?
   - [ ] What would be the signs of success or progress to you, your organization, or others?

APPENDIX E

# Universal Declaration on Archives

Archives record decisions, actions and memories. Archives are a unique and irreplaceable heritage passed from one generation to another. Archives are managed from creation to preserve their value and meaning. They are authoritative sources of information underpinning accountable and transparent administrative actions. They play an essential role in the development of societies by safeguarding and contributing to individual and community memory. Open access to archives enriches our knowledge of human society, promotes democracy, protects citizens' rights and enhances the quality of life.

**To this effect, we recognize**

- **the unique quality** of archives as authentic evidence of administrative, cultural and intellectual activities and as a reflection of the evolution of societies;
- **the vital necessity** of archives for supporting business efficiency, accountability and transparency, for protecting citizens' rights, for establishing individual and collective memory, for understanding the past, and for documenting the present to guide future actions;
- **the diversity** of archives in recording every area of human activity;
- **the multiplicity of formats** in which archives are created, including paper, electronic, audio visual and other types;
- **the role of archivists** as trained professionals with initial and continuing education, serving their societies by supporting the creation of records and by selecting, maintaining and making these records available for use;
- **the collective responsibility of all**—citizens, public administrators and decision-makers, owners or holders of public or private archives, and archivists and other information specialists—in the management of archives.

**We therefore undertake to work together in order that**

- appropriate national archival policies and laws are adopted and enforced;
- the management of archives is valued and carried out competently by all bodies, private or public, which create and use archives in the course of conducting their business;
- adequate resources are allocated to support the proper management of archives, including the employment of trained professionals;
- archives are managed and preserved in ways that ensure their authenticity, reliability, integrity and usability;
- archives are made accessible to everyone, while respecting the pertinent laws and the rights of individuals, creators, owners and users;
- archives are used to contribute to the promotion of responsible citizenship.

*Adopted at the General Assembly of the International Council on Archives, Oslo, September 2010. Endorsed by 36th Session of the General Conference of UNESCO, Paris, November 2011.*

# Bibliography

Adams, Susan. "Why We Need to Meet in Person." *Forbes Magazine*, February 11, 2011. www.forbes.com/sites/susanadams/2011/02/11/why-we-need-to-meet-in-person/2/#705211c92626, captured at https://perma.cc/7NJN-7UYF.

Adkins, Elizabeth W., and Karen Benedict. "Archival Advocacy: Institutional Archives in Corporations." In *Many Happy Returns: Advocacy and the Development of Archives*, edited by Larry J. Hackman, 45–66. Chicago: Society of American Archivists, 2011.

Allen, Beverly B. "Power to the People: Building the Colorado Chicano Movement Archives." *Archival Outlook* (September/October 2014): 6–7, 32.

Allison-Bunnell, Jody, Elizabeth Yakel, and Janet Hauck. "Researchers at Work: Assessing Needs for Content and Presentation of Archival Materials." *Journal of Archival Organization* 9, no. 2 (November 2011): 67–104.

Altman, Burt, and John Nemmers. "The Usability of Online Archival Resources: The Polaris Project Finding Aid." 64 (Spring/Summer): 121–131.

American Alliance of Museums. "About Us." https://aam-us.org/programs/about-aam/, captured at https://perma.cc/AJ8G-YPN5.

———. "Advocacy Resources." http://aam-us.org/programs/advocacy/advocacy-resources, captured at https://perma.cc/9PSB-2WLX.

———. "Center for the Future of Museums." www.aam-us.org/programs/center-for-the-future-of-museums, captured at https://perma.cc/55FQ-BMG7.

___. "Policy Issues." http://aam-us.org/programs/advocacy/policy-issues, captured at https://perma.cc/3RR6-WEYW.

American Library Association. "Advocacy, Legislation & Issues." www.ala.org/advocacy/, captured at https://perma.cc/2NYJ-DL5G.

___. "Celebration Weeks & Promotional Events." Updated June 2018. www.ala.org/conferencesevents/celebrationweeks, captured at https://perma.cc/MY8Q-E46B.

___. "Preservation Week." www.ala.org/alcts/preservationweek/sponsors, captured at https://perma.cc/NJC7-DTG4.

American Library Association Advocacy Institute. *The Advocacy Action Plan Workbook.* Chicago: American Library Association, 2009. www.ala.org/advocacy/sites/ala.org.advocacy/files/content/advleg/advocacyuniversity/advclearinghouse/Advocacy%20Action%20Plan%20-%20revised%2001-09.pdf, captured at https://perma.cc/Q5W3-TJWK.

American Society of News Editors. "Sunshine Week." 2019. http://sunshineweek.rcfp.org/, captured at https://perma.cc/D2L9-J7PH.

Amidei, Nancy. *So You Want to Make a Difference: Advocacy Is the Key.* 16th ed. Washington, DC: OMB Watch, 2010.

Archival Metrics, https://sites.google.com/a/umich.edu/archival-metrics, captured at https://perma.cc/A5XC-8WHZ.

"Archives on the Hill." 2018. www2.archivists.org/am2018/attend/archives-on-the-hill, captured at https://perma.cc/WFK7-U7Y9.

"Archivists Declare a Week for Peering into the Past." *New York Times*, October 4, 1990. www.nytimes.com/1990/10/04/garden/archivists-declare-a-week-for-peering-into-the-past.html, captured at https://perma.cc/N33M-D48K.

Arizona Archives Alliance. "Support AZAA's Advocacy Work." https://arizonaarchives.org/get-involved/support-fazas-advocacy-work/, captured at https://perma.cc/LXR6-MY3T.

Bastian, Jeannette A., and Ben Alexander. *Community Archives: The Shaping of Memory.* London: Facet Publishing, 2009.

Baumann, Roland L. "Oberlin College and the Movement to Establish an Archives, 1920–1966." *Midwestern Archivist* 13, no. 1 (1988): 27–38.

Bearman, David. "Survey of the Archival Profession." *American Archivist* 46 (Spring 1983): 233–241.

Bell, Danna C. "The Jobs Thing . . ." *Off the Record* (blog). February 4, 2014. https://offtherecord.archivists.org/2014/02/04/the-jobs-thing/, captured at https://perma.cc/97T5-DQS8.

Bellardo, Lewis J. "Observations on Thirty Years of Advocacy." In *Many Happy Returns: Advocacy and the Development of Archives*, edited by Larry J. Hackman, 89. Chicago: Society of American Archivists, 2011.

Booth, Steven D. "Bridge Over Troubled Water: How the Archivists and Archives of Color Roundtable Created Change at the Center for Black Music Research." *Archival Outlook* (November/December 2012): 4–5.

Brigham Young University Library. *Special Collections Theatrical Trailer.* March 14, 2011. www.youtube.com/watch?v=GIUiH3PNOAE.

Brigham Young University, L. Tom Perry Special Collections. *Introduction to the L. Tom Perry Special Collections.* March 1, 2013. www.youtube.com/watch?v=tZ_VGEzwvDw.

Bronskill, Jim. "Military Faces Archival Search to Pinpoint Number of People Forced Out for Being Gay." *The Canadian Press/The Globe and Mail*, June 4, 2017. www.theglobeandmail.com/news/national/military-faces-archival-search-to-pinpoint-number-of-people-forced-out-for-being-gay/article35198686/, captured at https://perma.cc/YT4Z-GP3R.

Burns, Chris. "Sound and Vision: Using Video to Tell the Tales of Archives and Archivists." *ArchivesAWARE!* (blog). Society of American Archivists, Committee on Public Awareness. July 12, 2016. https://archivesaware.archivists.org/2016/07/12/sound-and-vision-using-video-to-tell-the-tales-of-archives-and-archivists/, captured at https://perma.cc/M955-53Z6.

Callcott, George H. "Antiquarianism and Documents in the Age of Literary History." *American Archivist* 21 (January 1958): 17–29.

Campaign Workshop. *The Complete Guide to Advocacy.* February 2015. www.thecampaignworkshop.com/complete-guide-advocacy, captured at https://perma.cc/YTG6-YU6J.

Carmicheal, David W. "The Georgia Archives Budget: An Unfolding Crisis." *Provenance, Journal of the Society of Georgia Archivists* 31, no. 1 (January 2013): 7–13.

Chernow, Ron. *Alexander Hamilton.* New York: Penguin/Random House, 2005.

Christian, Michele A., and Tanya Zanish-Belcher. "Broadcast Yourself: Putting Iowa State University's History on YouTube." In *A Different Kind of Web: New Connections Between Archives and Our Users*, edited by Kate Theimer. Chicago: Society of American Archivists, 2011.

Church, Michael A. "Archives to Earbuds: Podcasting Collections at the Kansas State Historical Society." In *The Interactive Archivist: Case Studies in Utilizing Web 2.0 to Improve the Archival Experience*, edited by J. Gordon Daines III and Cory L. Nimer. Chicago: Society of American Archivists, 2009. http://interactivearchivist.archivists.org/case-studies/podcasting-at-kshs/, captured at https://perma.cc/A4W6-BT49.

Coalition to Preserve the Georgia Archives. *Our Georgia Archives, Our Georgia History—Is It Worth Saving?* January 2013. www2.archivists.org/sites/all/files/GA_archives_deck_Jan-2013.pdf, captured at https://perma.cc/G3Q2-KLRG.

Conway, Paul. "Facts and Frameworks: An Approach to Studying the Users of Archives." *American Archivist* 49 (Fall 1986): 393–407.

Council of State Archivists. "Advocacy." www.statearchivists.org/programs/advocacy/, captured at https://perma.cc/2RRX-BCDV.

———. "Archives Month Posters." www.statearchivists.org/programs/archives-month/archives-month-posters/, captured at https://perma.cc/YUU6-CS8N.

———. *Directory of State Archives*, www.statearchivists.org/connect/resources-state/.

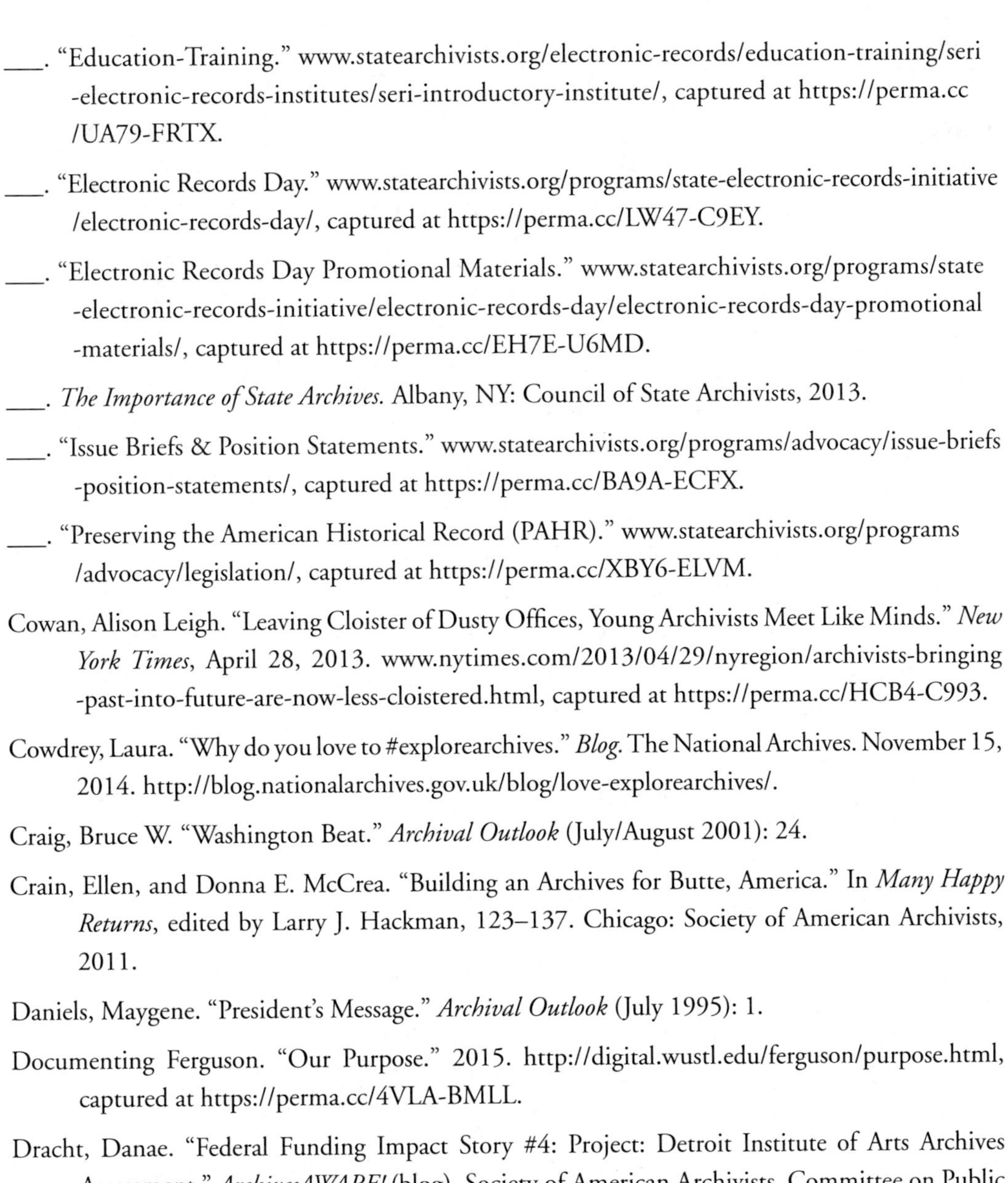

___. "Education-Training." www.statearchivists.org/electronic-records/education-training/seri-electronic-records-institutes/seri-introductory-institute/, captured at https://perma.cc/UA79-FRTX.

___. "Electronic Records Day." www.statearchivists.org/programs/state-electronic-records-initiative/electronic-records-day/, captured at https://perma.cc/LW47-C9EY.

___. "Electronic Records Day Promotional Materials." www.statearchivists.org/programs/state-electronic-records-initiative/electronic-records-day/electronic-records-day-promotional-materials/, captured at https://perma.cc/EH7E-U6MD.

___. *The Importance of State Archives.* Albany, NY: Council of State Archivists, 2013.

___. "Issue Briefs & Position Statements." www.statearchivists.org/programs/advocacy/issue-briefs-position-statements/, captured at https://perma.cc/BA9A-ECFX.

___. "Preserving the American Historical Record (PAHR)." www.statearchivists.org/programs/advocacy/legislation/, captured at https://perma.cc/XBY6-ELVM.

Cowan, Alison Leigh. "Leaving Cloister of Dusty Offices, Young Archivists Meet Like Minds." *New York Times*, April 28, 2013. www.nytimes.com/2013/04/29/nyregion/archivists-bringing-past-into-future-are-now-less-cloistered.html, captured at https://perma.cc/HCB4-C993.

Cowdrey, Laura. "Why do you love to #explorearchives." *Blog.* The National Archives. November 15, 2014. http://blog.nationalarchives.gov.uk/blog/love-explorearchives/.

Craig, Bruce W. "Washington Beat." *Archival Outlook* (July/August 2001): 24.

Crain, Ellen, and Donna E. McCrea. "Building an Archives for Butte, America." In *Many Happy Returns*, edited by Larry J. Hackman, 123–137. Chicago: Society of American Archivists, 2011.

Daniels, Maygene. "President's Message." *Archival Outlook* (July 1995): 1.

Documenting Ferguson. "Our Purpose." 2015. http://digital.wustl.edu/ferguson/purpose.html, captured at https://perma.cc/4VLA-BMLL.

Dracht, Danae. "Federal Funding Impact Story #4: Project: Detroit Institute of Arts Archives Assessment." *ArchivesAWARE!* (blog). Society of American Archivists, Committee on Public Awareness. May 23, 2017. https://archivesaware.archivists.org/2017/-5/23/federal-funding-impact-story-4, captured at https://perma.cc/M9L9-7RMR.

Duff, Wendy, Jean Dryden, Carrie Limkilde, Joan Cherry, and Ellie Bogomazova. "Archivists' Views of User-based Evaluation: Benefits, Barriers, and Requirements." *American Archivist* 71 (Spring/Summer 2008): 144–166.

Eberhard, Kim, and Colleen McEwan. "Spread the Word—and Support for—the Universal Declaration on Archives." *Archival Outlook* (January/February 2013).

Ericson, Timothy. "Choosing the Next Archivist of the United States." *Archival Outlook* (May 2004): 3, 19.

___. "U.S. Archivist Search Continues." *Archival Outlook* (May 1995): 10.

———. "Weinstein Confirmed as Archivist of the United States." *Archival Outlook* (March/April 2005): 6.

Errickson, Kaitlin. "An Independent National Archives." *Pieces of History* (blog). U.S. National Archives. March 29, 2016. https://prologue.blogs.archives.gov/2016/03/29/an-independent-national-archives/, captured at https://perma.cc/P4AN-LCGJ.

"Escape the Room . . . with Archives." *ArchivesAware!* (blog). Society of American Archivists, Committee on Public Awareness. March 8, 2018. https://archivesaware.archivists.org/2018/03/08/escape-the-room-with-archives/, captured at https://perma.cc/ZT6F-8VSV.

Fernández, Natalia. "Oregon's LGBTQ+ and Communities of Color: Community-Based Oral History Projects." Presentation at the SAA Annual Meeting, Portland, OR, July 28, 2017.

Finch, Elsie Freeman. "Archival Advocacy: Reflections on Myths and Realities." *Archival Issues* 20, no. 2 (1995): 115–127.

Finch, Elsie T. Freeman, ed. *Advocating Archives: An Introduction to Public Relations for Archivists.* Chicago: Scarecrow Press and Society of American Archivists, 1994.

*Finding Your Roots.* Season 2, episode 6, "Nas' Enslaved Roots: "A Receipt for a Human Being." Aired on PBS.org on October 27, 2014. www.pbs.org/video/finding-your-roots-nas-enslaved-roots-receipt-human-being/, captured at https://perma.cc/8TPY-DGWR.

Fletcher, Stephen. "A Priceless Gem for Only Ten Bucks." *A View to Hugh: Processing the Hugh Morton Photographs and Films* (blog). University of North Carolina, University Libraries, October 27, 2018. http://blogs.lib.unc.edu/morton/, captured at https://perma.cc/K7AX-T5QZ.

Fogerty, James. "Committee on Public Information Dispels Myths." *SAA Newsletter*, July 1989: 4–5.

Freer Gallery of Art Archives. *A Day in the Life of an Archivist.* August 13, 2010. www.youtube.com/watch?v=KqnsEz6OgRM, captured at https://perma.cc/GMP5-CQ6G.

Freivogel, Elsie Freeman. "Education Programs: Outreach as an Administrative Function." *American Archivist* 41 (April 1978): 147–153.

Fullwood, Steven G. "Always Queer, Always Here: Creating the Black Gay and Lesbian Archive in the Schomburg Center for Research in Black Culture." In *Community Archives: The Shaping of Memory,* edited by Jeannette Bastain and Ben Alexander, 235–249. London: Facet Publishing, 2009.

"The Giuliani Papers." Gotham Center for New York City History. February 16, 2002. www.gothamcenter.org/past-special-projects/february-21st-2015, captured at https://perma.cc/6WDQ-V8KZ.

Gottlieb, Peter. "#AskAnArchivist Day: A Tweet Success Archival Outlook." *Archival Outlook* (November/December 2014): 21.

———. "SAA and the U.S. Archivist." *Archival Outlook* (November/December 2009): 3.

Grabowski, John J. "Keepers, Users, and Funders: Building an Awareness of Archival Value." *American Archivist* 55 (Summer 1992): 464–472.

Gracy, David II. "Archives and Society: The First Archival Revolution." *American Archivist* 47 (Winter 1984): 6–10.

Greene, Mark A. "Putting Archives on the Agenda." *Archival Outlook* (July/August 2015): 12, 29.

Hackman, Larry J. "Archives Week in the United States?" *SAA Newsletter*, March 1991: 14–15, 20.

___. "Love is Not Enough: Advocacy, Influence and the Development of Archives." *Journal of the Society of Archivists* 33, no. 1 (2012): 9–21.

___, ed. *Many Happy Returns: Advocacy and the Development of Archives.* Chicago: Society of American Archivists, 2011.

Hager, Joshua D. "To Like or Not to Like: Understanding and Maximizing the Utility of Archival Outreach on Facebook." *American Archivist* 78 (Spring/Summer 2015): 18–37. http://americanarchivist.org/doi/pdf/10.17723/0360-9081.78.1.18.

Ham, F. Gerald. "The Archival Edge." *American Archivist* 38 (Winter 1975): 5–13.

Hathaway, Heather. "Creating Value for Internal Audiences." Presentation at the SAA Annual Meeting, Portland, OR, July 27, 2017.

Haws, Barbara. "Advocating with the Institution: Twenty-five Years for the New York Philharmonic." In *Many Happy Returns: Advocacy and the Development of Archives*, edited by Larry J. Hackman, 189. Chicago: Society of American Archivists, 2011.

Headlee, Celeste. *We Need to Talk: How to Have Conversations That Matter.* New York: Harper Wave, 2017.

Hendry, Julia. "Primary Sources in K–12 Education: Opportunities for Archivists." *American Archivist* 70 (Spring/Summer 2007): 114–129.

Hensen, Steven L. "Call to Action on Executive Order 13233." 2001, updated November 10, 2010. www2.archivists.org/news/2001/call-to-action-on-executive-order-13233, captured at https://perma.cc/TH78-PFHZ.

Hensen, Steven L., William E. Landis, Kathleen D. Roe, Michael Rush, William Stockting, and Victoria Irons Walch. "Thirty Years On: SAA and Descriptive Standards." *American Archivist* 74, Supplement 1 (2011): 706: 1–36.

History Associates, Inc. *The Business Case for Archives: How History Can Bolster Your Bottom Line.* Rockville, MD: History Associates, Inc., 2013. www.historyassociates.com/resource/guides/the-business-case-for-archives-how-history-can-bolster-your-bottom-line/, captured at https://perma.cc/JC8M-FTNZ.

Holt, Kaitlin, and Jen Hoyer, "The Way for Student Success: Lessons in Education Outreach," *Archival Outlook* (January/February 2018): 8, 29.

International Council on Archives. *International Archives Day 2017.* www.youtube.com/watch?v=XGx6UIs3WGs, captured at https://perma.cc/N2RU-YE2F.

___. "Universal Declaration on Archives." 2016. www.ica.org/en/networking/unesco/unesco-officially-endorses-uda, captured at https://perma.cc/KW7R-JM5Y.

___. "Why Archiving?" 2016. www.ica.org/en/why-archiving, captured at https://perma.cc/VT5B-UMRW.

International Council on Archives, Section on Professional Associations. "Film Festival 2016." www.ica.org/en/film-festival-2016, captured at https://perma.cc/Z8FN-F6KQ.

Jaaffar, Norehan. "Repurposing Archival Content for Advocacy at the National Archives of Malaysia." International Council on Archives International Congress, 2016, Seoul, South Korea. www.ica.org/en/3-use-records-and-archives-justice-advocacy-and-reconciliation-work.

James, Russell D. "Press Kits and News Releases." In *Public Relations and Marketing for Archives*, edited by Russell D. James and Peter J. Wosh, 250. Chicago: Neal-Schuman Publishers and Society of American Archivists, 2011.

James, Russell D., and Peter J. Wosh, eds. *Public Relations and Marketing for Archives*. Chicago: Neal-Schuman Publishers and Society of American Archivists, 2011.

"Joint Statement on 'Qualities of a Successful Candidate' for Archivist of the United States." Society of American Archivists. December 19, 2008. www2.archivists.org/statements/joint-statement-on-qualities-of-a-successful-candidate-for-archivist-of-the-united-states, captured at https://perma.cc/WQ2U-JVHZ.

Kenney, Anne R. "From the President's Desk." *Archival Outlook* (May 1993): 3.

Kirmer, Jennifer, and Sonya Rooney. "Documenting Ferguson: Capturing History as It Happens." *Archival Outlook* (November/December 2014): 3, 24–25.

Koerber, Jennifer. "Live from the Library." *Library Journal*, April 10, 2017. https://lj.libraryjournal.com/2017/04/marketing/live-from-the-library/, captured at https://perma.cc/GJ6Q-JWMB.

Lasewicz, Paul. "Forget the Past? Or History Matters? Selected Academic Perspectives on the Strategic Value of Organizational Pasts." *American Archivist* 78 (Spring/Summer 2015): 59–83.

Lawrimore, Erin. "The Big Picture: Effective Advocacy through Institutional Alignment." *Archival Outlook* (July/August 2013): 3, 25.

———. "Collaboration for a 21st Century Archives: Connecting University Archives with the Library's Information Technology Professionals." *Collaborative Librarianship* 5, no. 3 (2013): 189–196. http://libres.uncg.edu/ir/uncg/listing.aspx?id=15271, captured at https://perma.cc/B65F-VWZY.

———. "Effective Media Relations for Your Archives." *ArchivesAWARE!* (blog). Society of American Archivists, Committee on Public Awareness. June 13, 2016. https://archivesaware.archivists.org/2016/06/13/effective-media-relations-for-your-archives/, captured at https://perma.cc/3YH6-XMKE.

Leland, Waldo Gifford. "John Franklin Jameson." *American Archivist* 19 (July 1956): 195–201.

Leonard, Kevin B. "Blogs and Blog Marketing: Bringing New Users to the Northwestern University Archives." In *The Interactive Archivist: Case Studies in Utilizing Web 2.0 to Improve the Archival Experience*, edited by J. Gordon Daines III and Cory L. Nimer. Chicago: Society of American Archivists, 2009. http://interactivearchivist.archivists.org/case-studies/blogs-at-nu/, captured at https://perma.cc/8BKA-RYV8.

Levy, Sidney J., and Albert G. Robles. *The Image of Archivists: Resource Allocators' Perceptions.* Chicago: Social Research, Inc., 1984. https://babel.hathitrust.org/cgi/pt?id=mdp.39015071447299;view=1up;seq=3, captured at https://perma.cc/DD9L-VBNE.

Lowell Observatory. *What Is an Archivist?* October 10, 2016. www.youtube.com/watch?v=tg54sP3bXaI, captured at https://perma.cc/MN2H-2FB5.

Mason, Philip P. "Economic Status of the Archival Profession 1965–66." *American Archivist* 30 (January 1967): 102–155.

___. "Preserving Labor's History." *American Federationist* 71 (January 1964).

McSpadden, Kevin. "You Now Have a Shorter Attention Span Than a Goldfish." *Time Magazine*, May 14, 2015. http://time.com/3858309/attention-spans-goldfish/, captured at https://perma.cc/HBH7-F9E5.

Mecagni, Giordana. "Starting the Archives for Women in Medicine: Advocacy in Creation, Survival—and Beyond?" In *Many Happy Returns: Advocacy and the Development of Archives*, edited by Larry J. Hackman, 200–214. Chicago: Society of American Archivists, 2011.

Meissner, Dennis. "Bare Necessities." *American Archivist* 80 (Spring/Summer 2017): 6–18.

___. "Leadership Plenary." SAA Annual Meeting, Cleveland, OH, August 21, 2015.

Miller, Page Putnam. "Fighting for a Qualified, Non-Partisan U.S. Archivist: What We've Learned." *SAA Newsletter*, September 12, 1988.

Minchew, Kaye Lanning. "Lessons Learned While Saving the Georgia Archives." *Provenance, Journal of the Society of Georgia Archivists* 31 (January 2013): 16–21.

Monroe, Alden. "Thomas Owen and the Founding of the Alabama Department of Archives and History." *Provenance, Journal of the Society of Georgia Archivists* 21 (2003): 22–35.

Montgomery, Bruce P. "Presidential Materials: Politics and the Presidential Records Act." *American Archivist* 66 (Spring/Summer 2009): 102–138.

Murphy, Nora. "Your Perfect Pitch: Elevator Speeches from the Field." *Archival Outlook* (January/February 2014): 6, 25.

The National Archives UK. *Explore Your Archive.* Updated October 8, 2014. www.youtube.com/playlist?list=PLddhSH7bW0pW97staCfFGDFgLF6zI0aMI.

National Humanities Alliance. "Advocacy Resources." www.nhalliance.org/advocacy_resources, captured at https://perma.cc/6SNX-HM46.

Neal, Donn C. "From the Executive Director's Desk." *SAA Newsletter*, July 1989: 3.

New York Public Library. "The Schomburg Center for Research in Black Culture Acquires Papers of Renowned Literary Icon James Baldwin," news release, April 12, 2017. www.nypl.org/press/press-release/april-12-2017/schomburg-center-research-black-culture-acquires-papers-renowned, captured at https://perma.cc/X9S9-W9US.

New York State Archives. *A Manual for Documentation Planning in New York State.* Albany: New York State Archives and State Education Department, 2002, revised 2010. www.archives.nysed.gov/publications/manual-documentation-planning-new-york-state, captured at https://perma.cc/T3UB-4YUW.

Oostveen, Lauren. "Social Media." In *Public Relations and Marketing for Archives*, edited by Russell D. James and Peter J. Wosh, 33–54. New York: Neal-Schuman Publishers and Society of American Archivists, 2011.

O'Toole, Dennis A. "The Gift of History." *AASLH Technical Leaflet #252. History News*, 65, no. 4 (Autumn 2010): 1–4. www2.archivists.org/sites/all/files/AASLH_Tech+Leaf+252.pdf, captured at https://perma.cc/JV2H-TESE.

Pearce-Moses, Richard. "Finding Our Voice: Pleading the Value of Archives." *Provenance, Journal of the Society of Georgia Archivists* 31, no. 1 (2013): 4–6.

PGAV. *Storytelling: It Can Change Your Mind.* St. Louis, MO: PGAV Destinations, 2014.

Prom, Christopher. "Using Web Analytics to Improve Online Access to Archival Resources." *American Archivist* 74 (Spring/Summer 2011): 158–184.

Reich, Howard. "A Blow to Black Music in Chicago." *Chicago Tribune*, March 5, 2012.

Rhee, Hea Lim. "Reflections on Archival User Studies." *Reference and User Services Quarterly*, 54, no. 4 (June 2015): 29–42. www.researchgate.net/publication/279183209_Reflections_on_Archival_User_Studies, captured at https://perma.cc/9SQK-SJJL.

Robertson, Walter Jr. "NARS: The Politics of Placement." *American Archivist* 39 (October 1976): 485–492.

Roe, Kathleen D., "A Recent Opportunity to Raise Awareness of Archives," *Off the Record* (blog), September 5, 2014, https://offtherecord.archivists.org/2014/09/05/a-recent-opportunity-to-raise-awareness-of-archives-4/, captured at https://perma.cc/L93N-X4Z8.

"SAA, Coalition Partners Meet with Obama Transition Team." *Archival Outlook* (January/February 2009): 4.

Schooley, Jenny. "Coca Cola Connects Past and Present at Public Event." *Archival Outlook* (May/June 2010): 12.

Shelley, Fred. "The Interest of J. Franklin Jameson in the National Archives: 1908–1934." *American Archivist* 12 (April 1949): 99–130.

Shroder, John F. Jr. "2009 GSA Public Service Award." The Geological Society of America, 2009. www.geosociety.org/awards/09speeches/psa.htm, captured at https://perma.cc/6CBT-JEKX.

Sinek, Simon. "The Art of Inspiring People to Take Action." *Elite Daily*, June 20, 2013. http://elitedaily.com/money/the-art-of-inspiring-people-to-action/, captured at https://perma.cc/A8EE-KXH3.

———. *Start with Why: How Great Leaders Inspire Everyone to Take Action.* New York: Penguin Books, 2009.

Society of American Archivists. "American Archives Month 2010." www2.archivists.org/initiatives/american-archives-month-the-power-of-collaboration/american-archives-month-2010, captured at https://perma.cc/BUV5-SJ7M.

___. "American Archives Month 2015." www2.archivists.org/initiatives/american-archives-month-the-power-of-collaboration/american-archives-month-2015, captured at https://perma.cc/Z7WC-GKLE.

___. "American Archives Month: The Power of Collaboration." www2.archivists.org/initiatives/american-archives-month-the-power-of-collaboration, captured at https://perma.cc/4A62-CPGX.

___. *Archives Change Lives.* Updated March 28, 2016. www2.archivists.org/advocacy/archiveschangelives, captured at https://perma.cc/F4WZ-9EAJ.

___. "Archives, Public Policy & You: Advocacy Guide." Updated September 26, 2018. www2.archivists.org/advocacy/advocacy-guide, captured at https://perma.cc/E9JG-GM45.

___. "Archivist Nomination Politicized?" *SAA Newsletter,* September 1986: 1, 3.

___. "Backgrounder: Funding for the National Historical Publications and Records Commission." June 15, 2017. www2.archivists.org/statements/backgrounder-funding-for-the-national-historical-publications-and-records-commission, captured at https://perma.cc/2P4F-TNH4.

___. "Call to Action #9: #Archivesin5words." A Year of Living Dangerously for Archives. 2015. www2.archivists.org/living-dangerously/archivesin5words, captured at https://perma.cc/B2WY-AA6M.

___. "Celebrating the American Record with Young People." *American Archives Month Public Relations Kit.* October 2007. http://files.archivists.org/advocacy/AAM/YoungPeople.pdf, captured at https://perma.cc/79HZ-BVME.

___. "Council Resolution." *SAA Newsletter,* July 1986: 16.

___. "I Found It in the Archives!" October 2012. www2.archivists.org/initiatives/i-found-it-in-the-archives, captured at https://perma.cc/AR2H-T7MQ.

___. "Issue Brief: Presidential Records Act of 1978." 2014. *Society of American Archivists.* www2.archivists.org/statements/issue-brief-presidential-records-act-of-1978, captured at https://perma.cc/A62A-ZWS4.

___. "National Archives Independence a Reality at Last." *SAA Newsletter,* November 1984: 1.

___. "National Coalition for History Launched." *Archival Outlook* (January 24, 2003).

___. "Outreach," *A Glossary of Archival and Records Terminology,* 2005. www2.archivists.org/glossary/terms/o/outreach, captured at https://perma.cc/9TU6-QMAB.

___. "Preservation Week: Saving Heritage and Memories." Updated April 26, 2016. www2.archivists.org/initiatives/mayday-saving-our-archives/preservation-week-saving-heritage-and-memories, captured at https://perma.cc/8V7T-8DBP.

———. "Preserving the American Historical Record." Updated March 26, 2016. www2.archivists.org/initiatives/preserving-the-american-historical-record, captured at https://perma.cc/QS32-3ESS.

———. "Public Policy." Updated February 8, 2018. www2.archivists.org/advocacy/publicpolicy, captured at https://perma.cc/5S4U-Y4N3.

———. "Robert M. Warner Named Archivist of the U.S." *SAA Newsletter,* July 1980: 1.

———. "SAA Public Policy Agenda (2015–2017)." Updated November 7, 2017. www2.archivists.org/initiatives/saa-public-policy-agenda, captured at https://perma.cc/H9Q9-86W2.

———. "Sample Op-Ed Piece on Presidential Records Act Amendments of 2007 and Executive Order 13233," at www2.archivists.org/sites/all/files/Op-EdonPRA-EO.pdf, captured at https://perma.cc/Z6UN-AK3L.

———. "Selecting an Archivist of the U.S." *SAA Newsletter,* March 1987: 3.

———. "Senate Testimony Transcript Regarding the U.S. Archivist." *Archival Outlook* (July 1995): 6–7.

———. "Statement on the Nomination of Allen Weinstein to Become Archivist of the United States." April 14, 2004. www.archivists.org/statements/weinstein.asp, captured at https://perma.cc/U9U4-RYJK.

———. "U.S. Archivist Nominated." *SAA Newsletter,* March 1986: 1.

———. "U.S. Archivist Wilson Sworn In." *SAA Newsletter,* January 1988: 1.

———. "Word of the Week: inreach." *Dictionary of Archives Terminology.* 2014. http://us3.campaign-archive2.com/?u=56c4cfbec1ee5b2a284e7e9d6&id=9cd3d5044d, captured at https://perma.cc/2UHV-AVL6.

———. "Word of the Week: value." *Dictionary of Archives Terminology.* 2016. http://us3.campaign-archive1.com/?u=56c4cfbec1ee5b2a284e7e9d6&id=11c3422d1b, captured at https://perma.cc/2VAT-PKZX.

Society of American Archivists, Business Archives Section. Advocating Business Archives Toolkit. www2.archivists.org/groups/business-archives-section/advocating-business-archives-toolkit, captured at https://perma.cc/N867-R363.

———. "BAS Advocacy Success Stories." www2.archivists.org/groups/business-archives-section/bas-advocacy-success-stories, captured at https://perma.cc/XB9Y-F4FE.

Society of American Archivists, Committee on Public Awareness. Nick Pavlik, ed., *ArchivesAWARE!* (blog), https://archivesaware.archivists.org/, captured at https://perma.cc/JBZ9-LK6D.

———. "#AskAnArchivist Day." Updated September 12, 2018. www2.archivists.org/initiatives/askanarchivist-day, captured at https://perma.cc/Q8WF-HMGT.

———. "Crafting Your Elevator Speech." Updated December 15, 2017. www2.archivists.org/advocacy/public-awareness/elevator-speech, captured at https://perma.cc/8YG7-YKTT.

Society of American Archivists, Issues and Advocacy Section. Advocacy Toolkit. https://issuesandadvocacy.wordpress.com/advocacy-toolkit/, captured at https://perma.cc/WJU5-PU94.

Society of American Archivists, Regional Archival Associations Consortium. "Projects and Activities." 2018. www2.archivists.org/groups/regional-archival-associations-consortium-raac/projects-and-activities, captured at https://perma.cc/K6VC-YA9H.

Society of American Archivists, SAA-ACRL/RBMS Joint Task Force on Public Services Metrics. "Standardized Statistical Measures and Metrics for Public Services in Archival Repositories and Special Collections Libraries." Updated June 26, 2018. www2.archivists.org/standards/standardized-statistical-measures-and-metrics-for-public-services-in-archival-repositories, captured at https://perma.cc/CP4Y-S32A.

"Special Issue on Advocacy." *Provenance, Journal of the Society of Georgia Archivists* 31, no. 1 (2013).

Spindler, Rob. "#WhyIAmAnArchivist." *Archival Outlook* (March/April 2015): 13. www.bluetoad.com/publication/?i=251532, captured at https://perma.cc/6FJ4-U5K8.

Task Force on Archives and Society. "Archivists' Resource Allocators: The Next Step." December 9, 1985. http://files.archivists.org/governance/reports/Image-of-Archivists-Levy1984.pdf, captured at https://perma.cc/C7LF-NK7V.

Taylor, Tomaro I. "Connecting to Marginalized Groups through Web 2.0." University of South Florida Scholar Commons. *Academic Services Faculty and Staff Publications* 67 (2010). http://scholarcommons.usf.edu/tlas_pub/67/.

Traverso, Vittoria. "How 'Photo Detectives' Have Helped Reveal Irish History." *Atlas Obscura,* November 2, 2017. www.atlasobscura.com/articles/photo-detectives-ireland-irish-history-archives-exhibition-crowdsource, captured at https://perma.cc/LPV6-9LVV.

University of Iowa Special Collections. *Staxpeditions 6: Exploring Mystery Boxes: Manuscripts Edition!* November 6, 2013. www.youtube.com/watch?v=xbhDIerW2u4, captured at https://perma.cc/54CZ-HRRG.

UNLV University Libraries, Special Collections. *What We Do with Your Donations.* March 27, 2015. www.youtube.com/watch?v=llmF6g3n5gc&t=78s, captured at https://perma.cc/Z7WM-XXL7.

U.S. Internal Revenue Service. "'Direct' and 'Grass Roots' Lobbying Defined." www.irs.gov/charities-non-profits/direct-and-grass-roots-lobbying-defined, captured at https://perma.cc/8KNQ-N8P6.

___. "Lobbying." https://www.irs.gov/charities-non-profits/lobbying, captured at https://perma.cc/MKG9-29HG.

U.S. National Archives. "National Archives Virtual Genealogy Fair 2018." www.archives.gov/calendar/genealogy-fair, captured at https://perma.cc/8CYA-NGVW.

U.S. National Archives, Office of Government Information Services. "Sunshine Week." www.archives.gov/ogis/outreach-events/sunshine-week, captured at https://perma.cc/69RZ-RF6U.

Wakimoto, Diane, Debra Hansen, and Christine Bruce. "The Case of LLACE: Challenges, Triumphs, and Lessons of a Community Archives." *American Archivist* 76 (Fall/Winter 2013): 438–457.

Walch, Victoria Irons, Nancy Beaumont, Elizabeth Yakel, Jeannette Bastian, Nancy Zimmelman, Susan Davis, and Anne Diffendal. "A*CENSUS (Archival Census and Education Needs Survey in the United States)." *American Archivist* 69 (Fall/Winter 2006): 291–419. www2.archivists.org/sites/all/files/ACENSUS-Final.pdf, captured at https://perma.cc/6AN6-Y3DN.

Walton, Rachel. "Looking for Answers: A Usability Study of Online Finding Aid Navigation." *American Archivist* 80 (Spring/Summer 2017): 30–52.

Warner, Robert M. *Diary of a Dream: A History of the National Archives Independence Movement, 1980–1985.* Metuchen, NJ: Scarecrow Press, 1995.

___. "Secrecy and Salesmanship in the Struggle for NARA's Independence." *Prologue* 37, no. 1 (Spring 2005). www.archives.gov/publications/prologue/2005/spring/archivist-warner.html, captured at https://perma.cc/499S-ZTXC.

White, Leland J. "Controversy over Proposed 'Destruction' of Interior Department Records Explained." Latest News. National Coalition for History. October 27, 2018. http://historycoalition.org/2018/10/27/controversy-over-proposed-destruction-of-interior-department-records-explained/, captured at https://perma.cc/VZ6S-6JF3.

___. "Hearing Focuses on Challenges Facing Next U.S. Archivist." *Archival Outlook* (July/August 2009): 19.

___. "NCH Washington Year in Review." *Archival Outlook* (January/February 2008): 17.

Williams, Kathleen. "The NHPRC: Extending the Archives' Reach." *Prologue* 41, no. 2 (Summer 2009). www.archives.gov/publications/prologue/2009/summer/nhprc.html, captured at https://perma.cc/FLG2-XQDZ.

Williamson, Felicia, Scott Vieira, and James Williamson. "Marketing Finding Aids on Social Media: What Worked and What Didn't Work." *American Archivist* 78 (Fall/Winter 2015): 488–513.

Wong Smith, Helen. "Leadership Plenary." Presentation, SAA Annual Meeting, Cleveland, OH, August 21, 2015.

Wosh, Peter J., Richard Cox, Charles J. Dollar, and Rebecca Hirsch. "Founding Brothers: Leland, Buck, and Cappon and the Formation of the Archives Profession." *American Archivist* 74 (January 2011): 1–27.

Yakel, Elizabeth, and Helen Tibbo. "Standardized Survey Tools for Assessment in Archives and Special Collections." *Performance Measurement and Metrics* 11, no. 2 (2010): 211–222. https://doi.org/10.1108/14678041011064115.

Yakel, Elizabeth, Wendy Duff, Helen Tibbo, Adam Kriesberg, and Amber Cushing. "The Economic Impact of Archives: Surveys of Users of Government Archives in Canada and the United States." *American Archivist* 75 (Fall/Winter 2012): 297–325.

Zajac, Andrew. "How Giuliani Tried to Control His NYC Legacy." *Chicago Tribune*, October 28, 2007.

# Acknowledgments

Writing this manual has been a humbling experience. At perhaps too many points, I thought about starting over and taking an entirely different approach. At other times the challenges included deciding what to put in and what to leave out and finding effective examples of practice. Through it all, however, I heard the voices of those who have provided welcome collaboration, support, and energy and who have reminded me that I needed to get something out there—if only as a starting point from which someone else could revise or expand in the future.

Although all responsibility for any inadequacies is entirely my own, I am so fortunate to have good colleagues and friends to thank for their many roles in helping bring this volume to fruition. David Carmicheal, State Archivist of Pennsylvania, has been an inspiring and energetic co-conspirator in advocacy efforts for years. His creativity, eloquence, and great heart have been essential to my own development as an archival advocate and to bringing essential learning to the archives profession. I also extend my profuse gratitude to Nancy Beaumont, SAA's executive director, who generously shared her own considerable knowledge and editorial skills, provided unswerving support for my fixation with advocacy and awareness during my tenure as SAA president, and proved to be a great companion as together we spent "A Year of Living Dangerously for Archives."

A number of SAA colleagues deserve acknowledgment for the many ways in which they have contributed to my own understanding of advocacy and awareness and, ultimately, to bringing this volume to fruition. Dennis Riley of the New York State Archives has championed archival issues and done the sheer hard work—as a member and then as chair of SAA's Committee on Public Policy—of helping to move our profession forward (as well as listening to me rant over many lunches and cups of coffee). Peter Wosh, the editor of SAA's Archival Fundamentals Series III, has been generous with his insights and encouragement as I wrestled with particularly bedeviling portions of the manuscript. I am endlessly thankful for the superior comments from "unnamed reviewers" Steven DeJuan Booth of the Barack Obama Presidential Library, Christopher Burns of the University of Vermont, and Anna Trammel of Pacific Lutheran University. Their suggestions and observations were spot-on and improved this volume considerably. Thanks also to Samantha Winn of Virginia Tech University and Louis Jones of Wayne State University, each of whom located and shared some much-needed but elusive information when it was essential.

Much of what I have learned about advocacy and awareness was literally "on-the-job" training. During my career at the New York State Archives, then-state archivist Larry J. Hackman provided a superior model of both the skills and the persistence needed to advocate for and accomplish great things for archives. Bruce W. Dearstyne, then director of external programs, also was generous in sharing his knowledge and energy for advocacy and awareness. Christine Ward, recently retired as state archivist, has been a longtime colleague, friend, and cohort in many advocacy venues. Cynthia Woodside, former federal liaison for the New York State Education Department, provided essential advice and shared generously her contacts to help me learn to advocate in the wild world of Congress.

Colleagues from the Council of State Archivists (CoSA) have also been essential partners at the national level in tackling advocacy and awareness for archives. I have benefited greatly from the friendship of Barbara Teague, former state archivist of Kentucky and current CoSA Executive Director, as well as former New Jersey State Archivist Karl Niederer, former Delaware State Archivist Tim Slavin, former CoSA Executive Director Victoria Walch, and many other CoSA members. The archives profession has benefited greatly from their willingness to do the unheralded hard work of advocacy with Congress.

I am deeply indebted to two individuals for guiding me in the archives profession. Dr. Philip P. Mason has had a long and distinguished career as an astute archivist and educator. When I studied in his archives program at Wayne State University, he conveyed in clear, compelling ways why archives are of value and why archivists' work is important. I have never forgotten those lessons, and his continuing mentorship has been a great gift. Geneva Kebler Wiskemann, my first "boss" at the Michigan State Archives, was profoundly inspiring as she both taught me basic practices and talked about why what we do matters. Any achievements I have made in this profession are deeply rooted in the incomparable wisdom and generosity of these two individuals throughout my career.

Finally, it is fitting to acknowledge my beloved, long-suffering husband, James Corsaro, former head of Manuscripts and Special Collections at the New York State Library, and my astonishing daughter, Katherine Roe Corsaro, a musical theatre actress and archival advocate in her own right. Not only have they provided support for my advocacy and awareness work and my career, but they have enriched my life in ways beyond measure.

KATHLEEN D. ROE
Troy, New York

# Index

# About the Author

Kathleen D. Roe is a graduate of Michigan State University (master's in history) and Wayne State University (master's in library science/archival administration). She recently retired from the New York State Archives as director of Archives and Records Management. As president of the Society of American Archivists (2014–2015), she emphasized the importance of archival advocacy through "The Year of Living Dangerously for Archives" initiative. She is a Fellow of SAA and has served on various committees, most recently relating to public policy and advocacy. She is past president of the Council of State Archivists, where she has been involved in advocacy and federal legislative issues. Roe has written and taught on a range of archival issues, including advocacy and awareness as well as arrangement and description.